Two Shakes

of a

Lamb's Tail

A Memoir

By Robert Hesselberth

Two Shakes of a Lamb's Tail

TWO SHAKES OF A LAMB'S TAIL

Published by Artisan Quest Books
www.ArtisanQuestBooks.com

Copyright © 2014 by Robert J. Hesselberth
The publisher's colophon is a trademark of Artisan Quest Books

"Sunset Over the Vineyard" was originally published in *Athenaeum* in 2005. A draft version of "Running Under the Fan" was used, with the author's permission, as a training aid by the radiation oncology department of a Rochester, New York hospital, and by a prostate cancer support group in Sarasota, Florida.

Some names in this memoir have been changed and some conversations have been condensed. Otherwise, all of the events herein actually happened, although George Frazier denies having any memory of our using his Boy Scout sheath knife to cut almost through the string of a tampon belonging to his big sister.

RJH

For Marianne, David, Mary Jo, and Susan

Introduction

Scientists will someday prove that our short-term memory resides in our hair follicles. If not, why such a high positive correlation between my growing forgetfulness and the size of my bald spot? As further evidence, I note that my wife's short-term memory is much better than mine, and she isn't nearly as bald as I am.

Each chapter of this book is a record that abandoned its follicle, migrated to one of the many empty corners of my brain, and took up permanent residence there. If the afterglow of an experience has drilled its way deep into my skull, I can rerun it in my mind indefinitely, whenever I need shelter from the press of a busy life.

When I was growing up in a small Midwestern town that hosted a large university, a book by Norman Vincent Peale came to our house as a Book-of-the-Month Club selection. It was *The Power of Positive Thinking,* and we devoured it from cover to cover. Given my parents' nature, the book was preaching to the choir. There was plenty of positive thinking to go around without additional help. The positivity that they exuded seeped into my psyche and made possible much of what is told in this book.

That I would go to college was a given. Once on my own, I just decided to learn to fly; of course it was possible. Start an electronics manufacturing company from scratch? Ditto. Once decided, it was just a matter of time, total commitment, and three years of unplanned poverty.

All the fun and adventure to be had along the way made the time go by like lightning, leaving in its wake the sweet ozone smell of memories recorded here.

The older a person gets, the faster time passes. For example: At five years old, waiting one month for Santa Claus used

$1/60^{th}$, or almost two per cent of my life to date. At 50 years old, that same wait of a month used only $1/600^{th}$, or less than *two tenths* of one per cent of my entire life to date. I grow more patient as I age because a wait of one month, in *relative* time, gets shorter, causing the months to fly by at warp speed.

Time is the only thing I can think of that can't be defined in terms of what it *is*. We can define *time* only in terms of itself, or its effect on us, or our reaction to it, or what it is not. My dictionary devotes several column-inches to the definition of time, using cryptic terms like *a non-spatial continuum in which events occur*, or *a system by which intervals are measured*. Presumably the latter would be intervals of time, which reduces the definition to the circular: "*Time is a system by which time is measured*." Is this a definition? I prefer the first definition, but for me it provides no insight.

Whatever time is, it moves faster and faster, generating whirlwinds within hurricanes and calmness during an Indian summer, while my eyesight dims and memories now and then percolate to the surface. Where did it all go?

Wherever it went, I agree with George Frazier, my childhood friend and Boy Scout buddy, who, as he approached retirement, said "It's been a great ride."

If there is sadness here, it is only in short segments that are far outweighed by the good humor and decency of the folks around me. No one has been more fortunate than I in my selection of parents, spouse, family, and friends, who have added sparkles to the ride. They are all on my mind as I write this book.

Two Shakes of a Lamb's Tail

Contents

I Steely Street at War/9

II The Wonder Years/91

III Learning to Fly/139

Contents

IV The Spectracom Saga/195

V Sunset over the Vineyard/281

I

Steely Street At War

Backward, turn backward, then time in your flight,
Make me a child again just for tonight.
Mother, come back from the echoless shore,
Take me again to your heart as of yore.

A.M.W. Ball

The more we live, more brief appear
Our live's succeeding stages;
A day to childhood seems a year
And years like passing ages.

Thomas Campbell
A Thought Suggested by the New Year

Chapter 1

Feeding Dirt to Worms

On most days, I didn't see the CEO of the company I worked for except when I passed him in the hallway or answered his questions in a product or market development review meeting. But today I had been told by my boss that *his* boss, Bill Stolze, the CEO, wanted to see me in his office.

The last time I was in his office alone with him was to ask if there were any new opportunities in the company now that I had received my MBA degree from the University of Rochester. Six years of night school had given me a lot of new training. More importantly, the business schooling had changed my aspirations, and at 37 the fire in my belly was impossible to ignore.

As I climbed the stairs to the second floor, I tried to imagine what he might want. I got all the way in through the marketing department to his secretary's desk without figuring it out, but I had always been comfortable with Bill in the past and had no thoughts of anything bad about to happen. There was no one else in his office, and his secretary waved me in. His desk was clear of clutter with only a lamp, a phone, the logbook where he took notes during phone calls, and the usual photos of his wife and kids off to one side.

"Have a seat," Bill said.

He got right to the point. "I hear you're starting a company. Is that so?"

He looked right at me with no expression on his face.

My heart skipped a couple of beats and I said, "I'm looking at a lot of possibilities."

Which was true, but it was also my lame attempt to evade his question. I had been to a couple of job interviews, but my real desire was to start my own company, and I had written a business plan, was looking for a backer, and was working nights and weekends with two other engineers in the company to develop a product. It now appeared that I had shown the business plan to someone with a big mouth, who went right to Stolze with the story.

"We're going to have to let you go," he said. "Go back to your office and clear out your desk, and then see the personnel manager before you leave."

"Will I get the $5,000 separation pay I was promised if I didn't move to Long Island with my division of the company?" I asked.

"We can't give you that now," he said. My ten-year career with the company was over. In his calm, matter-of-fact way it was just business as usual. In the past, when *I* had to fire someone, I felt terrible and wanted to cry. But Bill was a much more experienced manager.

My head buzzed as I left his office. I had never been fired before. I suppose I cleaned out my desk and visited the Personnel Department as instructed, and I do remember that before leaving the building, I phoned Marianne to give her the news. I didn't want to surprise her and suddenly show up at home in the middle of the day.

I had begun my ten years with the company as the 50th employee at RF Communications, a two-year-old startup in Rochester, New York, and I was leaving when the company had grown to 1000 employees and had become a division of Harris Corporation, a powerhouse in the electronics industry.

Now my life would change.

In the days that followed my departure I reflected on the career path that had ended so abruptly, and the childhood and motivations that had led me to such an abrupt end of my job.

✦

Forty-five years earlier in 1927, the euphoria of the jazz age was about to end, and Adolf Hitler published his book *Mein Kampf*. My father, Wilfred "Duke" Hesselberth decided to leave the family farm in Illinois, against his parents' wishes, and be the first in his family to get a college education. He was fascinated by the new field of radio electronics, and wanted a career in it.

Duke met Merno King, the daughter of a small-town mailman, in the fall of 1930, when she arrived on the University of Illinois campus from Trenton, Missouri. Merno was a member of the first graduating class at the newly established Trenton Junior College (now North Central Missouri College). She had stayed at home to teach in the local grade school for three years while saving the money to complete her Bachelor's Degree at Illinois.

The Great Depression still had the country in its grip. After graduation in 1931 from the University of Illinois with a Bachelor's Degree in Electrical Engineering, Duke was unable to find a job. Only one of his 29 electrical engineering classmates found employment, and it was a non-technical position. Duke's solution to this dilemma was to remain as a part-time short-order cook, the job that had financed his degree, and continue in college to get a Master's Degree the following year.

Duke and Merno both lived at the same off-campus rooming house, which was owned and run by a cousin of Merno's mother. They began dating, and both got their degrees in the spring of 1932; she a bachelor's degree, and he a master's degree. I never thought to ask them if her presence had played a part in his decision to stay for the graduate degree instead of returning to the family farm on the Illinois prairie near Minonk.

Economic conditions were no better in Europe during the Depression, and Americans heard radio reports that events there turned in a different direction. Hitler was able to exploit the hyperinflation and unemployment to rise to power. While he was climbing toward the position of Chancellor of Germany, life was calm in university towns in the US. Merno taught in a Champaign, Illinois grade school, and Duke found a research job in West Lafayette, Indiana in the basement laboratory of the Purdue University Electrical Engineering building. His boss was the brilliant Roscoe George who had, the previous year, invented the synchronization technology that made all-electronic television possible. Duke's job consisted of making tiny metal parts and blowing glass bulbs with which to build experimental electronic vacuum tubes. He bought a motorcycle and commuted on weekends between West Lafayette and Champaign to see Merno.

During a Christmas vacation trip to Trenton in 1933 to visit Merno's family, the pair made a "spur-of-the-moment decision" to marry. Merno's father, Joe King, somehow found an available minister who married them in the Kings' living room on the day after Christmas. Knowing no one else in Trenton, and not having time to invite out-of-town family, Duke had no best man, and Merno had only her family and a personal friend or two in attendance.

Was the quick decision to suddenly marry influenced by the seemingly endless worldwide depression and the uncertainty it brought? The terror and uncertainty wrought by the Nazis in Europe was probably too far removed to scare Merno and Duke into such precipitous action, but whatever external motivations surrounded them, they were in love and there was no need to wait.

Meanwhile, in Germany, Hitler and his minions were learning to persecute Jews, practicing for when their talents would be needed for more serious atrocities across Europe.

When Christmas vacation was over, Merno had the remainder of her teaching contract to fulfill back in Champaign. The school administration allowed her to finish the school year, but no more, since she was now a married lady and would be supported by her husband. She rented an apartment in Champaign, and Duke continued his motorcycle commutations until the spring semester ended in 1934, when they moved into their own apartment in West Lafayette.

Then, three weeks before I was born in April of 1935, Adolph Hitler violated the Treaty of Versailles by introducing military conscription in Germany. That fall, the Nuremberg Race Laws deprived German Jews of their rights of citizenship, giving them the status of "subjects" in Hitler's Reich. Jews were forbidden to marry or have sexual relations with Aryans or even to employ young Aryan women as household help.

By 1935, over one-third of births in the US occurred in hospitals instead of at home. My birth at the Home Hospital in Lafayette, Indiana was followed by my mother's and my standard two-week hospital stay. Soon afterward, my father's quest for a better paying job took us to Chicago, where, after a year, his employer's bankruptcy forced another move, this time to Silver Spring, Maryland, followed by yet another employer's bankruptcy.

During this sojourn, my mother's incessant search for vitamins and elixirs that would guarantee good health led her to give me, via eye dropper straight from a tiny medicine bottle, a few drops of cod liver oil before meals. To adults the stuff was smelly and vile-tasting enough to gag a maggot, but I didn't see it that way. My mother had used her penchant for positive thinking on me, and the result was magical: I *liked* cod liver oil. Each day at the appointed time, the first thing I called for when

14

settled in my high chair at the table was "Oy-Oy!... Oy-Oy!... Oy-Oy!" which Mother gladly gave me, if only to shut me up. Dad thought it was hilarious. Later in life, he never let me forget that I was probably a mutant, born with the taste buds of a cat.

According to Mom, I learned to talk when I was just over one year old. In a department store, seeing a Mickey Mouse doll from my stroller, I smiled, pointed at it, and exclaimed, "Mickey Mouse!" causing a case of the vapors in the store clerk, who couldn't believe that a baby was speaking as clearly as an adult.

In the spring of 1938, Dad's summer technician's job at Kansas State College (now Kansas State University) took us to Manhattan, Kansas.

"Daddy," I said, "What do worms eat?"

"Dirt, I guess," he replied, and went on with whatever he was doing.

He later found me crying in the yard, holding an earthworm. "What's wrong?" he asked.

"The worm won't eat any dirt," I said through my tears. The story was repeated for me as I grew up, until it seemed to be part of my own memory: the day Bobby tried to make an earthworm eat some dirt. I was three years old.

Half a continent to the east, and across the Atlantic Ocean, a madman was charming and inflaming his people, feeding them his own special brand of dirt.

Hitler's war against the countries of Europe in general, and against Jews in particular, continued. Austria was annexed and then Czechoslovakia. Along the way, all ten-year-old German boys were conscripted into the Hitler Youth.

At three years of age in the summer of 1938, I wasn't aware that my name was German, or that three of my four paternal great-grandparents were mid-19th-century, Protestant Christian immigrants from Germany. (The fourth was from Switzerland.) I suspect that my German immigrant ancestors, had they lived long enough, would have been ashamed of their homeland.

But in 1938, while I tearfully tried to force-feed earthworms, American adults had their own problems. The Great Depression was still forcing everyone to concentrate on finding jobs, or to worry about staying employed.

Dad's summer job in Kansas ended in the fall of 1938, and he took us back to Purdue, where, this time, he was a glassblower in the Physics Department and began working on his PhD in electrical engineering. He moved us into a small rented house at 125 Steely Street near the southern edge of West Lafayette, where we were separated from the New York Central railroad tracks by a large cow pasture owned by the Purdue School of Agriculture. One of the denizens of that pasture was a big brown bull with a viewing hole in its side, perhaps six inches in diameter, through which agricultural researchers could peer or, presumably, reach in with a soup ladle, take a sample, and analyze the contents of one of the animal's stomachs. I never learned which one. The hole cover that the researchers had fashioned was not always firmly in place, and occasionally semi-digested grass, having entered the bovine at the front end, spilled from the side hole midway in its conversion to an altogether different substance during its journey to the output end. If this happened when the herd was near our yard, albeit on the other side of the pasture fence, I watched—a small boy mesmerized by animals that did nothing but munch grass and were too big and scary to pet.

Being an obedient kid, I never climbed the fence to stray into the pasture unless Dad was with me. When he took me exploring to see what was on the other side of the pasture, it was only after teaching me to avoid the cow pies deposited there by the herd. This talent served me well in future years during our visits to the Illinois farms where my dad's brother and sister, Uncle Albert and Aunt Sue, lived with their families. While running through their fields and barnyards with my cousins, I never once stepped in any such surprises.

On the far side of that pasture, train whistles and steam engine chuffs supplemented the clock on our kitchen wall. The *James Whitcomb Riley* passenger train from Cincinnati went by at suppertime, announcing its trip to Chicago with a mournful whistle blast.

"There goes the Riley," Mom would say, as I helped her set the dinner table.

At dusk, with the cattle home in their barn, whip-poor-wills called to each other from somewhere across the empty pasture, and after I was in bed, chuffing noises from a long freight train lulled me to sleep as it moved out of the station in Lafayette, straining like the "little engine that could" to chug its way up the long slope from the bridge over the Wabash River. Then a sudden slip of its drive wheels gave new meaning to the word "choo-choo." The chuffing sped up until the engineer got the wheels to grab the track again and the train with its warm, comfortable noises continued chugging and faded into the distance, into my dreams.

Chapter 2

Let's Name Him John

"Mommy, don't get on the bed, John's under there! You'll squish him!"

The far side of my parents' bed was against the wall, and to change the sheets my mother had to climb onto the bed to tuck them in. "OK, but you should get him out of there so I can finish making the bed."

It was 1938, and I was too young to be aware of Hitler's barbarous assaults on his Jewish citizens. We had recently moved into our rented house on Steely Street in West Lafayette, Dad had a new job back at Purdue that was to prove quite secure, and our family was surviving the Depression. We had a 1937 Plymouth in the driveway, and the ice man delivered blocks of ice right to the house to cool the food in our icebox. With all the amenities we needed, our small town in the middle of the country felt safe.

I crawled under the bed, sliding on my stomach under the springs, among the dust bunnies and between the dangling cobwebs to where John had hidden, way back in the corner. Grabbing his hand, I pulled him out of danger and took him into the hall.

"OK, Mommy, you can get on the bed now," I said. John then got a tongue lashing and some advice about safe places to play.

John was my friend who had come to live with us a few weeks earlier. I played with him nearly every day, but he was in constant danger from grown-ups, none of whom could see him. Protecting him was a high-priority task, ranking right up there with teaching him how to play.

I don't know how long John lived with us or why he disappeared, but I suspect that he felt abandoned when I found other friends among the kids on Steely Street and in Miss Schrock's Nursery School.

Events in Germany got nastier. Jewish-owned shops were destroyed, synagogues were vandalized and burned, and sacred Torah scrolls were destroyed. In 1940 the Nazis began bombing England in what became known as the Battle of Britain. Later that year, President Roosevelt signed a military conscription bill, and a few weeks later he was re-elected for a third term as president. Dad was fortunate. He had been too young for military service in World War I, and he was too old for the draft in World War II. I was oblivious to all this. We were shielded in our Midwestern, college-town cocoon. With very few Jews living in West Lafayette, those problems in Europe remained very far away.

Meanwhile, I had a more important event to think about. Mom explained to me why she was getting a bigger tummy, and that I would soon have a new baby brother or sister to help take care of.

In early 1941, when I was almost six and Mom was spending two weeks in the hospital, Dad said "What do you think we should name your new little brother?"

"I don't know," I said.

"We could name him after your imaginary friend, John—do you remember him?—that you used to play with. Would that be OK?"

I considered this possibility. My proprietary rights in the name "John" were minimal. After all, I hadn't invented the name, nor had I bestowed it on him. It was already his name when he first came to play with me.

"Umm…OK," I said. At age five, eloquence wasn't my strong suit.

Each day Dad went to the hospital to visit Mom and John, but I wasn't allowed to go with him because I might give the new baby a cold or spread other bad germs. I either stayed with a neighbor for the hour that Dad was away, or he went while I was in school. One time he took me along, but I had to sit in the car until he came out to go home. He parked the car on the street outside the big brick building where I could look up to see the third-floor window of Mom's room.

"Now if you watch that window, I'll ask Mom to wave to you from her bed," he said. "Just keep watching until you see her wave."

My eyes were riveted to that window forever, it seemed, until a few minutes later I finally saw an arm move across the window a couple of times.

When the two weeks had passed, Dad brought Mom and my new brother, John, home from the hospital. A two-week stay for having a baby was normal in January of 1941. By then, most new babies were born in hospitals. In 1907, my father had been born at home, and *his* mother had been born in the middle of an Illinois cornfield because *her* mother couldn't get back to their house on the prairie quickly enough on that July day in 1867 when she felt her first baby coming. *Her* mother-in-law, my Great-Great-Grandmother, was also working in the field on that day, and came over to help when Great Grandma lay down between the knee-high corn rows, but she ordered her mother-in-law away because the two women didn't get along. The family's oral history didn't include the details of that confrontation, but it's not likely that there was a polite conversation between the two strong-willed, pioneer immigrant women (German and Swiss) in those circumstances.

The massive migration from Europe to the new world was continuous in the latter half of the 19th century. In the US, even the common folk could own land. Those immigrant farming families must have been enormously proud of their farms and their new lives. Having a baby in the middle of a cornfield was just a minor inconvenience that went along with the freedom to control their own destiny.

Both the baby and her mother survived the cornfield ordeal, and the latter went on to produce thirteen more children. Four of them died as infants, including a pair of twins. The surviving ten offspring grew up to produce three dozen children, one of whom was my dad, who had the mind-boggling good fortune of having thirty-five siblings and first cousins on his mother's side.

Two generations after the cornfield nativity that began the family's American pullulation, John was still wrinkly and red when he came home, in spite of his extended hospital stay. All he did was cry, suck on his bottle, and fill his diapers. Well, he did give us a smile now and then. We liked that the best. How could anyone have guessed that he would someday become a DuPont vice president, a PhD chemical engineer in charge of all the research and development for the four-billion-dollar nylon-producing division of the company? But then, how many invisible playmates do?

Chapter 3

Post-Potty Training

When I was three and had moved to Steely Street in West Lafayette, I'm pretty sure I was already potty trained. By 1938 parents didn't need to spend so much time raising their food and could concentrate more on raising their children. Dr. Spock hadn't yet appeared on the scene, and conflicting theories on child rearing were more plentiful than diaper pins. Should we be strict or indulgent? Breast or bottle feeding? Pick up the baby when it cries, or leave it alone so it learns not to cry? If a six-year-old misbehaves, should he be spanked or reasoned with? I was spanked, but only on extremely rare occasions, when my sin was suitably egregious. My wife would now say that it warped my personality, but I'm doubtful.

Poor potty training was a major parental sin, the price of which was a damaged psyche and a life of misery for the child. That's why I'm sure that I was properly trained to make my deposits in accordance with disciplined free will, and not randomly wherever they wanted to occur. Mom wouldn't have had it any other way. In her firm, positive, and cheerful way she would have given me no other choice.

While violence against Jewish shops, department stores, and synagogues in Germany reached a frenzied peak, and their police and fire departments stood by and watched, Steely Street was my training ground. On our quiet little street, Mom could impress upon me, and later on my brother, all of the important bits of knowledge and abilities that made for a happy and successful life. While the Battle of Britain began and the United States Congress passed a military conscription bill. Mom, positive in her faith that things would work out well, focused on teaching me to behave appropriately, preparing me for after the war. A good bit of that teaching was done by doing her best to set good examples.

When my parents argued, it was so unusual that the impression stayed with me permanently. We had recently moved to West Lafayette, and Dad had begun his new part-time job as a glass blower in the Physics Department at Purdue while he worked on a PhD in Electrical Engineering.

Job availability in the U.S. was nearly non-existent. The Great Depression had eliminated job opportunities for several years and had resulted in Dad's annual job hops from Chicago to Silver Spring, Maryland, to Manhattan, Kansas after getting his Master's Degree at the University of Illinois in 1932. The Chicago and Silver Spring jobs had evaporated as small companies went bankrupt and jobs all over the country went up in smoke. Times were not good.

In addition to the lingering economic disaster in the US and the turmoil in Europe, the head of the Purdue Physics Department, Dr. Karl Lark-Horovitz, after his approval of Dad's hiring, suddenly decreed that Physics Department employees could not work on advanced degrees in other departments: Dad had to get his degree in Physics if he was to remain a Physics Department employee. "Larkie," as he was sometimes referred to, reneged on his commitment and changed the rules in the middle of the game.

The stress must have been considerable as Dad began course work leading to a PhD in Physics to hang on to his job. He wasn't happy working on a Physics degree when his entire purpose in leaving his home farm country as the first ever in his family to attend college was to learn the new field of electronics.

The argument at home between Mom and Dad took place in our living room on Steely Street, voices escalating until both were yelling and I couldn't take any more of this brand new means of communication. Standing to the side of them as they vented about whatever it was that got them so agitated, I stamped my foot and screamed, "Stop it!" Mom looked at me in surprise and immediately knew they had committed an example-setting no-no. She grabbed me in a big hug while she wiped my tears and apologized over and over.

Never, ever again did I hear my parents raise their voices to each other.

(Decades later my newly divorced secretary said that her marriage had failed because they just didn't get along and were always yelling at each other. As she grew up, her parents had behaved the same way, so "I thought that's what husbands and wives did: Yell a lot at each other." The examples that parents set for their kids count for a lot in later life.)

As the Japanese bombed Pearl Harbor, and the Andrews Sisters' recording of "Boogie Woogie Bugle Boy" was played on the radio, Mom taught me about colors that may or may not be worn together: Blue and green don't go together, nor do brown and blue. If I really wanted to offend others and consign myself to everlasting shame and degradation, I would wear pink and red together. Small boys didn't ever wear pink and seldom wore red, but I learned that lesson anyway, just in case. When I was more mature and could absorb more complex thoughts, she added plaids with stripes to the list of banned combinations.

As the Japanese attacked the Philippines, Wake Island, Guam, Malaya, Thailand, Shanghai and Midway, Helen O'Connell and Jimmy Dorsey recorded "Wonder When My Baby's Coming Home" and Kate Smith's recording of "The White Cliffs of Dover" hit the top of the charts. On Steely Street at five or six years old, I wasn't aware of either the war or the popular music of the day; Mom was teaching me how always to make hospital corners when I made my bed. Years later, during army basic training, I learned that some young men had never heard of hospital corners on beds. The drill sergeant had to teach them what their mothers had not. The practical use of this knowledge, for which I'm ever grateful to my mother, later enabled me to make the blanket stretch so tightly across the bunk that the drill sergeant could drop a quarter on the bed and see it bounce. If it didn't bounce, the consequences were fearful: Aside from the clear and present danger to national security if the quarter didn't bounce, the sergeant would tear the bed apart, forcing me to remake it from scratch. Hospital corners helped me avoid this humiliation.

As the Allied and Axis powers were declaring war on each other, and over 5,000 Americans died on Bataan during Japan's infamous Death March, I learned that when out on the street with Mom or any other lady, I was always to walk on the curb side to protect her from the traffic. This tradition was said to have originated in Europe, where chivalry demanded that the man walk on the side most likely to receive any splashed mud or horse droppings from passing carriages, or any garbage or other waste heaved from a window into the street by residents of upstairs apartments. To this day, I'm uncomfortable walking on the inside, leaving the lady exposed to the dangers that lurk near the curb. Even though trends toward sexual equality have erased this custom from our culture (women are now equally capable of shielding their men from those curbside indignities), I still surreptitiously move to the outside of the female, unless it would attract too much attention to force my way over there. I'm still waiting for the opportunity to protect a lady companion from splashed horse droppings caused by a passing carriage or a speeding automobile. If the occasion arises, I'm well trained and ready to do my duty.

The man always lets the woman go through a door or get into a car first, and he opens the door and holds it for her while she does so. The woman goes first through any crowded passages, including up a set of stairs. (Later in life I realized that the man's view is sometimes enhanced by this arrangement.) An exception to this rule requires the *man* to lead when going *down* stairs, so he can catch her if she falls. I have never been obliged to catch a woman who fell downstairs behind me. Perhaps the mere knowledge that I was in position to protect her from falling was enough to deter such clumsiness.

Mom must have had a view of sexual equality that was way ahead of its time. Making a bed, setting a table properly (knife on the right next to the plate - cutting edge facing left, spoon on the outside of the knife, fork on the left of the plate), and clearing the table after the meal were traditionally women's work, but she taught them to me. Had she, in years past, witnessed such good examples set by her father, and wanted to pass them on to me? Or had her father been lax in these areas, instilling in her a need to break a hereditary chain of male slothfulness? Perhaps, having been taught by her mother to be compulsively proper, she felt that her son should also be proper. At any rate, her early instruction saved me, later in life, from the embarrassment of wearing pink and red as part of the same outfit.

Chapter 4

Of Mice and Young Men

Vernon Walters, an older boy who lived at the west end of Steely Street, had a part-time job in the Purdue School of Agriculture where they experimented on white mice. He showed me the room full of cages where he fed the animals, kept their water bottles full, and cleaned their cages. The mice were large, their bodies perhaps four inches long with soft, pure white fur, and a pink tail that matched their eyes and was as long as their bodies. Vernon reached into a cage and grabbed one, and held it by the tail as he put it into my hand and showed me how to hold its tail so it couldn't get away. When I let go of the tail, it scurried up my arm where it sat on my shoulder. Long white whiskers on either side of its pink nose vibrated as it snooped around, sniffing at my ear.

Just to show off, Vernon demonstrated how he killed a mouse when a fresh corpse was needed for experimentation: He picked it up, held it firmly in his hand and dashed it, head first, against the concrete floor. When the stunned mouse tried to crawl, he picked it up and again threw it at the floor, even more vigorously. This time it stayed still. The university apparently had more mice than they needed.

While universities in the US experimented on mice and cattle to improve America's food supply and knowledge of nutrition, the Nazis, during the war, were damaging body parts and injecting diseases into their human cattle against their will. And in June of 1942 the mass murder of Jews by gassing began at Auschwitz. In our secure little corner of the world in central Indiana, researchers were merely concerned with such mundane investigations as the digestive processes of cows.

Back at home, I begged my parents to let me have a white mouse for a pet. "Please, Vernon said he could give me one," I pleaded. My parents eventually relented, and Vernon brought one home for me. I named it Snoopy. Dad came up with an old birdcage from somewhere, and Vernon gave me a water bottle that, when mounted upside down in the cage, let the mouse get drops by putting its mouth against the open end of a small protruding glass tube.

For the several weeks that I cared for Snoopy, I kept his water bottle full and put wheat or oats into his cage. But the attention span of small boys is limited, and I eventually ran out of friends to show him to. This early experience with pet rodents was to prove invaluable when, years later, I became a parent.

I have no memory of how my association with Snoopy ended, but there are several possibilities. Mom was not a fan of Snoopy. Her nurturing instincts did not extend to mothering mice, but I very much doubt that she would have engineered his "disappearance." He might, however, have escaped and disappeared. Or, given his probable lack of a balanced diet, he might have died and been buried somewhere in the wilderness of our back yard, perhaps beneath the wild cherry tree that held my tree house, his grave affording him an ideal view of the cow pasture that abutted our back lot, and the opportunity to spend his eternity watching much larger four-legged critters chew their cud.

Chapter 5

Stepping on Cracks

I n early 1940, while rationing was beginning in Britain due to Nazi blockades of shipping supply channels, I was learning to follow rules. On the way to and from school, I was told by the other kids that if I stepped on a crack I would break my mother's back. The peer pressure associated with this rule kept all the sidewalk cracks in town safe from any possibility of being covered by my shoe soles.

As the Nazis invaded France, Belgium, Luxembourg, Denmark, Norway, and the Netherlands, and Winston Churchill became the British Prime Minister, the wisdom of the ages was floating in the air around us, like perfume, and kidspeak became our language. The adults stood on the periphery, hiding amused smiles. We learned to follow the rules because everyone did, didn't they?

In July, as the Battle of Britain began, when instructed to take two giant steps forward, I never, ever did so without first asking, "Mother, may I?" In September the U.S. Congress passed the military conscription bill, making males between the ages of 21 and 30 eligible for the draft, while on Steely Street we followed the rule that said a game of tag had to start with choosing someone to be IT: One potato, two potato, three potato, four; Five potato, six potato, seven potato, more—

You're IT!" No one ever argued with the outcome unless the kid doing the counting messed up and didn't do it right.

As the political campaign wore on through the summer, resulting in Roosevelt's re-election for a third term as president in November, we hid in the bushes next to someone's front porch, not coming out until the cry went out: "Alley, Alley Ox In Free!!"

Now and then, though, the adults generated the rules.

When I was told by my mother to stop crossing my eyes because they might get permanently stuck that way, it was a long time before I took an enormous and rebellious risk and crossed them again. We avoided germs by not drinking out of other people's glasses. When my farm cousins and their families all drank water from the same tin cup that hung on a hook by the back yard water pump, we were amazed that they remained healthy. Their day would come.

When the US entered the war, new rules governed the availability and use of everything that contributed to the war effort. Soon after the Japanese sneak attack on Pearl Harbor in late 1942, rationing began in the US. Tires, cars, fuel, shoes, sugar, coffee, and many additional food items were rationed, and we all had to abide by a host of new rules. Hoarding these items was unpatriotic, and our consciences prevented it. When paper became scarce, signs appeared on restroom paper towel dispensers, instructing us to "Blot, don't rub." If we blotted the water from our hands, more water would be absorbed and fewer paper towels would be required.

New rules were everywhere, and nobody complained; everyone followed the rules. When I asked for something that was in short supply, Dad said, "Don't you know there's a war on?" He participated in this training in more unorthodox ways. He told me that if you wanted to catch a bird, you first had to put salt on its tail. I guess I didn't follow that rule, because I never caught one. Or maybe I just didn't use enough salt.

Chapter 6

Two Shakes of a Lamb's Tail

I don't remember exactly how I first became aware of the passage of time. I suppose most children are affected by it when, as babies, they become hungry and start crying for food. It's unlikely that those memories stay with us, though. I know I haven't remembered any of them, at least not until I was a few years old and began to equate boredom with hunger. If I didn't have anything to do that would lengthen my short attention span, eating came to mind.

When I said, "Mom, I'm hungry," she knew that until the next meal was served, the best food was distraction.

"Would you like me to read you a book?" she asked.

"No, I'm hungry," I said.

The standard fussing and negotiating continued until she could get me motivated to do something, anything that would take my mind off my misery, my boredom, and my universal cure-all, food.

"Let's go build a road in your sandbox!" If that got my attention, to the sandbox we went, where a road was duly built for my toy car, but not until after we had combed our fingers through the sand to find any surprises the cat had buried there.

If it was almost time for a meal, her usual response to my declaration of hunger was, "I'll have lunch ready in two shakes of a lamb's tail."

Two Shakes of a Lamb's Tail

Everybody knew that "two shakes of a lamb's tail" was a pretty short amount of time, seeing as how lambs' tails moved back and forth very quickly. Her use of the phrase, though, had clever but sneaky aspects: First, it generated an image in my head that distracted me from the vacuum in my stomach, and secondly, it was non-specific; I couldn't complain that she had passed her promised deadline.

She used the lamb's tail time scale for a variety of purposes. If we were going to the store and Dad said, "Let's go get in the car," Mom might reply, "I'll be there in two shakes of a lamb's tail," as she hurried off to get her purse or go to the bathroom.

If I asked her to tie my shoe because it took too long for me to do it, she said, using her perpetually positive demeanor, "You can do it! It'll only take two shakes of a lamb's tail." No task was impossible, and those that were nearly so just took a little more confident optimism.

There was one situation, though, that required a lot more time and patience than two shakes of a lamb's tail. I was almost six when my brother, John, was born. We spent the first few weeks trying to make him smile, and feeding and bathing him.

John was born with limited skills that included sucking on his bottle and filling his diaper. Crying hard was another major talent. Whenever Mom changed his diaper, his face got red, his eyes squinched shut, and his squalling could drown out a motorcycle. We noticed at those times that his scrotum swelled up and got bigger than an egg.

"The doctor says that he was born with a hernia," Mom said. "The swelling happens because he strains when he cries, and some of his insides go down there and need to be pushed back up inside."

At first, she showed me how she did it, pressing gently and all the while trying to calm him so he'd stop crying. Then she taught me how to do it, slowly, gently, while being really nice to him. "It's okay, John. Don't cry….. It'll be okay."

When he was about ten months old and could stand up in his crib, the doctor decided that it was time for him to have an operation to repair the hernia. He would be away from us in the hospital across town for two whole weeks—the same amount of time that Mom and he had been in the hospital when he was born. The worst part of it was that we wouldn't be able to visit him. Even Mom couldn't visit him, because if she did, he would probably cry when she left to go home, and the strain it would put on his stitches could tear them open. That would be very bad, and we couldn't risk it.

At the hospital, I had to stay in the car while Mom and Dad took John in. While a nurse held him and played with him, Mom and Dad sneaked out of the room and back to the car. I'm sure the next two weeks were not easy for Mom, but she never let on. Her positive demeanor kicked into high gear and she was sure that everything would be all right, never for even a moment letting me feel any anxiety or loneliness. My biggest fear was that, with all the smothering attention he was getting to keep him from crying, he would be spoiled rotten by the time he came home. I doubt if I thought of this by myself. It's possible that Dad planted that seed in my mind during one of his humorous wise cracks designed to take Mom's mind off the dangers of the ether anesthetic and the operation.

The operation went well. Afterward our only concern was making it through the two-week recuperation period without his crying, and then getting him home.

When we were past the halfway point in the two weeks, Mom's friend, Dolores Gregg, whom John had learned to call "Doh," took Mom and me to the hospital to sneak a peek at John. The idea was that while we could see him, we couldn't allow him to see us because he might cry when we left. We were to stand in the hallway, and peek around the edge of the doorway to see him in his crib. I was told to make no noise, and under no circumstances was I to let him see me.

We tiptoed up to the door of his ward, and the nurse furtively pointed out the location of his crib. As I peeked around the door frame, I saw his crib ten feet away, against the wall. Mom and Mrs. Gregg stood behind me, and with their heads above mine and against the doorframe, did their own peeking.

John was standing cheerfully in his crib, holding onto the side rail, wearing a diaper and an underwear top, watching the other activity in the room as though he hadn't a care in the world. Just as each of us got a good look at him, he looked our way, and with a bright smile, said, "Hi, Mommy! Hi, Doh! Peekaboo!" Mortified, we ducked back behind the wall and retreated down the hall as though he could come after us.

We stopped and listened. No crying. His short attention span had served him well, and he had found something else to occupy his mind. The expected outburst didn't happen. We breathed a collective sigh of relief and left the hospital, pleased with our view of him that had lasted exactly two shakes of a lamb's tail.

Several days later John was home with us, healthy and happy, and with his stitches intact.

Chapter 7

Are We There Yet?

The scenery on the trip across western Indiana and into central Illinois in our 1937 Plymouth wasn't the most captivating, especially for a seven-year-old boy, but Mom, in her perpetual positive thinker's mode, made the trip bearable. Her bag of tricks to minimize boredom included counting cows, looking for Burma Shave signs, and finding the entire alphabet in the proper sequence on road signs, one letter at a time. After John abandoned his bassinet beside me on the back seat and started to read, he joined in the contests, which then got more competitive.

Each series of Burma Shave signs kept boredom at bay for at least a minute or two as I repeated what we had just read:

> **Burma-Shave**
> *Was such a boom*
> *They passed*
> *The bride*
> *And kissed the groom*

Or,

> *To kiss a mug*
> *That's like a cactus*
> *Takes more nerve*
> *Than it does practice*
> **Burma-Shave**

The lessons that resulted from those sign sightings were invaluable.

"Mom, why would anyone kiss a mug?"

The verses were in two general categories that promoted either the use of Burma-Shave shaving cream, or traffic safety.

> *Give hand signals*
> *To those behind*
> *They don't know*
> *What's in*
> *Your mind*
> **Burma-Shave**

A third category during the war had patriotic themes, promoting the sale of war bonds or making fun of Hitler or the "Japs." Some of the cleverest signs combined two themes:

> *Soldier*
> *Sailor*
> *And marine*
> *Now get a shave*
> *That's quick and clean*
> **Burma-Shave**

The Burma Shave signs became everyone's favorite advertising campaign as drivers around the country were entertained and kept awake on the road. The campaign began in the late 1920s and ended in the 1960s.

In Mom's eyes, the alphabet game was better because it kept us distracted for much longer. The first one to get all the way to Z won the game. We had to find each letter in sequence, somewhere in any sign along the road. X was not easy to find, but it might appear in the word "next" if we stayed alert. Q was the hardest letter to find, but we got past it if we spotted a gas station that sold Quaker State Motor Oil. Keeping quiet until someone shouted "Z!" gave us opportunities to fudge and skip a few letters that we hadn't really seen, but in our family cheating was unthinkable, and we never did.

These and other manifestations of Mom's positive thinking made the miles shorter, and the endless corn fields and cow pastures and occasional barns and tractors flew to our rear and out of mind. About halfway to our destination, where railroad tracks ran beside our road for miles, we passed sidings holding swarms of empty freight cars awaiting harvest time to descend on local grain elevators and haul to market their contents.

Pauses in our trip were now and then caused by the need for a rest room rather than by breakdowns or flat tires. If a gas station wasn't in sight and bladder capacity was minimal, or if John was screaming for a diaper change, we stopped by the roadside as far from any farmhouses as possible and tried to drown a few weeds or the timothy grass that grew there. The wind that rattled the corn leaves in the field beside the road spun the windmill on a distant farm as it pumped well water into a trough for the cows. The whine of an occasional car going by on the highway switched to a lower pitch as it passed us. Then the hum faded into the distance.

We climbed back into the car, leaving behind the meadowlarks singing to each other from power lines and fences, as the crows on telephone pole crossbars laughed at us for trying to hide between the open car doors as we relieved ourselves.

"Mom, I'm hungry."

"Grandma will give us some lunch when we get there."

> *She kissed*
> *The hairbrush*
> *By mistake*
> *She thought it was*
> *Her husband Jake*
> **Burma-Shave**

"Why would anyone kiss a hairbrush?"

"It's just a joke. His beard was so scruffy it looked like a hairbrush."

"Oh."

On one of these trips, a driver, whose car had a flat tire, waved us down. He needed a jack. Dad stopped, and used our jack to help the man change his tire.

"How much do I owe you?" the man said as he reached for his wallet.

"Nothing," Dad said and waved his hand at the man. "Just do the same for someone else sometime."

These semi-annual highway trips into Illinois to see Dad's family, and the annual ones on into Missouri to visit Mom's family, provided opportunities for serious conversations between my parents and me.

"What's that sticker on the windshield?" I asked.

"That's a gasoline rationing sticker."

"What's a rationing sticker?"

"It tells the gas station attendant what kind of rationing stamps we need to give him."

"Why do we need to give him stamps?"

"Because there's a war on."

"When will the war end?"

"Soon, we hope."

"Will I get to be alive in the year 2000?"

Mom and Dad thought about it. "He'll be 65 then," Mom said.

"We won't get to see it, but you might," Dad said.

During one trip, the discussion turned to the distinction between acceptable and unacceptable behavior.

"Always do what you think is right," Dad said. "You'll usually be correct."

> *"At ease," she said*
> *"Maneuvers begin*
> *When you get*
> *Those whiskers*
> *Off your chin"*
> **Burma-Shave**

"Dad, what's a maneuver?"

As we approached Minonk where my grandparents lived we all tried to be the first to spot the huge power line towers that stretched across the prairie a couple of miles outside of town.

As a tower peeked over the horizon above a corn field, the most alert among us won the contest by sing-song gloating:

"I see the highline! I see the highline!"

Looming over the horizon on the other side of town was the local "jumbo."

As the Native Americans who had roamed the prairie in the early 19th century were replaced by Polish, German, English, and Irish settlers, Minonk became home to those ethnic groups.

Many Poles became coal miners, Germans became farmers, and Irish worked on the railroads. As the mine seams were worked to their end over the decades, each mine closed, leaving behind a mountain of slag from the miles of underground tunnels . These "jumbos" were scattered about the central Illinois landscape, each next to a vertical coal mine shaft, separated from the next one by a few miles of corn or soybean fields. The jumbos, sometimes a hunting ground for fossil hounds where Dad once took me on an unsuccessful search, were generally invisible to the local population, no more annoying than a large barn or windmill. They were just there, unnoticed by most; isolated pimples on the endless, flat prairie.

Later, in 1989, the jumbos at Minonk and up the road at Rutland disappeared, their thousands of tons carried off to provide base material for interstate highway roadbeds and interchanges.

The high lines and the jumbo on the horizon told me that Grandma and Grandpa were just minutes away. I didn't need to ask: We were there.

My paternal grandmother, Ida Marie Emma Klesath, had first married a drunk named Tjark Hinrichs. They had two sons, Harma (pronounced "harmy") and Eddie. In 1902, when the boys were 10 and 7, they were left without a father when Tjark drank himself to death.

My paternal grandpa, Frederick Hesselberth, had first married Clara Lincoln. After a few years Grandpa divorced her for adultery after she ran off with his business partner. They had no children. In 1903, Frederick married Emma and they went on to have three children of their own: My Uncle Albert, born in 1904; my dad in 1907, and Sophia (so'-fee), known as Aunt Sue, in 1912.

I never met Eddie Hinrichs, who had left home early, and rarely if ever came back. Dad never talked about Eddie, but when I was older, Mom told me that Dad had never forgiven Eddie for not coming back to Minonk for his own mother's funeral.

Uncle Harma married Aunt Rachael and they had one daughter, Doris Ann, who was quite a bit older than I, so I never knew her well. She was a beautiful, quiet young lady who married and had one child after moving to Chicago. When I was twelve, my dad got a phone call from Harma after I was already in bed. I only heard part of one side of the conversation, but when Dad exclaimed, "Doris Ann!" I sensed that something bad had happened, but it wasn't until the next day that I found out she had died of a sudden heart attack. She was 25 years old.

Uncle Harma was a telegrapher for the railroad that ran through Minonk. The time or two that I visited his office, the clickety-clack of the telegraph key fascinated me. By then I had learned Morse code as a Cub Scout, but it was the version that used dots and dashes sent as a tone. These magic clicks that the railroad used were a mystery to me. Not only was the code different, but I couldn't understand how you knew which click began the dot or dash, and which click ended it. Dad told me that Harma was so good that he could send a message with one hand on the telegraph key at the same time he wrote down an incoming message with a pencil in the other hand.

With no radios or cell phones for communicating with the engineers of trains that didn't stop in Minonk, Uncle Harma had to pass messages to the speeding train by using a long pole. The paper message was attached to a loop of string that was held open by the Y-shape at the end of the pole. As the train approached, Uncle Harma held the pole up so the engineer could lean out from the window of his steam engine and put his arm through the loop of string as he whizzed through the station. If all went well, the pole remained with Uncle Harma, and the message, still attached to the loop of string, ended up in the engineer's cab. The information in the message was never revealed to me, but my imagination could provide possible contents: *You're ten minutes ahead of schedule, so you have time to stop your freight train at the next station to go to the bathroom.*

Entering Minonk (pop. about 2000), we drove over brick-paved streets for four or five blocks to Grandma and Grandpa's house. Grandpa (Dad called him "Pop.") usually didn't have much to say, but when he tried to give me a hello kiss, his mustache tickled me and I resisted, giving everyone something cute to chuckle about. Grandma greeted me with a hearty "My goodness, you're growing too fast! I'm gonna put a stone on your head!" I assumed that was a German saying that she had learned from her immigrant parents.

Entering the house from the front door put us in the sitting room with few chairs and the icebox-sized kerosene heater that kept the house warm in cold weather. It was placed in the sitting room so its output could migrate into the surrounding bedrooms and kitchen. When I first entered, the house had a peculiar odor that diminished as I grew used to it. In the corner was Grandpa's leather-cushioned Morris Chair, an early predecessor of today's Laz-E-Boy, that reclined if its resident pushed a recessed button in one of its wooden arms. When Grandpa wasn't around, my cousins and I took turns sitting in it, reclining it carefully so as not to knock over the brass spittoon that sat beside it.

The door to the attic stairs was in one corner of the sitting room and led to a dusty treasure trove of magical and mysterious items stored there. The stairs were ladder-like, so steep my parents wanted to be there to catch me if I fell. At the top was a jumble of old furniture, trunks and boxes containing mysteries that young boys weren't allowed to inspect, toys that my dad had outgrown, and a life-sized plaster phrenology head with sections of the brain engraved and labeled on its surface.

Phrenology was the science of the brain, whose originator, Franz Joseph Gall, in the late 1700s, theorized that the brain consisted of 27 separate "organs," each controlling a basic function of personality and intelligence such as affection and friendship, pride and arrogance, memory of words, kindness, poetical talent, and religion. As late as the early 1900s models of the human head were marked with each of these 27 areas of the brain, giving people maps so that they could locate the areas they wanted to develop more fully.

Grandma and Grandpa's bedroom was to the left of the front door, through a door next to the Morris Chair. To the right of the front door was the dark and rarely-used living room where Dad's old rocking horse had been put out to pasture to await the arrival of grandchildren. Behind the living room was a guest bedroom, and yet another bedroom beyond that, both previously used by my dad, Aunt Sue, and my uncles when they were young. The beds held large, straw-filled mattresses, and beside each was a night jar which avoided the need for nighttime trips to the back yard outhouse. Dad sometimes liked to activate Mom's sense of propriety by calling the night jar a "thunder mug."

Behind the sitting room was the kitchen with its corn-cob and coal-fired cook stove and a kitchen counter that Grandma called the "zink." I thought she was pronouncing "sink" with a German accent but later thought it equally likely that the metal counter top really was made of zinc. Beside the sink was a hand pump that furnished water from under the house where the cistern collected rain water from the roof, allowing the family to avoid the vile-tasting town water that came from wells in the area. During dry spells when the cistern was empty, we had no choice but to drink the town's smelly sulfur-water, which prompted Mom to bring with us a supply of odorless and tasteless West Lafayette water.

Under the large kitchen table was a metal wash tub that was pulled out for Saturday night baths, but only when we weren't visiting. Baths were a major undertaking. Water had to be heated to boiling on the cook stove and mixed in the wash tub with more cold water carried from the pump. I never learned the more intimate details. Did they flip a coin to see who got to use the bath water first? Did one of them bathe while the other poured cold water to wash away the soap? It seems only logical that they scrubbed each other's backs. And if they skipped their baths for a week or two because it was so much work, were there consequences?

Asking these questions didn't occur to me until I was much older and had deduced a probable cause for the strange fragrance in the house. But, as a small boy, when I asked my parents about it, they denied smelling anything unusual, and I thought no more about it. In later college years, when I had summer jobs in Peoria, Illinois, I noticed a similar smell when the breeze was in a certain direction on warm evenings—a sort of yeasty smell but not as pleasant as baking bread—that the locals thought might come from the local Hiram Walker distillery. Decades later, on a business trip to Peoria, I again noticed the odor, and was instantly transported back to my grandparents' house by the memories it triggered. By then I knew enough about the world to decide that the smell in my grandparents' house was that of people who didn't frequently bathe.

For the first few hours in Minonk we sat in the sitting room while the adults discussed boring stuff: What was new with the neighbors in Minonk? Who had moved, who was sick, and who had married whom? Farm talk, the corn crop, and of course the weather and how it affected the corn crop. As soon as I could beg Dad into it—anything to avoid the boring adult conversation—he took me out to "The Shop"—out the back door, past the summer kitchen to the back of the property near the outhouse, where there once had been a street with a store and a blacksmith shop, but was now just an alley with some abandoned buildings. One of those buildings was now—and by the look of it—had been since the dawn of civilization, Grandpa's Shop. Exploring it gave me the same feeling that I get as an adult when exploring a hardware store: a combination of exhilaration and wonder that such a diversified conglomeration of magnificent old tools and bins of gadgets and doodads could exist in one place. After a few minutes it was Dad's turn to get bored. He had been there before. He had grown up there and didn't need to explore that dusty old building full of unused furniture and abandoned junk. He finally convinced me to return to the house by bribing me with a few glass swirl marbles I had found in a cabinet drawer.

The dinner gathering on the first day in Minonk usually included only the Hesselberth side of the family—about 18 people in all.

The next day before we went to the Klesath family reunion in Dana, we stopped at Uncle Harma's and Aunt Rachael's home where I got to play with their little black Scotty dog. The obsessive mutt's favorite plaything was a number ten tin can with the ends cut out. Running at breakneck speed, the dog rolled the can across the lawn with its nose. If a bump in the lawn pushed the can off-center, the dog did a tight U-turn, came back to the can, and again zoomed over the lawn, nose to the ground against the can, pushing it ahead of him. We stood there watching in hilarious awe as the dog exhausted himself in joyful, single-minded, manic enthusiasm. The only way Uncle Harma could get the animal to stop was to pick up the can and hide it. As I petted the panting dog while he cooled down, I saw a callus on the top of his nose from rubbing on the rolling can, similar to the one Louis Armstrong developed on his lip from playing the trumpet.

At the Klesath family reunion (Klesath was Grandma's maiden name) we encountered a blizzard of Dad's cousins, their spouses, and their offspring. The big event was usually held at the town park or schoolyard in Minonk or Dana. All those noisy farm folks with their spouses and children had quite a time at the gatherings, but they managed to scare the dickens out of the meek little "city boy," as they thought of me.

During the war years, we went to Minonk only when we could save enough rationing coupons to make the 280-mile round trip to Illinois from our home in Indiana. Most of the men of my dad's generation were too old to be drafted, and their offspring were far too young, so nearly everyone attended. Dad's cousins included Bill Marston, who had attended the University of Illinois with him, and who later went on to become Chicago's commissioner of streets and highways under Mayor Richard Daley. Then there was Ronnie Coons, who was married to Dad's cousin Juanita. He was likely to say anything that popped into his head, and he said it loudly whether it was ordinary or scatological, without regard for whoever might be listening.

One cousin, Gayle, was confined to a wheelchair. He was unable to hold his head up or even feed himself, although he always seemed to be in good humor. His parents could understand his speech, but I couldn't. He died while still in his twenties or thirties. I can still see the reclining wheelchair, which must have been built in the early part of the century and was mostly made of wood and wicker.

The picnic meal at those events was always spectacular, putting today's restaurant Sunday brunches and buffet meals to shame. It was a potluck dinner, and each of the women brought two or three dishes that were set out on long tables. Those who had just butchered a cow or killed and cleaned some chickens brought meat dishes. The rest brought far too many salads, vegetables, fruit, and deserts. My farm cousins were big eaters. They put away about four times as much as I could in half the time and then teased me about being such a light eater.

While the women prepared the meal, my cousins and I played on the playground merry-go-round, teeter-totters, and swings. The dads talked about their Chevy automobiles and their John Deere or Farmall tractors and whether they would pull a four-bottom or six-bottom plow. Those machines were especially well-cared-for during the war, due to limited availability of new ones.

After dinner there was always a business meeting where letters from absent cousins were read, new births and marriages were announced, and the family whose turn it would be the following year to host the reunion was named. Then any children whose mothers could cajole them into reciting a poem or performing in some other manner would entertain for a while. When I was about six, my mother taught me "The Owl and the Pussy Cat," and I actually got up in front of all those strangers and recited the whole thing.

By the time I was in upper high school and then college, I lost interest in attending the reunions. I was well over 40 by the time I started attending again when my wife, Marianne, and I became interested in genealogy. After researching the life of my immigrant great grandfather, John (Johann) Klesath, I prepared a presentation for the Klesath family reunion. I tracked his travels while in the Union Army during the Civil War. No one in the family had done that before, at least partly because they couldn't find his trail. When he had volunteered in 1861, they signed him up as John "Clezott" and that was how he was known until his discharge five years later. His name had been recorded as some clerk heard it spoken in Great Grandfather's German accent. It was only by accident that I found his name in his unit personnel list.

The trail started in Illinois, went down the Mississippi with Grant's army to Shiloh and then to a hospital in Memphis when he got sick. From there, he was transferred to the Washington, DC-based "Invalid Corps" (later to be known as the Veterans' Reserve Corps) where he guarded the White House and the Secretary of War's house. My one-hour presentation was a popular success, and for two or three more years I returned to present my latest research findings. By then the attendance at the events was falling off as fewer and fewer of the original 36 cousins were still alive.

My presentations included how he met his wife, the daughter of another member of his army unit, in Washington DC at the end of the Civil War, where her family had come from in Switzerland, and the fact that my father's mother had been named after one of her aunts who had also come from Switzerland. (No two related people could possibly be named Ida Marie Emma unless the younger one was named after the older one.) We also found that the family name had been Klevesath in Prussia. The immigrant's shortened and newly invented name explains why there are no unrelated Klesaths. The couple returned to the Illinois farm and produced fourteen children, ten of whom lived past infancy. Nine of those children produced the thirty-six first cousins, including my dad. The chart showing descendants of John Klesath and their spouses now contains hundreds of people, dozens of different names, and reaches down to the seventh generation.

As the reunion gathering broke up and the relatives headed for home, we too said our goodbyes and drove back across the endless prairie farm country to our home in West Lafayette.

Steely Street at War

Don't stick
Your elbow
Out so far
It might go home
In another car
Burma-Shave

Car in ditch
Driver in tree
Moon was full
And so
Was he
Burma-Shave

Altho
We've sold
Six million others
We still can't sell
Those coughdrop brothers
Burma-Shave

Chapter 8

Farming Facts of Life

For a few summers in the 1940s my country cousins put up with their Indiana "city boy" cousin on their central Illinois farms for a week at a time. It was like a week of summer camp before I was old enough for summer camp, and I begged my parents to leave me there and come back for me a week later. During those summer interludes, my cousins trained me in the obligations and delights of rural living. I, like Mark Twain, learned right away to tell a cow from a horse, and I was anxious to learn more.

American farmers were making big strides in food production techniques in the 1940s and were learning to rotate crops to avoid "wearing out the land." Corn was still the primary crop in the region, but as soybean yields improved with the help of plant breeders at major Midwestern universities, rotating between the two crops became the norm. Uncle Albert was mightily impressed by the new strain of disease resistant soybeans that had been developed by Dr. Al Probst, a Purdue professor of agronomy who lived across the street from us in West Lafayette after we left Steely Street.

At the farm, I shared a double bed with my cousin Fred, but his room had no curtains or shades on the windows. I was troubled by this exposure to the public, even though the nearest house that might contain any public was a mile away, and it was unlikely that anyone would wander past the farm to see what a city boy looked like in his skivvies. Still, Fred's sister, Margie, and his mother, my Aunt Zora, were somewhere around the house, and what assurance was there that one of them wouldn't accidentally peer into Fred's second-floor bedroom while climbing around on top of the hen house? Fred wasn't concerned about this risk.

Before we got ready for bed, we had to visit the two-holer outhouse. If the sun had already gone down, a flashlight was a required accessory and made it easier to read the Sears, Roebuck catalog that was a permanent fixture lying beside the seats, always handy in case we wanted to order something from it. At first I was puzzled by the many pages that had been torn out of it, but soon figured out why. For those who might wonder in these days of ubiquitous toilet tissue, the catalog pages were not non-skid as has been widely reported, but were definitely non-absorbent. It was rumored on the farm that corn cobs not needed as fuel for the kitchen cook-stove were available for emergency use in the outhouse. I never personally saw a supply of them there, although I suspect that the origin of the simile "as rough as a cob" stems from this usage. If not, why would anyone even notice a corn cob's roughness? My mother, learning refinement as the wife of an assistant professor at Purdue, brought her own supply of toilet tissue when we visited Dad's Illinois relatives.

A few miles away, the outhouse on Aunt Sue's farm had a classy feature: beside the requisite two seats was a smaller third one, lower to the floor, for small children. It was the ultimate in modern farm luxury and a testament to Uncle Raymond's craftsmanship. A three-year-old could use the facility at the same time as a parent, and the parent, relieved of responsibility for preventing the child from falling through the larger adult seat into the abyss below, could concentrate on his or her own reason for being in the building.

Early on I learned to take deep breaths before entering the outhouse, and to avoid breathing while inside. The feculent aroma that lived in the building made eyes water and assaulted olfactory nerves in ways never encountered by a city boy accustomed to indoor plumbing. I needed no instruction to avoid loitering in there.

Each cousin, when he got old enough, was assigned "chores" that had to be done at the appropriate times, no matter what else was going on. Fred had to feed the chickens, which had the run of the barnyard, by throwing grain around on the ground for them to peck at and fight over. If they ingested barnyard grit and dirt in the process, that was ok, too. It just went into their craw to help grind up the grains of corn or oats they found. Fred had to gather the eggs that were provided each day by the more generous of the hens. When I helped him gather eggs I had a problem to solve if a hen was sitting on one and didn't want to get off. Fred knew just how to handle the situation, but I got pecked by the hen. Chickens are not the brightest creatures in the barnyard, but motherly instincts are pretty basic. The gloomy interior of the henhouse was lined with shallow boxes attached to the walls where the hens could nest. After my eyes adjusted to the dim light, I saw a few hens that watched me with suspicion.

If there was a hen in its nest, there were good odds that there was an egg under her. One or the other of her beady yellow eyes, one on each side of the head, saw everything. When I tried to sneak my hand under her, she spotted it right away, cocked her head to focus the nearest eye on it, and prepared to defend her territory.

She had an attitude that said, "This is my egg, I saw it first, and you can just get out of here! If that hand gets any closer, it should prepare to be seriously perforated."

Fred, the bold, confident farm boy, either shoved her off the nest amid flapping of wings and lots of clucking and squawking and just took the egg, or else he inserted his hand under her and nabbed the egg before she could peck him. He got what he had come for before the hen realized what he was up to; whereas I, the timid city boy, thought first to protect my hands and forearms from lifelong scars and pockmarks and thereby forfeited the advantage of surprise.

I best liked collecting eggs from nests on which no chicken sat, but I still had to learn the difference between a "china egg" and a real one. Each hen had its own favorite nesting box in the hen house. Being creatures of habit, the hens always came back to the same nest to lay their eggs, so it was easy to identify the birds that were not productive. The occupant of a nest in which no eggs appeared for a few days was at risk of being cooked by Aunt Zora and eaten. But first, an inducement was offered: China eggs were fake ceramic eggs that were put into a less productive nest to fool the hen into laying more. The farmer who used them hoped that mama hen would see an egg already in the nest, forget that she hadn't actually produced it herself, and think up a second one to keep the first company.

Out in the barn, major adventures awaited. First I had to help Fred bring the cows home from their pasture where, after their morning milking, they had taken a twelve-hour lunch while they contemplated and ruminated. When we got out to the pasture, the herd was already waiting patiently at the gate, having been told by an internal timekeeper somewhere deep in their lethargic brains that it was time for their evening milking. When the gate was opened for them they took a bucolic stroll back to the barn on the other side of the next field. After the last cow cleared the gate and Fred had closed it, we followed along behind the herd, being careful not to step in any gifts they left for us. Uncle Albert's cows had never exhibited a need in their diet for stool softeners. The cows waited at the barn for Fred to open the door. Inside, each cow headed for a vacant milking station and upon arrival put her head through a locking device that, when closed, kept her submissively standing in one place eating hay or chewing her cud until after she was milked.

The milk from the eight or ten cows was accumulated in ten-gallon milk cans and taken to the basement of the house. The family drank some of the fresh, unpasteurized milk before it was separated. I didn't appreciate its raw taste, but if I was thirsty, my primary alternative was to drink the farm's smelly well water. They separated the remaining milk, took the cream into town, and sold it to the grocery store. The less valuable skimmed milk became pig food.

The job of milking each of the cows was shared by Uncle Albert and his older children, but most of the actual work was done by Albert. Sitting on his low stool beside the stern end of the cow, his forearms bulging like Popeye's, building muscle power as he alternately squeezed and pulled, squeezed and pulled—left, right, left, right, until the bucket under his hands was nearly half full. Then, being an equal-opportunity milker, his hands moved over to the other pair of teats (Each cow was required to have four, but Fred told me that a neighbor had once owned a cow with six. He didn't tell me whether she produced fifty percent more milk.) and exercised them until the bucket was filled. I watched, awash in a variety of barn aromas, mostly sour milk with a tangy edge of cow manure, and overlaid with just a hint of eau de hay. I stood among an assembly of barn cats that materialized out of the gloomy, hidden corners of the building as soon as the milking began. They were more intensely mesmerized than I by the unceasing rhythm of his hands and the musical notes produced by the milk streams when he started with an empty bucket. The notes became lower as the bottom was covered, until all that remained of them was rhythmic gurgling as the bucket slowly filled.

To amaze me even more, Albert stopped filling the bucket and aimed the udder in his right hand at the head of a watchful cat and squeezed. As the stream of milk reached the cat, its mouth opened and it rapidly lapped and swallowed, working its way upstream toward the source. When the stream stopped, the cat waited for more, but Albert wasn't one to waste milk. The cat's next meal would be a mouse or a rat caught in a dark corner of the barn.

When I confidently asked if I could try milking, Albert moved off his stool and put an empty bucket under the cow. I sat down, grabbed two of the cow's handles and squeezed them alternately, but nothing happened.

"Here, let me show you," Fred said.

He reached in, grabbed a teat, and produced a strong stream and a perfectly pitched A-flat as it hit the bottom of the bucket. I tried again. This time I both squeezed and pulled down, coaxing three reluctant drops into the bucket. The cow looked back at me and frowned. I was a failure as a milker.

Years later, after I had studied physics and hydraulics, I knew the reason for my lack of talent: The hands must do more than just squeeze and pull. Since the cow doesn't have four built-in check valves, the milker's hands must also provide that function, allowing the liquid to move only one way—downstream but not upstream. I guess Fred and Uncle Albert didn't have time to teach me those subtleties, or else they were afraid that my lack of sensitivity and hand-eye coordination would annoy the cow so much that she would go dry.

The hay mow was a wondrous place in the upper level of the barn, where we could hide behind straw bales and shoot imaginary guns at Japs, Germans, or each other, or climb to the top of stacked bales and play king of the mountain. One year I stayed at the farm of my Aunt Sue and Uncle Raymond, at least partly because their well water tasted marginally better than the vile, mineral-laden water that Aunt Zora and Uncle Albert's well produced. My cousin Ray and I played longer than we should have in their hay loft, and I spent a sleepless night sneezing and wheezing from the resulting case of "hay fever." After that, I stayed out of hay lofts.

I envied my cousins because of all the farm machinery they got to play with. Fred and his older brother, Bill, learned how to drive the family's 1938 John Deere tractor as soon as their legs were long enough to reach the clutch and brake pedals. My cousin, Ray, was equally fortunate and got to drive Uncle Raymond's 1939 Allis-Chalmers. When Fred and Uncle Albert let me try it, I wasn't strong enough to depress the clutch pedal to put the tractor in gear. It was probably just as well — I might have put the tractor into the creek and frightened the catfish that lived there. Fred and I once caught some of those fish under the bridge where the road crossed the creek, and Aunt Zora cooked them for supper.

The meals cooked by both Aunt Zora and Aunt Sue were the best ever tasted by a young city boy, especially at family gatherings where there were far more dishes to pass than there were people to eat their contents. Aunt Sue's creamy coleslaw with its perfect blend of magical seasoning is still the standard by which I judge coleslaw quality, and finding an equal has been an elusive goal.

Much of the food eaten on the farm was produced right there in the fields and gardens surrounding the house. When meat was needed for dinner, the family killed a chicken. The biggest problem was catching the chicken. Once caught, its head was held down on the chopping block between two ten-penny nails that prevented lateral movement while someone operated the ax that removed it. The chicken holder needed to keep a tight grip on the animal for a while after the deed was done. If the chicken slipped away, it would run around headless in the barnyard for a while, leaving a trail of blood here and there before it finally collapsed. Grandma Hesselberth had legendary ability to behead a chicken without the use of ax or chopping block. She just picked up the chicken and without blinking wrung its neck with her bare hands, unfazed by its squawking remonstrances and flapping wings. The squawking stopped as soon as its head was off in her hand, but the flapping subsided later as Grandma held the bird away from her by its neck stub to keep from getting blood on her dress.

A more special occasion was the butchering of a cow. A couple of male relatives or neighbors showed up on the appointed day to help. They led the cow out of the barn into the barnyard with a rope around its neck and a second rope was attached when it arrived at the designated execution spot. One man held the rope on the cow's left, and another man held the rope on the right so that the cow's head couldn't move.

My cousin Ray told me that he always turned away before the cow was shot. He didn't consider it a pleasant spectator sport, but, of course, I wanted to watch since I had never witnessed such an event.

The two men on either side of the cow pulled their ropes taught, looking like they were having a stationary tug of war, the winner of which would get the cow's head. The cow, unable to move and not liking this at all, obligingly lowered its head until its chin nearly touched the ground. Uncle Albert walked up in front of the cow, carefully aimed his rifle down at the cow's forehead with the muzzle inches away, and fired a single shot. Simultaneously with the crack of the rifle, the cow's legs collapsed, the shot echoed off the barn wall, and the animal hit the ground with an earthshaking thump as clouds of dust rose from the barnyard dirt underneath. Then all was quiet as the dust settled.

It was then clear to me why Ray didn't like to watch a large animal die. I turned and walked away, hoping no one saw the tears in the corners of my eyes. I stayed in the house while the men skinned and butchered the cow.

A few pigs were raised on the farm, but I never saw one butchered, which suited me just fine. They were not very sympathetic animals, making a terrible mess of the pen where they lived. One of the daily chores was "slopping the pigs" wherein the household garbage, skimmed milk, spilled grain, and any other miscellaneous detritus that had once been alive, was put into the feeding trough. The pigs then acted like pigs, sometimes climbing right into the feed trough to wallow and root around in the delectables found there.

Fred once asked me if I had ever seen pigs "do it." By then I was old enough to know what he referred to. I had never seen pigs so engaged, so he explained to me that once started, they continued, on and off, for hours with endless enthusiasm. The activated male member was "very long and skinny" with a "crook" in the end of it, the purpose of which was unknown. I pondered this information with a proper amount of wonderment and disbelief, but could add no supposition or theory to explain the puzzle. I later posited that, after such unmitigated usage, the organ might have worn out and broken, and then, lacking a splint or a cast, had healed badly. I was unable to verify this, but much later I did confirm Fred's description by reference to a more formal authoritative source.

The "crook" that Fred described is more accurately called a twist, similar to a partial twist of a drill bit or an auger. The sow's cervix is especially suited to receive and lock onto this anatomical anomaly as it is inserted with a twisting motion by the amorous boar who can, only then, achieve fulfillment. It is believed, by those familiar with this quirk of nature, that this was the origin of the common and salaciously descriptive usage of the verb, "to screw."

If my stay at the farm coincided with the run of the Illinois State Fair in Springfield, my parents gave me ten dollars to spend there before they left to go back home for the week. The trip was less than two hours away in Uncle Raymond's 1938

Chevy, or, after the end of the war, in his 1948 Hudson with the "step down" body. My ten-dollar bill was gone well before the day was over.

The midway dazzled me with its strange characters and tempting ways to donate my money. In the background the steam calliope promoted a festive atmosphere, while barkers lured people into tents to view freak shows featuring a dog-faced boy, a sword swallower, a pair of Siamese twins, a fat lady, or someone who was half man, half woman. Other barkers tried to get me to spend my money on a kitchen tool that slices and dices, or a ring-toss or rifle-shooting gallery where it was nearly impossible to win a stuffed animal. The bumper cars were my favorite ride, and absorbed most of my cash. My cousins and I weren't allowed into the "hoochie-koochie" shows, but we were fascinated by the pretty ladies who stood outside to lure customers while the barker pointed out their features and abilities with his cane and his patter. I really didn't mind being barred from their show tent — it couldn't have been as much fun as giving my cousins whiplash in a bumper car.

At the end of an exhausting day we returned to the farm, dozing in the back of the car, our dreams filled with ring-tosses and bumper car crashes, and our stomachs with hot dogs, cotton candy, and snow-cones.

Each summer, at the end of my week on the farm, my parents returned to Illinois to bring me back home to Indiana, where, for the remainder of the year, I studied the three Rs instead of cow milking and pig anatomy.

Today that central Illinois farm country is a different place. You can drive for miles and never see an animal on any farms, except for an occasional dog in a yard or a woodchuck beside the road. The fertile farmland produces such prodigious amounts of valuable field corn and soy beans that the labor-intensive raising of cattle, pigs, or chickens is no longer economical. Because the animals are gone, farmers can take vacations, and fences are no longer needed. Getting rid of the fences eliminates the need to control the weeds along them, and allows crops to be planted right out to the drainage ditches beside the roads.

The corn grows to ten or twelve feet in altitude and is planted, fertilized, and harvested by enormous $300,000 combines with air conditioned, stereo-enhanced cockpits suspended ten feet above the ground over monster, six-foot diameter tires. Automatic transmissions have eliminated the need for clutch pedals that small boys can't depress, and computerized GPS satellite receivers tell the pilot where and how much to fertilize in each section of a field based on last year's grain production in that section. The soil is no longer plowed, so that less of it washes down the Mississippi River and into the Gulf of Mexico. When corn and soy beans are harvested, only the grain is collected by the combine, which then grinds the remainder of the plant into fragments and deposits it back on the soil, leaving the farmland richer. Barns are replaced by huge metal buildings that house machinery instead of cows, and their interior fragrance is markedly improved.

Chapter 9

Pride Goeth

It was beautiful. Maroon with cream-colored trim; no one had ever seen such a beauty. The tires were fat, the electric horn was loud and resonant, powered by a dry-cell in the tank in front of the seat, and the coaster brake was smooth and whisper silent. A coil spring shock absorber was mounted prominently where the front wheel fork connected to the frame, giving the rider some isolation from bumps, potholes, and curbs that got in the way, and the chain guard prevented the rider's pants cuff from getting caught in the front sprocket and causing a wreck. It was the latest in Schwinn high-tech cycling, and was my very first bicycle.

Arnold, Schwinn and Company had captured a large part of the growing U.S. bicycle market in the early part of the twentieth century, and by the beginning of World War II was the most famous bike manufacturer in the country. Bicycles became a more important mode of transportation as gasoline was rationed and the automobile manufacturers produced tanks, jeeps, and airplanes during the war. The Schwinn brand in the 1940s was aggressively promoted by ads showing nearly every famous movie star in Hollywood riding their Schwinn and touting its smooth ride, its high quality, and its easy pedaling: Dorothy Lamour in shorts, emitting glamour as she held the handlebars of her Schwinn; Ronald Reagan and Jane Wyman taking a ride together on their his and hers Schwinns; and Roy Rogers on his bike, telling his horse, "Next to riding you, Trigger, there's nothing like riding a Schwinn."

Mom and Dad had resisted buying me a small beginner's bike, pointing out that I would soon outgrow it. Why not just wait until I was big enough to ride a full-sized 26-inch bicycle, and save the expense of buying a small one? *Wait until I was big enough? That could take forever.* They had condemned me to riding my tricycle that I had already outgrown, and to begging for rides on the bikes of older friends. But somehow Mom's positive demeanor prevailed, and I accepted my fate. When my own bike finally arrived on my ninth birthday the next year, the world turned brighter. I bounded out of bed with more enthusiasm every morning, and it took longer to go to sleep at night.

Dad held the bike upright and kept it calm while I climbed on. He ran beside us as we wobbled down the sidewalk in front of our house. At first he held on to the back edge of the seat to prevent an immediate wipe-out. As the bike grew used to me on top of it, my confidence grew, and Dad released his grip for a few seconds at a time, then longer, and finally, as I began to lose patience with him for hanging on so much, he let go and stood watching. The bike was bigger than I was, so getting on and off was no simple matter. Sure, I could keep going for a while if Dad held the bike for me as I got on. But then what? Our Steely Street front yard was banked where it met the sidewalk, offering the equivalent of a landing step where I could put my foot down as we stopped and tipped over, as well as a soft place to fall if I didn't coordinate the process.

Getting up and onto the bike by myself was more complex. The bike much preferred that I get onto it from the left side. If I tried mounting from the right side, it shied away and threatened to tip me off. With my left foot on the left pedal, I set the bike in motion by pushing off with my right foot and swung it up over the rear wheel, over the chest-high seat, and finally over the "crotch-killer" bar to the right side, where it would, if I was lucky, find the right-side pedal before the crash came.

The protections against injury while riding a bike were minimal. Some bikes had no chain guard, and to forget to wear your pants clip, or at least roll up your pants leg, was to invite serious trouble. A pants cuff caught between the chain and the sprocket was the equivalent of having your right ankle suddenly and tightly handcuffed to the frame, leaving the rider unable to pedal or brake. The only solution was to fall off the bike, hopefully to the left where your free leg and foot could cushion the landing. My chain guard protected me against that disaster.

The bar that ran from below the center of the handlebar to just below the front of the seat presented a significant risk. Toe clips and straps on the pedals had not yet been invented. Woe be unto any rider who allowed his foot to slip off the pedal without the seat firmly underneath him. Girls weren't exposed to this risk as their bikes had no such bar. It never made much sense to me that boys, who had the most personal equipment at risk, were subjected to this danger, while girls were not.

Helmets were for football players and soldiers only. Only race riders wore helmets on a bike, and any sissy who wore one on a street bike would have been laughed out of town.

Bicycles were not completely devoid of safety protections. Many bikes had a bell or a horn that warned others that you were in their vicinity. In later years, after the expensive battery was depleted, I had a mechanical ah-oogah horn on my handlebar. Chain guards were becoming standard equipment on all the new bikes, and rear view mirrors were an accessory mounted on many.

About the time I started riding without the benefit of my dad's assistance, he took me to the town hall to get the bike licensed. We registered it with the police, in return for which I got my own tiny license plate to mount on the rear of the bike, either under the back of the seat, or on the rear fender. I was required to obey the same traffic rules as cars, use my hands to signal turns, and have my light on if I rode after sundown.

My bike became my primary mode of transportation. I got a padlock with a long shackle to fasten a wheel so it wouldn't turn, in case someone else took a liking to it when it was parked at school, in front of a store, or in someone else's driveway.

Then I saw someone else riding their bike without holding the handlebars. Of course, I had to try it too. I began by keeping my hands almost touching the handlebars for a few seconds at a time. Then longer. I found that I could steer without holding the handlebar by leaning my weight slightly left or right, being careful not to over steer. As long as I was moving fast, it was easy to ride with no hands.

I grew bolder. When all the neighbor kids were out playing in the street before sundown on a warm autumn evening, I raced down the block, taking advantage of the slight downhill slope of Steely Street, my arms stretched wide and the wind in my face, in a perfect showoff version of "Look Ma, no hands!"

"Wheeeeee!" I sang as my bike and I became one, flying through the universe without a care, observed by the rest of the world for whom I performed.

Georgianne May had hold of my feet and one of the other bigger kids held my shoulders. I was howling in pain as I was carried back up the street to my house where Mom applied first aid to the bleeding scrapes all over my face. Merthiolate stung. As my crying subsided, I remembered flying down the street and then nothing more until I was carried home. I had done a face plant on the pavement when I lost control of the bike, with no serious damage to my body except my face.

Every boy falls down and skins his knee or his elbow at one time or another. It's what knees and elbows are for as you grow up. Few boys skin their face in eight or ten places, and then have to live with humiliating disfiguration for the next several weeks while the scabs decide to fall off. I couldn't very well walk around with a bag over my head, so I just had to endure.

"What happened to you?" a classmate asked.

"I fell off my bike," I said, and for a while my anonymity was erased.

"Ooooh! Did it hurt?" she asked.

My beloved bicycle miraculously was spared this mortification, the only serious damage being misaligned handlebars which Dad easily straightened. From then on, I was more careful about holding the handlebars, and the bike never again threw me off.

Chapter 10

Grandma and Grandad King

My mother's father was Joe Wilbur King, a mailman in Trenton, Missouri. We saw him only once each summer, when we made the all-day drive of 350 miles in our 1937 Plymouth from West Lafayette, Indiana to Trenton to visit him and Grandma King for a week. To make the all-day automobile trip go faster we played our usual road sign alphabet games, counted cows, and kept our eyes peeled for Burma Shave signs.

When Mom once took me to Trenton by train to visit her parents, we went from Lafayette to Chicago and then changed trains for the longer part of the trip to Missouri. The overnight part of the trip was spent in bunks that folded out where our seats had been. The restrooms on the train had a rule that the toilet couldn't be used when the train was stopped in a station because when flushed, the toilet dumped right down onto the tracks.

The Kings had married in the summer of 1906, and the following spring started having babies. Grandad was earning fifty cents a day carrying the mail in Galt, Missouri, and my mother was their first daughter. They named her Merno, because Grandma had liked the name when she met someone with it.

In 1915, the Kings moved 14 miles west to Trenton when Grandad accepted an appointment as city mail carrier there.

They raised their four daughters at 1706 Moberly Street, the house where we always visited them.

Grandad King was the strong, quiet type, who was amused by most of life. A hint of a smile lived on his lips most of the time, except when the conversation was about Harry Truman.

Harry Truman had begun political life in Kansas City, just 100 miles southwest of Trenton, and Grandad had been aware of him for decades. Those decades included the political successes and excesses of the Pendergast machine, the back-room bosses that controlled the Democratic Party in Kansas City. Grandad considered them all to be crooked, and he hated Truman because he was a part of that machine and wouldn't have been elected to the U.S. Senate without the machine's blessing.

In Grandad's spare time he raised a few chickens on his two-acre lot at the edge of town, and each year he planted a large garden beside the house. The tomatoes were magnets that attracted my dad. After we arrived in Trenton and unloaded the car, Dad made a bee-line for the tomato patch, salt shaker in hand, to find the ripest, reddest tomato, which he ate like an apple. First, he had to lick a wet spot on the tomato skin so the salt would stick before he took his first bite. Grandma's part of the garden had several rows of Zinnias as high as my head that covered the entire red-yellow-white part of the spectrum. Between the rows there were always two or three large spider webs, each home to a big black and yellow "garden spider" that lurked in the center, patiently waiting to jump out at small boys and inject their bodies with painful poison before wrapping them in a cocoon of silk thread so that newly-hatched baby spiders could suck the juices from the trapped boy.

If I brushed the zinnias on my way down the aisle, it jiggled the spider web, setting off warning signals that told the spider to vibrate the web back and forth like a vertical trampoline. If the bug didn't come right into the web, the spider would move the web to the bug. Terrifying business for the surprised boy who wanted only to look at the flowers, not get trapped and have his juices sucked out.

The ground under the pear tree was another dangerous part of the yard. Fermenting fallen fruit attracted bees and wasps that gathered there and didn't want to leave. The ripe fruit still on the tree was delicious but could be sampled only after a grab-and-run maneuver to avoid getting stung by a drunken bee.

A safer part of the yard was the thicket of asparagus that grew each year next to the steps at the back door of the house. Grasshoppers by the dozen gathered there among the feathery foliage, presumably finding food and shelter, but also pairing off to copulate with abandon. Finding a pair of grasshoppers locked in carnal embrace, I risked getting tobacco juice¹ stains on my fingers when I pulled them apart to see what would happen and then felt guilty about ruining their day. Looking back on it, I can imagine the grasshoppers scowling at me as they spit their brown juice, saying "Hey, pervert, you're interrupting something important here!"

The multi-purpose building back by the alley housed several chickens, the one-holer privy, and the grandparents' Pontiac. It was Grandad's pet peeve that sparrows (the scourge of the earth, matched in depravity only by Harry Truman) liked to eat the grain they found in the chicken house. His solution to the mess they made while stealing their meals was to sneak up on the chicken house when the sparrows were inside and slam the door shut. Slipping inside, he caught the hapless birds, pulled their tail feathers out, and let them fly away without their rear stabilizers, wobbling like drunken sots.

---

¹ Grasshoppers spit "tobacco juice" as a defense mechanism. It stains the skin of small boys who catch grasshoppers in their hands. I became adept at grabbing the insect by its folded wings and held it away from me as it spat.

"That'll teach 'em," he said.

The privy was abandoned right after WWII, when an indoor bathroom was installed. That summer, the highlight of our visit was the new indoor toilet in what had been a closet next to the kitchen. We no longer had to use the chamber pot beside the bed if we had to go in the middle of the night. Even better, no one had to empty those pots the next day.

The water supply in Trenton was notable for its high chlorine content. Turning on a faucet brought forth the odor of a swimming pool. Even with this smell, Trenton water was far more drinkable than Minonk, Illinois water, where my other grandparents lived. Here in Missouri there was no sulfur-laced mineral smell and taste to make me gag.

Another difference we encountered in Trenton was the use of coins that divided the penny into tenths of a cent. Minted by the state of Missouri, they were denominated in two values: one mill and five mills. One mill was one one-thousandth of a dollar. At first, the coins were made of cardboard the size of a milk bottle cap, and later either plastic, red for one mill and green for five mills, or a grey metal, probably zinc, about the size of a nickel but thinner. The five-mill metal coin had a distinguishing hole through its center.

Production of these coins was started in 1935 when the state's 1% sales tax law was enacted, causing retailers to charge customers fractions of cents for low-priced items. The mill coins enabled more exact amounts to be charged, eliminating rounding errors. They were called "sales tax receipts" to get around the federal law that restricted to the federal government the minting of money. Their use continued until 1961. By the time I used them, the only ones in common use were plastic and metal.

The garage part of the outbuilding had housed the family cow when my mother was young. The milk donated by the cow was skimmed for its cream which was then poured over fresh strawberries that grew in the garden. Later, owning a car became more important and less work than keeping a cow, and since there wasn't room in the building for both, the car replaced the cow. Grandma learned to drive, but Grandad didn't feel the need. His feet could take him anywhere in town, just as they did every day when he delivered the mail. When he had been younger, just starting out as a mailman in Galt, Missouri, his feet had been just as important, even though he used a horse and buggy on rural routes and to deliver packages in town at Christmas time. When I knew him in Trenton, he walked all over town and knew everyone by name.

The family considered Grandad's feet to be the most important organs in his body, or so it seemed to me. One evening in the sitting room the discussion wandered to the importance of healthy feet. My feet and Mom's feet were narrow and required A-width shoes, which were hard to find in shoe stores. Mom sometimes needed AAA, or extremely narrow shoes if she wanted them to fit properly, and she even needed arch supports at times. Grandad's feet were ideal. The miles and miles of daily walking for his job kept them in perfect shape. He took off his shoes and socks to show us how fit his feet were.

"My feet have to be in good shape; I walk so far with the mail every day," he said.

"Just look at how his toes grip the floor," Grandma said.

We all looked at how his toes gripped the floor. Mom marveled at the way the end joints of his middle toes bent backward because his toes gripped the floor so hard.

Across the alley from the garage, Grandad had mounted a wren house and a bluebird house on the fence, and we were entertained during our summer visits by the birds that lived there.

Once in a while a stray hound dog wandered up the alley. It rarely got farther than the garage, for by then Grandad was shouting and throwing a stick or a corn cob at it.

"That's nothin' but an old skillet hound," he said. The definition of a skillet hound remained a mystery. Was it a dog that deserved to have a skillet thrown at him? Or perhaps a dog that came begging for the scraps left in the skillet at the end of a meal? I never found out.

One summer, when I was old enough to hold a fishing pole, Grandad took me fishing at the town reservoir. After a short while I was too bored with the whole process to stick with it, though Grandad continued to fish until I got *really* bored, but neither of us caught anything.

Over the years, I gradually became aware that Grandad chewed. Tobacco. Or probably snuff. Now and then he would get up out of his favorite chair and saunter out to the front porch to stand at the railing. I never saw him actually chew anything, or put any brown stuff into his mouth, and I never saw him spit. There were no spittoons in the house like my other grandfather had. There were no strange smells in the house, except for the chlorine smell of the water that came from the faucet, and no stains on his shirt, but when I got older, Mom admitted that her father used tobacco, but that he was very secretive and polite about it. Looking back, I have wondered how he managed to hide it when we were fishing at the town reservoir. Did he spit into the water so no one would step in it on the bank? Maybe he just swallowed when there was no porch railing to spit over and no bushes to keep small boys from stepping in it.

Grandma had been born Minnie Grace Mitchel in Urbana, Illinois in 1888. When I knew her, she painted for a hobby. Her oil paintings included several meticulously detailed pictures of sunflowers in a vase, and she painted a picture of a southwestern mission building from a post card. Her attention to detail carried over into the kitchen, where, after breakfast, she carefully tied shut with a piece of string each box of Wheaties and Grape Nuts cereal before putting it back in the cupboard.

My parents were mildly amused by these painstaking efforts to preserve the crispness of the cereal. Maybe the Wheaties required this protection from the elements, but who had ever heard of a limp Grape Nut? There must have been a practical requirement for keeping the cereal boxes closed, because manufacturers now build a closure into the box-top flaps of each and every brand of breakfast cereal, and today, at home, we carefully close each box before putting it back in the cupboard. I guess Grandma was on to something as she led the way for General Mills and Kellogg decades before they followed.

Grandma had an under-bite that caused her lower front teeth to close in front of her upper front teeth. It didn't hamper her speech or her eating, and I wouldn't have known about it if Mom hadn't told me. Grandma played the harmonica very well, but I never knew whether her underbite affected her virtuosity on the instrument.

During one of our summer visits, while I helped Grandma dry the breakfast dishes, she told me of something she had heard through the window over the kitchen sink. Grandad was working in the shrubs under the window, when he was threatened by an angry bee.

As he tried to brush it away, he muttered, "Damn bee!"

"It tickled me because he never swears," Grandma said, still chuckling about the event.

Arriving for another summer visit, we found that tendonitis in Grandma's forearm had become a problem. To avoid the pain, she stopped using that arm. The arm got weaker and eventually useless as it "froze" against her waistline where it stayed for most of every day. The next summer we arrived in Trenton to find an old flatiron rigged up with a rope and pulley between the colonnades that separated the front room from the sitting room.

In the 1940s electric irons were becoming common, and the old ones that were heated on the stove were often used as doorstops. Following instructions from the doctor, Grandad had rigged up one of those irons as an exercise weight for Grandma, and her arm was almost back to normal. Over the next few weeks and months she regained full use of the arm.

In 1952 Grandma contracted what is now called lymphoma, but then was reported to us as "lympho blostoma," a cancer of the lymph. At least that's what we understood it to be. She was bedridden and was reported to be doing very poorly, so we made our annual trip to Missouri a few months earlier than usual to see her. On arrival as we went up to the door we were surprised to see her looking hale and hearty as she opened the door to greet us. As we got closer we saw that it wasn't Grandma after all. It was Mom's Aunt Jenny, Grandad's sister, who had come to the house to sit with Grandad and help tend Grandma, who was in a coma. Grandma died that night before my bedtime. We had arrived just in time to help with the funeral arrangements.

Not knowing what I could do to help in such a sorrowful situation, I went to bed before the adults. After a while Mom came into my darkened room and, thinking I was asleep, allowed herself to break down and sob for a while. I wanted to comfort her, perhaps hold her hand, but knowing that she wouldn't want me to see her cry, I remained still as a mouse until she left the room.

Grandad sold the house and moved into an efficiency apartment in the Plaza Hotel in Trenton. He then spent his winters in Pomona, California to be near his two middle daughters who lived there a few houses from each other. During those 18 years Mom convinced him to come by train to visit us in West Lafayette a couple of times. He would never stay more than a week because, he said, "I have to get home to Trenton to check my mail." We figured he was not only bored and didn't want to intrude on us at our house, but that my brother and I probably drove him a little nuts with all our activities and comings and goings. He thought I was crazy for running laps around the tennis courts to stay in condition for tennis season.

He was known to enjoy "shaggy dog" jokes, but when we begged him to tell us one, he resisted, relenting only once:

"A family was at their Sunday dinner table," Grandad said, "passing the dishes of food around, when Uncle Jim put the bowl of mashed potatoes down in front of himself, picked up a wad of the gooey potatoes with both hands, and proceeded to rub them into his face. Everyone stared at him for a moment, then someone asked, 'Uncle Jim, what in heaven's name are you doin' with those mashed potatoes?' Uncle Jim looked around the table, then said, 'Oh... I thought they was parsnips.'"

Each morning at our breakfast table Grandad used a spoon to put copious amounts of jelly or jam on his toast. Mom had taught me to use a knife and to spread my jam thinly over my toast. She probably hadn't learned that from her father. He used so much jam that the rest of us looked at each other and rolled our eyes when he did it, but it wouldn't have been polite to say anything about it.

While he was there, he told me a story about how he got his name. His father was working on the railroad in Missouri when he was born, and named him Jose, after a much-admired Mexican co-worker. As Grandad got into school he was teased by the other boys who made fun of his name and mispronounced it "Hosie," and "Josie" as though he were a girl. The teasing prompted him to start going by the name "Joe." Grundy County, Missouri had not yet begun issuing birth certificates in 1880 when he was born, so no one could prove otherwise, and he remained Joe for the rest of his life. He had never spoken to his family regarding his early embarrassment about the name Jose, so my telling of his story was the first time they had heard it.

Joe King died of a stroke in his hotel room in 1970, less than three months before his 90th birthday.

Chapter 11

Dr. Frasch

He was short, pleasantly middle-aged, older than my parents, and bald except for a white fringe at the back and sides. Although it was probably a little oily, his soft, kindly voice was what the cliché author had in mind when he thought up "bedside manner." Think Liberace with no hair and no piano.

Upstairs in the Lafayette Life Insurance building, his sister Gwendolyn was his receptionist and secretary. She may have doubled as his nurse when one was needed, but I was never in his office when he needed one. He gave me my shots and vaccinations himself. He weighed me and measured my height himself. If Mom said I seemed a little listless, he took a blood sample by puncturing my finger himself with a little blade that looked suspiciously like the X-Acto knife blade I later used to build model airplanes, squeezed out a large drop of blood, and then matched it with a printed color chart to see if I was anemic. As we left his office, Gwen collected two dollars for the office call, wrote a receipt for Mom, and then went back to polishing her nails as she passed the time of day with other patients in the waiting room.

Never married, Dr. Frasch lived with his sister in a big house in an older neighborhood in Lafayette, Indiana. My parents learned that he had come out of medical school at the top of his class a few years before they moved to town and made him their doctor. It was in the days before medical specialists were common. An eye doctor and a dentist were the only other specialists. A medical doctor treated everything else. Dr. Frasch delivered me, and later removed my tonsils, reporting that they were "soft and mushy." He came to the house to take my temperature, thump my chest, prescribe aspirin, and to make me gag when he stuck his tongue depressor down my throat. He lanced my boils until Dad figured out that he could do it himself just as well with a sterilized razor blade or one of Mom's darning needles.

One of my more unusual childhood diseases was pleurisy, an inflammation of the double membrane that lines the chest cavity and surrounds the lungs. It can be caused by a viral or a bacterial infection and sometimes occurs in the aftermath of a cold or pneumonia. But it can also occur spontaneously for no known reason. My pleurisy came with no known cause.

Dr. Frasch came to our house to see me writhe in pleurisy-induced pain when I coughed or turned over. He gave me a penicillin shot in my buttock with a needle the size of a fencer's foil, and then he wrapped adhesive tape around and around my upper torso to reduce the painful movement when I took a deep breath or turned over in bed. Aspirin was also prescribed, and a few days later I was cured.

Trench mouth was another of my exotic diseases, which got its name during WWI when the soldiers in the trenches of Europe contracted a bacterial form of gingivitis due to poor hygiene and lack of tooth brushes. As far as I know, we had good hygiene in our house on Steely Street, and my mother certainly made me brush my teeth, but it didn't matter; I still got the trench mouth sores in my mouth. Dr. Frasch had me gargle with peroxide and sentenced me to a few days in the hospital for this one, giving me a lot of time to read books and magazines which then had to be sterilized by baking them in the oven before they could be used again at home. Several books with scorched pages remained in my bookcase for years, reminding me of that dreaded infection, and the taste of peroxide lingered almost as long.

Throughout my school days, Dad referred to the doctor as "your boyfriend" when he was talking with Mom. When Mom had an appointment with Dr. Frasch, Dad teased her about going to see her boyfriend. When she was diagnosed with a "floating kidney" her boyfriend prescribed a girdle with a built-in bulging pad that pressed against her to help hold the kidney in place. She knew Dad was just teasing, and ignored his comments.

Today, family doctors have their own specialty: internal medicine. Problems beyond that category are farmed out to other specialists like a hand surgeon, a dermatologist, or a hematologist. Dr. Frasch and his black bag are just memories.

Chapter 12

Victory Garden on the Wabash

The Wabash River meanders across the land, winding its muddy way through wide, shallow valleys and around occasional hills. It starts as a collection of trickles in western Ohio that merge, until big enough to have been named by Indians or settlers. Twenty-eight miles later the Wabash crosses into Indiana, and another 200 miles downstream it's joined by the Tippecanoe River near Delphi. At the little town of Battleground, where two Shawnee brothers, Tecumseh and the Prophet, were defeated by William Henry Harrison in the battle of Tippecanoe in 1811, the Wildcat Creek joins the flow just before West Lafayette, where I spent most of my childhood. Several miles downriver from town, the Wabash absorbs the waters of Sugar Creek before heading south to become the border between Indiana and Illinois. Then it blends into the Ohio River, flows into the Mississippi, and eventually empties into the Gulf of Mexico, where it contributes its mud and silt to the Louisiana delta.

During World War II, the fertile farmland on the banks of the Wabash River was ideal for victory gardens. Tracts were rented to families that wanted to contribute to the war effort by being as self-sufficient as possible, leaving commercial food production available to support our troops fighting in Europe and in the Pacific.

Two Shakes of a Lamb's Tail

At eight years old, I was too young to contribute much effort to my parents' victory garden, but I did help harvest the results. After Dad came home from work on hot summer evenings, with cicadas buzzing in the trees along the river, I learned to tell when tomatoes were ripe and how to pick pea pods and green beans from the vines without pulling up the entire plant. The other vegetables were handled by my parents: Kohlrabi, peanuts, Brussels sprouts, carrots, and potatoes, harvested by hand or with a spading fork larger than I was.

Rusty Knauer and I both "helped" in our respective families' victory gardens. The first name Russell and a head of bright red hair made his nickname "Rusty" inevitable. When the tedium of gardening became too boring for young boys to endure, we wandered off into the brush and trails along the river bank, skipping stones into the river, looking for frogs and fish, or exploring for new kinds of natural wonders. One of those wonders was a dead cottonmouth snake longer than we were tall. At least we were 90 percent sure it was dead. A few pokes with a long stick changed the percentage to 100, and we picked it up with our bare hands. After coiling it on the ground, we propped its head up on a rock so that it looked about to strike and then called Rusty's mother to come see what we had found. When she saw the coiled snake staring at her in the middle of the trail, her bloodcurdling screams probably rattled all the classroom windows on the Purdue campus back in town.

Wanting to calm his mother, Rusty picked up the snake by its neck and said, "See, Mom, it's okay. It's already dead," but Mom was not calmed. Her intensified hysterical screams attracted other gardeners, including my parents, who made me go sit in the car until they were ready to go home. The shock we had induced in Mrs. Knauer was the topic of a stern lecture delivered during the trip home.

The vegetables grown in our victory garden and canned by Mom and Dad fed us for many meals the following winter, although their direct contribution to the war effort was probably overshadowed by the feelings of involvement and teamwork on the part of the gardeners, who bought war bonds, endured gasoline rationing, and saved tin foil and bacon fat to help win the war. My parents bought a pressure cooker to use in canning vegetables grown in the garden. In 1943 alone, over 300,000 pressure cookers were purchased in the US. In the summer of 1944, as the D-Day landings gave us new hope for an end of the war, it was estimated that 50 percent of the vegetable production in the US came from 20 million victory gardens.

The family that lived next door to us on Steely Street contributed more than their share to the war effort. Lewis Sisson, a doctoral student at Purdue, was called to active service in 1942 and became an Army Air Corps fighter pilot and then a flying instructor who taught Indian pilots at Karachi, India. As a captain in March of 1945, he was reported missing in action when his P-38 fighter plane disappeared during a mission over Burma, behind the Japanese lines. Six weeks later the area was freed and his plane was found, but no signs of him or his remains were ever found. His young wife and two daughters, ages five and one, were left without a father.

In later years, the wilderness along those Indiana rivers and creeks was our wild frontier. As Boy Scouts, Rusty and I with a few friends became Lewis and Clark, going where only Indians had been and where Huckleberry Finn might have traveled if he had explored upstream in the tributaries of the Mississippi. We learned the names of trees and wild flowers, identified birds, and cooked our meals from provisions carried in our backpacks. At night we slept under war surplus pup-tents in sleeping bags still damp from shooting rapids on the Wildcat or Sugar Creek.

But by then, the war was over, the Great Depression was just a memory, and a golden age had ended the need for victory gardens.

Chapter 13

Uprooted

"I don't know, Mom… I wanted to wake up." I tried to hold back the tears.

"I know you're trying. Just be sure to go to the bathroom right before you go to bed every night," she said.

I was in the fourth grade in Greenwich, Connecticut, and I was wetting the bed nearly every night. At nine years old, the potty training I had received eight years ago was slipping away, forgotten during the night.

We were in Connecticut, a thousand miles away from Steely Street and my back yard tree house. I was playing with new kids in a new neighborhood and going to a new school. The map implanted in a groove of my brain would atrophy. It had led me to school—down to the end of Steely Street, then left on Grant Street, right on Harrison, left on Chauncey, and all the way across State Street where the sixth-grade patrol boy with the official white belt across his shoulder and chest held me on the curb until there were no more cars speeding down into the Wabash valley, and up the hill past the Methodist church and the town library to Morton School.

After six years with the Purdue University Electrical Engineering Department, Dad's talents were needed elsewhere, and he was taking a year's sabbatical. The new field of television beckoned, and CBS in New York City wanted Dad's experience in making vacuum tubes, including cathode ray tubes and television picture tubes. He would work for Dr. Peter Goldmark, the technical guru who was leading CBS Laboratories' way into the new technologies that would change the world.

Television. That magic word that would insert itself into everyone's vocabularies and living rooms hadn't yet been abbreviated "TV." Black and white television had been around for a while, and Purdue's EE Experiment Station had constructed a small television station, W9XG, (pictures only, no sound) on the hill beside the football stadium in 1931 for which Dad had later made tubes in his lab. He transmitted a still photograph of me and Lydia Heim, the daughter of co-worker Howard Heim, over the system and I got to see myself on a five-inch black-and-white screen in 1939. *Color* television was still a technical curiosity, although Peter Goldmark had invented and demonstrated the first such system in 1940 at CBS Labs. And now, in 1944, Dad would work for him.

The uprooting trauma was made bearable by the positive spin that Mom put on it: The adventure, the long trip, the new friends. And we would come back in a year.

The wartime national speed limit of 35 miles per hour caused the trip in our 1937 Plymouth to take 50 percent longer than it would have taken before the war. Dad normally drove at 50 or 55 miles per hour on long trips, but he had to restrain himself on the portion of the Pennsylvania Turnpike that was open by then. We had never been on a four-lane, limited access highway before. To us it was one of the wonders of the modern world, especially the long tunnels through the mountains.

We moved into a rented second-floor apartment in the Greenwich home of Mrs. Sweeney, a widow lady with a thick Irish accent, where we stayed for a few months until Dad could find a house that we could afford to rent. The neighborhood on Orchard Place came complete with a pack of rowdy kids and an abandoned haunted house in the back woods. The neighbor kids were probably much the same as those on Steely Street back in Indiana, but to me they were stranger, louder, and rougher. Arlene Waylon and her younger brother, who lived next door, were my closest friends during those months, but their parents were so strict they couldn't come out to play very often. When they did, they couldn't stray off their own property, and they weren't allowed to help me explore the haunted house that was practically right in our back yard. On warm evenings when windows were open, my parents and I could hear the Waylon kids crying and screaming as their father beat them when he got drunk.

Adjusting to a totally new environment didn't leave me with lasting impressions of trauma or hardship, but elements of them must have affected me. When I began wetting the bed at night, it wasn't due to rebellion or alienation. I just couldn't control my bladder through the night. My parents restricted my liquid consumption in the evenings. They put a rubber sheet over my mattress, and tried to train me to wake up to go the bathroom. I wasn't trainable. They offered me a nickel as a reward each morning that I woke up dry. I got very few nickels, but when I did get one, lavish praise accompanied it. There was never overt criticism, but I knew that fourth graders should have been toilet-trained long before fourth grade. And I had been. I hadn't been afflicted this way on Steely Street. Even my little brother, John, didn't wet the bed anymore. The rotten little kid was making me look bad. Why me? Why now?

I wanted in the worst way to get up when I had to go to the bathroom in the middle of the night. I wanted it so much, I dreamed that I *was* getting up, going into the bathroom, aiming at the toilet, and going. It was real. In my head I was right there in the bathroom, but my body was still asleep in bed. The bed and my pajamas were wet in the morning, and I cried because I had failed again.

Dad's long commute into New York City forced him to get up before sunrise, walk all the way to the center of town to catch the train, and return just in time for our 7:00 p.m. dinner. On Saturday mornings I took swimming lessons at the YMCA in Stamford, riding the train by myself in both directions. I was scared, but I went anyway.

Entertained by the train ride, I learned how to put my little ticket under a strap on the top of the seat back so the conductor could punch it as he came down the aisle. The adult commuters could have their ticket punched this way without taking their eyes off the newspaper as the conductor came through. Between trips up and down the aisle, the conductor called out in his New York accent the stations as they came into view: Cos Cob, Riverside, Old Greenwich, Stamford. At each stop, a new herd of people shoved tickets under the little straps, prepared for punching so they too could ignore the conductor when he came by.

The locker room and the pool at the Y were the scary parts of the trip. The other kids were big and loud and obnoxious, laughing and yelling and horsing around— rough kids with their eastern accents that continued their rough ways, naked, right out into the pool. Being naked in front of other splashing, cannonballing boys who didn't care about getting water in their eyes and ears and mouths was ok for them, but knowing each other made it easier. Motivated by fear, I was too occupied with staying unnoticed to get to know them. I just wanted to keep my head above water and get through the lesson.

Back in the locker room the threat of a paddling hung over us, and I rushed to be one of the first ones showered and dressed. The last one dressed learned the feel of "Big Bertha," the fraternity paddle wielded against his bottom by the instructor.

Then back to the safety of a seat on the train with my ticket under the little strap and the conductor's voice calling out the stations in reverse order. I was safe for another week.

At last my parents found a house in Old Greenwich that we could rent, so we left Mrs. Sweeney's upstairs apartment and moved again. This time there were empty lots on either side of our house and no neighbor kids getting whacked around by their drunken father. When school ended in the spring, two other Bobs came to the neighborhood for the summer and we collected and traded playing cards, played catch, and, in the empty lot next door, built a lean-to that substituted for my Steely Street tree house. Because we all had the same first name, the chubby one with thick glasses became Froggy, the other, more assertive one got to keep his name, and I became known as Hess. In the summer of 1945 my brother John, who was still learning to talk in plain sentences, started calling me Hess when he heard my friends call me that. Years went by before he learned that my name was really Bob. In the fall when school started, the other two Bobs went back home to the city.

Instead of returning to Indiana that fall when our year was up, Dad was asked by CBS to stay on for six more months, and I spent much of my fifth-grade year in the Old Greenwich grade school. One bitter winter morning after a nighttime blizzard, I walked the more than a half-mile to school only to find it closed and nobody there. Not knowing what else to do, I returned home. When Mom asked a neighbor about the closed school, we learned that the town fire whistle had blown a coded signal to notify everyone of the school closing. In Indiana we had never heard of school closings because of snow, and I was the only student to show up that cold morning in Old Greenwich. I got to go sledding that day on the big hill across the street from our house. Some daring older boys grabbed the rear bumpers of cars as they slowly made their way over the packed, snow-covered streets, sliding on the soles of their shoes as they squatted behind the car. If the car went over a clear spot in the road, the hitchhiker took a tumble on the pavement. When Dad got home that night, and I told him about it, he gave me a stern look and said, "Don't you ever try that. It's a dumb and dangerous trick." I never did.

Somewhere along the way my nighttime bladder control improved so that Mom could end the bribery and save her nickels. The Germans surrendered and the war in Europe ended on VE Day. President Roosevelt died of a sudden brain hemorrhage, and after hearing the news on the radio I ran into the back yard to tell Mom, who was there talking with a neighbor. She didn't believe me and went into the house to hear it for herself. A month later the atom bombs were dropped and the Japanese surrendered on board the battleship USS Missouri, ending the slaughter on those Pacific islands. The country was euphoric as rationing slowly ended and the troops began coming home. The USS Missouri came to New York harbor, and the public was invited to go on board to tour this revered monster machine of death and destruction that was now a hallowed memorial to the end of the war and to the brave men and women that fought it. Mom took me on the train into the City to tour the ship, and we stood at the very spot where General McArthur had accepted the Japanese unconditional surrender and signed the peace treaty. We went back home to Connecticut with an 8 x 10 souvenir photo of the ship.

In Mom's determination to expose me to the cultural sights and sounds of the big city while we lived in the area, she took me on another train ride to visit the Statue of Liberty. We climbed the stairs and looked out the windows that formed the headband of Lady Liberty's crown.

The Statue didn't yet exist when my ancestors came to these shores from Europe, but their immigration and new life is symbolized by the nation's focus on that inspiring statue and Emma Lazarus' brilliant poem, "The New Colossus" that is forever associated with it. At ten years old, my appreciation of the statue and what it stands for hadn't yet matured. But I took with me, back to Connecticut and from there to Indiana, the seeds of that appreciation—no, the seeds of that *intense admiration* for those forbears—those tired and poor, wretched refuse—who paved the way for my parents, my brother, and me to live in America with freedom and opportunities to succeed.

Although the CBS tube laboratory that Dad built was functioning by the time we headed back to Indiana, the CBS system of color television developed by Peter Goldmark was incompatible with existing black and white television, and lost out in the marketplace to RCA. Ironically, the Purdue research and development work by Roscoe George and his team, of which Dad was a member, didn't pay off for Purdue. RCA won a patent law suit against Purdue for control of the technology that the company had paid for, and went on to lead the way into America's living rooms.

Back in West Lafayette, we moved into a rental home at 415 Evergreen Street, nearer the campus and just five short blocks from the Electrical Engineering building, where Dad could easily walk to work as he resumed his teaching and research job.

When I walked into my public school fifth grade classroom in the spring of 1946, Ralph Johansen spotted me, stood up at his desk, and cheered while Mrs. Ulrich, who opened the class each day by leading us in the Lord's Prayer, tried to shush him. Rationing ended, but butter, bread, and toilet paper were still in short supply, and I volunteered to stand in line, instead of Mom, in the Piggly Wiggly grocery store at the west end of Evergreen Street to wait for those items to be put out for purchase. That year, the automobile manufacturers began making cars again instead of jeeps and tanks, and Studebaker introduced a new body design that made it difficult to tell whether the car was going forward or backward. The other car companies followed suit, and my friends and I had to memorize an entire new encyclopedia of automobile names and models and features so we could argue about which was best.

The war was over and we were back home among friends.

Two Shakes of a Lamb's Tail

II

The Wonder Years

The noiseless foot of Time steals swiftly by
And ere we dream of manhood, age is nigh.

Decimus Junius Juvenal

Lost, yesterday, somewhere between sunrise and sunset,
Two golden hours, each set with sixty diamond minutes.
No reward is offered, for they are gone forever!

Horace Mann

Chapter 14

Rip Van Winkle

The excitement of visiting the dog pound to choose a pet was better than Christmas, but some planning was necessary. We set rules for ourselves: We didn't live on the farm like my cousins who had a big collie named Queenie. A city dog had to be small, but not one of those tiny nervous ankle-biters. It had to have short hair. My mother didn't want long hair like Queenie's migrating onto the furniture, the rugs, and our clothing. We didn't want a purebred dog that got sick more easily. This requirement was probably financially motivated. Pound dogs were free, and they were rarely purebred.

We chose a soft, fluffy puppy a few weeks old that was coal black except for a vertical white streak down the center of his chest. The folks at the pound thought he was part beagle and part something else, but they weren't sure what. When we got him home, he slept most of the time, so after a few days of discussion we named him Rip Van Winkle, and called him Rip for short. For the first few nights, he was lonesome and howled and cried until he went to sleep. After the first couple of weeks he got over the separation from his siblings and became accustomed to our house. When Rip was indoors, he was confined to the kitchen during the daytime, and went to the cellar for the night when we went to bed. To train him to stay in the kitchen when all the family action was in the living room we closed the door that separated the kitchen from the dining room. As we left the kitchen, we squeezed through the door without opening it any farther than necessary. After his nose was bumped by the door a few times, Rip learned to stay away from it as we left the kitchen. After he learned to never leave the kitchen, we occasionally left the door open. Strong disapproval greeted him if he so much as put a single foot onto the dining room carpet. Eventually, we left the door open all the time, and Rip voluntarily remained in the kitchen when he wasn't tied to our clothesline in the back yard.

Rip learned to go to the basement when we were ready to go to bed, but he never learned to like it. If the family was in the kitchen, that's where he wanted to be. When he was young, my technique was to call him from part way down the cellar steps. Being eager and agreeable, he came bounding down the stairs to me. Then I beat a retreat back up the stairs, closing the door at the top. He eventually learned that he was to go down alone when we stood at the top of the stairs with the door open and gestured in the direction of the cellar. His speed was glacial, but became reckless if we threw a dog biscuit down the stairs ahead of him.

We taught Rip to come when called, not to use the kitchen floor as a toilet, and to speak for his supper, but not until after we poured it into his dish. Rolling over and sitting up were more difficult. Rip was smart, but not *that* smart. We got him to roll over a few times, with much coaxing, but eventually gave up. Rolling over was just too taxing for all of us. When I tried to lift the front part of him into the sitting-up position, his backbone turned to mush, and we eventually gave up. A few years later, Ed Sullivan had a hilarious dog act on his show, where the owner's boundless energy in motivating his dog to do tricks had no effect whatsoever on the dog. It just sat there watching this enthusiastic goofball emit enthusiasm. It was a reenactment of my teaching Rip to sit up.

Two Shakes of a Lamb's Tail

We moved into our new house out on the north edge of town when I was a sophomore in high school and we had to retrain Rip. My mother was *very* protective of her new wall-to-wall carpets, and now there were *two* doors from the kitchen into the rest of the house for him to learn not to use. Outdoors, there was much less traffic, so he could roam freely in the empty fields to the north. We no longer tied him to the clothesline in the back yard, but he always came home when called.

When I was feeling rambunctious, I pounced on Rip and we wrestled. This rough playing began when he was a puppy, and we developed it into an art form. Rip taught me to growl and bark, just like *he* did when we were roughhousing. When he was old enough to remember his ancestral hunting instincts, we added mutual sneaking and stalking to our repertoire. In the back yard, when our eyes met from twenty feet apart, we slowly moved into our stalking stances, all four paws on the ground, bodies and heads hunched down below the horizon so we wouldn't be noticed—two malevolent killer predators stalking each other, the loser sure to become dinner for the winner.

Floppy ears cocked forward, his eyes alert, Rip was a statue inching toward me in the jungle, one paw slowly moving past the other where it froze to the ground as his weight shifted ever so slightly in my direction. A guttural growl began in his throat and escaped past his bared teeth. I answered from deep in my own throat: G-r-r-r-r-r. If I twitched as though to begin my attack, he hunkered down even lower, ready for anything. Finally from ten feet away he uncoiled his body, the steel springs in his legs launching him at me, a black leopard pouncing on his prey.

I tripped him and shoved him over sideways. He rolled the rest of the way over, bared his fangs, growled ferociously, and then came at me to rip my throat open. I caught him in midair and spoiled his aim. Then we were both rolling on the ground wrestling and growling at each other: a vicious, snarling wild animal and Tarzan's Boy fighting for his life. Each time he got away and came at me again, I tripped, flipped, or dumped him. I got him in a bear hug and grabbed his snout to hold his mouth shut like an alligator wrestler. The fury of his struggle broke my death grip and he escaped. Then he got his front end low to the ground where I couldn't get underneath him. He snarled and snapped at my hands and arms when I tried to grab him...

"Bob, don't you have homework you should be doing?"

Darn Jane... Interfering just as I was ready for the kill.

"That's enough, Rip," I said, and the action was over. Rip relaxed as though nothing had happened, his life never in danger. "Good dog," I said, giving him a quick head pat. He grinned back at me, his tongue hanging from the side of his mouth as he panted to recover from the exertion of his near-death experience. The glint in his eyes told me, *You would have been dead meat if she hadn't butted in.*

The ribbons of shredded flesh healed, the puddles of blood evaporated, and I went into the house to wash off the leopard slobber.

Chapter 15

Extensor Carpi Radialis Brevis

It has a nice sound, doesn't it? A tintinnabulation that adds class to the conversation. Especially if you say it like an American with an Italian accent: *Extensor Carpi Radialis Brevis*. It could be the lyrics of a song by the same person who wrote "Mairzy Doates," or perhaps some words from a Catholic mass, asking God for an extra helping of fish next Friday. In the world of racquet sports, if you tell someone that it's the tendon in the fat part of your forearm that hurts when you have tennis elbow, it takes away the romance of the words but still elicits admiration for your eclectic vocabulary.

I realized at an early age that I wasn't much of an athlete, but I envied those who could dribble around me, drive for a layup, and score effortless baskets in driveway basketball. Catching a fly ball in right field (It was always right field) was beyond the limit of my talent except for once when, running at full speed and afraid the ball would hurt my hands, I relaxed them so the ball would pass through unimpeded on its way to the ground. I must have relaxed too much, because the ball fell miraculously into my hands in a totally stingless catch. Accolades from the other players, who were as surprised as I was, reverberated across the field and enlarged my heart to near bursting. "Good catch Bob! Way to go!"

In the seventh grade I became aware that the fans around me in the football bleachers, who showered admiration on the players, included girls—yelling and screaming girls who looked right through me as they launched compliments at the athletes, and deification at the quarterback. Maybe there was more to sports than I had realized. I decided to go out for eighth-grade football.

I was so skinny I was nearly invisible, so to avoid getting squashed by those big guys in the middle of the line, I went out for end. We had to furnish our own shoulder pads, which my mother helped me buy at J.C. Penney. Wearing those babies under my sweatshirt, I became visible and could believe I was the most ferocious end on the field. On defense the first day, I was cross-body-blocked by Deadrock, who was later to become the meanest, roughest lineman in central Indiana. The block folded my legs backward at the knees like a flamingo's. The next play I tried to tackle Tom Welton, who was doing an end run around me. Afraid of his high-kicking running style, and not wanting a face-full of cleats, I just faked it and fell on the ground.

The next day I quit the team.

In giving up my dreams of eliciting screams from the bleachers, I didn't give up my hopes of finding a sport at which I could excel. After school Jim Eaton and I played ping pong with each other in our basements. We got good at it, learning to call it "table tennis" while we practiced backhand and forehand topspin smashes, sidespin and backspin shots, and fast serves that were hard to return. But how much glory was to be found at home in the basement? If I could be that good with a table tennis paddle in my hand, maybe my sport was tennis, where someone might actually see me score a point. I could already hear the girls screaming.

In tenth grade Richie Bauman and I taught ourselves to play tennis. Every good-weather day found us on the Purdue intramural tennis courts after school. If one of us wasn't available, the other went to the courts and hit the ball against the practice backboard for an hour or so. We practiced serves and overhead smashes like we had seen Pancho Gonzales do when he and some other pros came to town for an exhibition match. Backhand and forehand shots, drop shots, crosscourt and down-the-line shots were practiced, all without the benefit of a coach. When we grew tired of practicing, we ran laps around the courts to improve our endurance. If the Purdue tennis team was playing a match up the hill on the team's courts, we took time out and watched to see how it was done.

At the start of our junior year in high school, we declared ourselves ready for the big time. We had heard that our biology teacher, Mr. Bush, played a little tennis, and we pleaded with him to start a tennis team and become our coach. After a few weeks of this pestering, he got the OK from the school administration, and we were off and running. Now, when someone wanted me to do something with them after school, I could tell them, "I have tennis practice." The words had a nice ring, like what I had heard the more famous jocks in my class say: "I have football practice." We were all in it together now, the football team, the wrestlers, the basketball team, and the tennis team, committed to a higher calling, making after-school sacrifices for the glory of West Side High and adoring glances from girls.

The tennis team had four matches that first season; a lot, considering that there weren't many schools in central Indiana that had tennis teams. Rich Bauman won the number one spot on the team, and I earned a solid number two position. Lower classmen rounded out the team in the number three, four, and five slots. In our senior year we had six matches during the season. The coach had found two more schools that would agree to play us. The season won-lost records were mediocre, split about 50-50.

When Rich and I entered Purdue we both went out for the tennis team. He made the team; I didn't. "Not aggressive enough," said the coach. I hung around as assistant student manager until the position of student team manager opened up a couple of years later, and I earned a letter jacket my senior year.

The lack of indoor tennis courts in those days drove us to visit the Purdue squash courts in the winter, where Rich and I taught ourselves to play that game, finding occasional matches with other students, and running laps on the indoor track in the field house. Also running laps were two FBI agents who were graduate students. They had become famous as world class distance runners in the early 1950s before they arrived at Purdue to earn advanced degrees.

On the squash courts, we met Bob Friend, a Pittsburgh Pirates pitcher who had received a twenty thousand dollar signing bonus when he graduated from West Lafayette High School four years ahead of Rich and me. When his signing bonus was announced in the Lafayette newspaper, the headline was, "When a Feller Needs a Friend." He took eight years to graduate from Purdue, thus eventually becoming our classmate by going to college in the fall semester each year and pitching for the Pirates in the spring and summer. To stay in shape he played squash in the winter. I got to warm him up on the court a time or two, but he was a much better player and would have blown me off the court in a match. One of his regular squash opponents was an assistant Purdue football coach, Hank Stram, who went on to become the head coach of the Kansas City Chiefs, where Lenny Dawson, a Purdue classmate of mine, was the quarterback. Friend spent his entire baseball career with the Pirates and eventually pitched in a World Series before his retirement.

Rich and I also occasionally played badminton with a Sunday afternoon group of Purdue students and staff in the women's gym. The organizer of the group was a women's physical education teacher who was ranked number three in the country in women's amateur badminton. We found competitive badminton to be, in many ways, more fun and exciting than tennis and squash. When hit with an overhead smash, the shuttlecock comes off the racquet at up to 200 miles per hour. Its feathers slow it down in the air, but the game requires very fast reflexes and agility. It's the most strenuous of all the racquet sports, and very few in the U.S. play it competitively.

After graduation from Purdue and my move to Rochester to work for General Dynamics Electronics Division, I kept playing tennis, but squash eventually became my favorite, as well as the only racquet sport to inflict injuries on me.

Racquet sports can be continued until you die or your joints give out, whichever comes first. The drive to win can cause injuries in any sport, but in racquet sports it rarely damages your opponent. We do it to ourselves. Pulled muscles and tendons are the most common afflictions, occurring when we reach down into our reserves of desperation and lunge for the ball just at that moment when all hope is lost: the ball is beyond our reach, and a mere mortal would say, "Oh, well, I'll get even by winning the next point." In mid-lunge, just as ball and racquet connect, it happens: I just tore my *extensor carpi radialis brevis*.

My first squash injury was a severed Achilles tendon that did its severing as I stepped back to allow my opponent room to hit the ball. In that sport, if you don't get out of your opponent's way and allow him an unfettered swing at the ball, you either lose the point or have to play it again, depending on the circumstances. So I stepped back to get out of the way, and fell to the floor in a painful heap, done in by politeness, and wondering who was behind me, swinging a hammer at the back of my heel. The pain lasted less than fifteen minutes.

It took me about that long to figure out what had happened. My Achilles tendon had been sore for several weeks, hurting each time I got up out of a chair or out of bed, but the soreness went away with some stretching. By the time I walked around for a few minutes exercising it, the pain didn't exist until the next time I hadn't walked for a while. But pain means something. *Ah ha! I guess I've broken my Achilles tendon.*

As I was helped to my feet after absorbing all the sympathy that was available in the vicinity, my left foot wouldn't move. I could put my weight on it, but if I lifted it off the floor, it just hung there drooping at the lower end of my leg. With all of my mental energy focused on the foot, it wouldn't move up or down. When my brain said, "Point your toes upward," nothing happened. It was as though the nerves were severed along with the tendon.

Someone brought me a bag of ice and a crutch, and I called my wife, who came to the tennis club and took me to the hospital. After a night in the emergency room, I was operated on the next morning. When I awoke after the anesthesia wore off, I found my lower leg in a cast with toes pointed down to prevent tension on the repaired tendon.

Crutches create strong arms and sore armpits, but I got good at using them. For six weeks they became part of me, accompanying me in the car and on airplanes across the country, leaving my side only to lie next to my bed when I slept. When the cast came off after six weeks, I wore a high-heeled shoe which was gradually cut down over the next few months as I stretched my tendon in physical therapy and in the hot tub at the tennis club. For several weeks I went to the tennis club every day and stood on the seat in the hot tub to warm my legs from thigh to foot, heating the tendon, but not the rest of my body so I could work longer at stretching the repaired part. The water in that tub was so heavily laced with chemicals that all the hair disappeared from my legs, growing back only after the dunking stopped. After six months of convalescence and rehab I was back on the squash court, with only a minor, but permanent, decrease in my foot's range of motion.

When the doctor told me I could start playing again, I was afraid of breaking the tendon again. "Not likely," said the doctor. "It's more likely that the other tendon will break."

"Why is that?" I asked, not sure I believed him.

"The repaired tendon is stronger than before because we made it thicker when we overlapped the broken ends before sewing it back together," he said. "But it's possible that some of the same strain and damage has occurred in your right tendon as well."

Not possible, I thought. This time, if a tendon starts hurting, I'll lay off playing squash until the soreness goes away.

Back on the squash court after six months of treatment, recovery, and physical therapy, I started playing, but very carefully. My high-heeled shoe and the other shoe, which had both its heel and sole built up to match so that I didn't list to starboard with a limp, had been gradually cut down to normal as the repaired tendon stretched back to near its original length. I gained confidence as the muscles gained strength, and soon I was playing with my usual enthusiasm and semi-competence, producing just as much exhaustion and as many mis-hits as before, but without a limp and free of soreness.

Then tennis elbow started. I had experienced tennis elbow in my earlier tennis playing days, but it never stayed with me for very long. But now I was older. Body parts didn't heal as quickly. On the squash court someone with a knife stabbed me, or so it felt, just below the elbow.

At forty years of age, my *extensor carpi radialis brevis* had torn when I swung at a squash ball. Until then I didn't know what *extensor carpi radialis brevis* meant. If I had known, I might have used it in a complete sentence: "Damn, I think I just broke my *extensor carpi radialis brevis*." But sadly, lacking that foreknowledge, I just went with the subject and left the predicate unstated, leaving the players on the next court to assume that my expletive marked only the loss of another point by an immature player who couldn't handle defeat.

For the next year, my orthopedist and I became even better friends as I helped put another of his kids through college. He taught me what an *extensor carpi radialis brevis* was, and that it was merely torn, not severed. We started with my arm in a cast for three weeks to immobilize it while the tendon healed, followed by a few weeks of physical therapy. Back on the squash court, it began hurting again. The therapists tried every trick in their book: Whirlpool baths, heat, cold, massage, exercise, and something they called electrical stim (short for stimulation) and I called electrocution. Electrodes are attached to body parts on either side of the injury, and pulsed with just enough juice to cause muscles to contract and relax, but not enough to kill you. The unit that produced the electrical pulses, called a TENS unit, was small enough to clip into my belt, a sort of pacemaker for my arm. Now I could walk around, go to work, or eat my dinner while being secretly stimulated.

The whole process reminded me of a handheld electrical gizmo that was in my grandparents' attic in Minonk, Illinois. It contained a small Tesla coil, and looked much like today's caulking cartridges. It produced a very high voltage and a static discharge that glowed blue at the business end where the probe was. If the doctor wasn't bothered by a little quackery, the device was probably safe to apply to an afflicted body part because little or no current passed through the flesh, and may have worked to cure mysterious afflictions only by scaring the patient. The device, called a *Violet Ray*, had long since been relegated to the attic by the time I was old enough to climb the grandparents' steep stairs to find it in the medical department, beside the phrenology head and the bedpan. Dad later used the device to detect leaks in the vacuum pump system in his vacuum tube laboratory at Purdue University. A microscopic leak in the glass tubing would glow bright blue as the vacuum sucked in the ionized molecules produced by the device. Similar devices are still used to detect leaks in neon signs, but medical use has been discredited, as has the more recent practice of using x-rays to cure my teenage acne.

When none of the therapy methods worked to cure my tennis elbow, the doctor tried injections of cortisone into the area where the tendon attached to the bone on the side of the elbow. He didn't find much flesh there, and it felt as if the needle bored right into the bone.

"There, that oughta do it," he said as he removed the needle for the fifth time.

When the bruise disappeared a few days later, the arm was cured. No pain or discomfort at all. Back on the squash court, it took six weeks for the pain to return. After a second injection, the pain returned in three weeks.

"Well, we can only do this one more time," the doctor said. "After that the cortisone starts to damage the tissue."

This time, the pain returned in only one week.

"We can surgically repair the damage," said the doctor. "It's a simple operation. We remove the tendon from the bone and reattach it a little farther down the arm. I only do two or three of these a year because it's rare that tennis elbow gets bad enough to tear the tendon, but I've never yet had a failure."

"Before you cut," I said, "let me try not using the arm for squash. I'll lay off for a year and then we'll decide."

The doctor agreed, and for exactly one year I didn't even pick up a squash racquet with my right hand. Instead, I learned to play left-handed for that year. I had to drop down from being a high C-level player to low D-level on the challenge ladder at the club, but as the awkwardness slowly disappeared and I stopped bumping my nose on the walls, I challenged my way back up to the top of the D-level. I was just getting ready to challenge a low C player when my year was up, and I started surreptitiously playing a few strokes with my right hand whenever I got behind in a match. Upon pulling ahead, I switched back to my left hand and continued to play. After few weeks of this subterfuge, I gained confidence in using my right hand without damaging the tendon again, and very quickly restored myself to my rightful place in the mid-levels of the challenge ladder. The surgery was never required.

A few years later, my other Achilles tendon gave way, twelve years after the first one had blown out. This time there was no early soreness to warn me, but it was only torn, not severed. Another six weeks in a cast, followed by more therapy, repaired it. As this is written many years later, there have been no further injuries more serious than getting hit in the rump or the thigh by the ball. If I had still lived with my parents, my dad would have asked me what lessons I learned from all those injuries...perhaps how to take better care of my body parts?

The only lesson I'm sure I learned was how to say *extensor carpi radialis brevis*.

Chapter 16

The Benefits of Boy Scout Training I

George and I stood in his driveway after school. "I found my sister's box of Tampax in the bathroom closet," he said. "D'you wanna see 'em?"

He was by now so immersed in his new family that he called Emily his sister. After their parents' car had been hit by a train, George and his younger brother, Ross, had moved to West Lafayette from Iowa to live with their aunt and uncle. The parents had waited at the crossing for a train to pass, and then started across the tracks without knowing that another train was coming from the opposite direction on the other tracks. The aunt and uncle who took the boys in already had two kids: John, who was away at college, and Emily, nearly ready to follow suit. George entered junior high school in my class, and Ross was two years behind us. Both joined my Boy Scout troop.

The two of them were as different as two brothers could be: George, dark-haired, and round-faced, was cheerful, aggressive, and opinionated. His attitude said, "Let's get some machetes and blaze a trail through the jungle." Ross, also cheerful, was red-headed, with a slim build and a milder manner, but both had a streak of devilment built in. Ross had once brought home a condom and entertained us by filling it with water in their basement laundry sink. It didn't break until more than a gallon of water had stretched it to cover the entire bottom of the sink.

I considered George's question thoughtfully for about two milliseconds before answering.

"Yeah, I guess so," I said, trying to be cool. "Is anyone else home right now?"

"Nope. C'mon."

We scampered on tiptoe up the back stairs of the empty house, through the kitchen, down the hall, and into the bathroom. Tucked behind some freshly laundered towels on the second shelf from the top was the blue box. George pulled it out and placed it reverently on the front of a lower shelf where we could get a better view. Opening the box, he pulled out one of the cylindrical objects and laid it on the shelf. Its white paper wrapper was folded at the ends, but not sealed. Unfolding the ends, he unrolled the paper and laid its contents back on the shelf.

There it was—an engineering marvel: Two concentric shiny white cardboard tubes containing a soft cottony firecracker with a long fuse dangling from one end. We gazed at it in awe as an entire library of images rolled through my mind. I had never been able to examine such a device this closely before, but I had learned the basic mechanics of its use, probably from my friends. My imagination revealed the arcane purpose of each of its components, and I saw right away that the string was an extraction feature.

"D'you s'pose... D'you s'pose the string ever breaks?" I asked.

"Looks pretty strong to me," he said. His eyes sparkled. "I guess...we could weaken it some."

The seed I had planted in George's mind had sprouted. As he gave voice to this creative possibility, more images came and went. "D'you think we should?" I said.

George gave me a look, his mind already made up. He was an action person, not an indecisive wimp like me.

"Stay right there," he said as he raced down the hall into his room. Three seconds later he was back with his Boy Scout sheath knife. The Scouts did a good job of teaching us how to handle knives and axes—how to carry them without endangering the nearby population, how to sharpen them without slicing off fingers, and how to tell when they needed sharpening and when they were sharp enough. George and I had developed knife and ax sharpening into an art form.

"Okay, this is tricky," he said. "You hold the string right near where it's attached down against the shelf so it can't move, and I'll cut part way through it."

George's visual-mechanical skills and planning ability were paying off. These traits and his leadership ability were to one day guide him into the executive vice presidency of a large engineering firm that built power plants around the world. He had already thought our clandestine project through to the desired end result, and it was his knife, so it was natural that he was the one to wield it. I was the nurse, making sure that the doctor encountered no distractions during the operation.

I did as I was told, being careful not to leave fingerprints. The knife had been so well sharpened using his Boy Scout Carborundum stone that it was impossible to see where metal ended and thin air began. George's knife-sharpening skills put Gillette to shame. The metal at the sharp edge was no thicker than a single molecule of high-carbon steel. With the steady hands of a surgeon he began to saw on the string, cutting one fiber at a time. He was operating a quarter of an inch from two of my fingertips, but I didn't flinch. If I lost a fingertip, my biggest problem would be what to tell my parents.

"I think I heard a car," I said.

"Naw, it just went by on the street," George said.

"You sure?"

"Will you shut up? I'm trying to concentrate."

Finally, the string had only a few uncut fibers. He stopped and resheathed the knife, as we had been taught. Never leave a knife where it might cut someone by accident. We reassembled the newly modified device, wrapped the paper around it, and carefully folded the paper ends using the original creases. Back in the box it went, the box was stashed back behind the towels, and with heartbeats running at about 200 per second we thundered down the stairs and out the back door. By the time George's Aunt Dorothy returned home a few minutes later, we were in the back yard, discussing our progress in earning Marksmanship merit badges.

In the days and weeks that followed, we would have appreciated some feedback on the success or failure of our caper, but information about the mysteries of young womanhood was far too tightly controlled. One of the basic tenets of intelligence gathering is that your target must not know that you know that she might have had a problem. George couldn't just casually ask his sister, "Oh, by the way, have you had any special problems lately?"

Knowledge of a final resolution was too much to hope for, and the outcome remained a figment of our fantasies.

Chapter 17

The Benefits of Boy Scout Training II

George had been introduced to rifle shooting back on the farm in Iowa. My own experience was limited to target range shooting at Scout camp, where I earned the Marksmanship merit badge. We learned target shooting, but with a heavy emphasis on safety: Never point the rifle at another person, don't carry it around loaded, and above all, don't peek down the barrel or put your body parts in front of the muzzle. Having earned the merit badge, I asked my parents for a .22 rifle for Christmas, but no firearms appeared in my stocking. My begging and pleading produced only a hint of compromise, leading me to believe that a .22 caliber *air* rifle was a possibility. I started saving my money.

Air rifles were also called pump guns or pellet guns. No simple Red Ryder BB guns, these: They had rifled barrels, and at close range they were just as accurate and could do nearly as much damage as a regular .22. They fired lead pellets propelled by air under high pressure. Beneath the barrel was a long cylinder similar to a tire pump that pressurized the air in a chamber. Pulling the trigger released the air into the barrel behind the pellet with a loud, satisfying ***pop***. The rifle I wanted was the Crossman with a magazine that held over a dozen pellets, and a pump handle that doubled as the handhold under the barrel. It looked very much like a rifle that fired real bullets.

George already had an air rifle. It was only an old .17 caliber Franklin, but I coveted it. While I waited to get my own rifle, George occasionally let me fire it at tin cans in the alleys around the neighborhood or in his backyard. We were careful not to use it out on the street where a grown-up or a policeman could see us. The Franklin's pump handle was a little knob under the muzzle end of the barrel. To pump the gun, the operator pulled the pump shaft straight out from the end of the barrel, put the pump handle on the ground, and used his weight to lean on the rifle, pushing it toward the ground to create one pump stroke. At least two strokes were needed to fully load up for the next shot. It wasn't the most convenient device to use, but it worked, and its ammunition was much cheaper than real bullets.

One evening, in an alley two blocks from my home, we practiced our marksmanship, shooting at tin cans with George's rifle. When it was my turn to shoot, I began pumping. Starting the second stroke, I reached for the knob under the muzzle to pull it out and shot myself in the hand. No one had told me that when I pulled the pump handle out with my left hand, I should take my right forefinger off the trigger. Being too dumb to figure that out for myself, I had squeezed the stock too vigorously with my right hand while grabbing the pump plunger at the end of the muzzle with my left.

When my Dad got me to a nearby doctor's house, the real fun began. With one of his torture tools the doctor probed nearly an inch into the fleshy base of my thumb while Dad put his weight on my forearm to keep it from moving.

Why do we have a genetic propensity to put a wounded finger into our mouth or to hold it against our chest? If I hit my finger with a hammer (always a finger on the left hand as I'm a right-handed hammerer), I immediately clasp it against my chest with my other hand. Never mind that this maneuver requires that you first drop the hammer, with high odds that it will fall onto an instep or big toe. A finger cut by a knife goes straight into the mouth, and only God knows where the knife will fall. I had no idea where George's pellet gun fell after doing its dirty deed on my left hand, but now, as the doctor tried to probe for my gall bladder by going in through my thumb, the thumb tried to move to my chest for comfort. Because Dad stood on my arm to keep the thumb away from my chest, my chest went to my thumb, which annoyed the doctor and prevented him from probing any deeper than my thyroid gland. With his free hand, Dad yanked my head back out of the way, allowing the doctor to continue vivisecting me.

Then it was over. The pellet, which probably hadn't penetrated any deeper than my armpit, was found and extracted. Dad relaxed his multiple hammerlocks on me, and the doctor, having neglected to anesthetize my thumb before removing the lead pellet, thoughtfully did so now, using a syringe with a needle the size of HB pencil lead before he installed a few stitches.

A few months later, I got to buy my Crossman auto feed .22 caliber air rifle. My parents figured that with all my Boy Scout training, I wasn't likely to hurt myself with it.

Chapter 18

Having a Good Time

After holding my head in my hands for a while, I threw a pillow at the wall of my bedroom, but it just went *phump* and fell to the floor, no hole in the wall or anything. Hitting the bedpost with my hand hurt a lot, but things were still the same. I spun around in place and tried to turn blue, but all I got was dizzy.

I had just accepted a telephoned invitation to be Sondra's date at the 1951 West Lafayette High School Girls' Club square dance the following week. It didn't matter that she wasn't the prettiest girl in the freshman class, or that she was two years behind me in school. It didn't matter that my dad and her dad both taught in the same department at Purdue and knew each other very well. I could handle those things. It didn't even matter that I could barely talk to girls. I wanted to learn. What really, *really* mattered was that Sondra was six inches taller than I was. I had accepted a date with a giant because I was flattered to be asked and too stupefied to say no.

When I told my mom that I didn't really want to go, she said one of those mom things that she always said when a major crisis threatened to wreck my entire future: "You'll just have to make up your mind to have a good time," she said. My own mother, all cheerful and sparkly, had consigned me to death by mortification. "I'm sure you'll enjoy it," she added, removing all hope of dispensation.

Back in my room I threw the pillow again, after a Bob Feller windup, intending it to go through the wall and into my parents' bedroom. Still no damage except to my hand, which, on the follow-through, hit the bedpost again.

My imagination led me through a labyrinth of hideous possibilities to come during the evening. At seventeen, I had developed considerable skills in conjuring up exciting fantasies regarding the opposite sex, even if I had no skill or experience to translate them into reality. Nice girls didn't kiss on first dates, and she was, if nothing else, a nice girl. Even if she wasn't a nice girl, I wouldn't have known what to do about it. But I could barely imagine the two of us at the end of the evening on her front porch, under the blinding porch light that her father had turned on while we were at the dance. (It was a known fact that fathers of teenage girls, before turning on the porch light, surreptitiously changed the 60-watt bulb to a 300-watt one, and then, to save on the electric bill, reversed the process after the daughter was safely in home in bed.)

As I move in for the kiss, rising on tip-toes, my head is back and my chin scrapes upward past her bosom and I stretch skyward to reach for those stratospheric lips. My heart thumps and my eyes close, partly to hide the passion of expectation, and partly to preserve my retinas from the damaging rays of the porch light, and then... the kiss lands squarely on her Adam's apple.

No way, Jose.

The big Friday night event in the school cafeteria approached with the determination of a steam engine that knew my foot was caught on the track. The engine chugged toward me, repeating "Gonna GETcha, Gonna GETcha, Gonna GETcha." Maybe I would be sick. The pleurisy I had had a couple of years before might put me back in bed, or I might strain my arm doing an American Twist serve on the tennis court. I couldn't square dance with my arm in a sling, could I?

In the end, I couldn't even conjure up a case of terminal acne.

On the appointed evening, I picked up Sondra in our family's dark blue 1949 Plymouth four-door sedan with the extra brake light in the middle of the trunk lid. She seemed taller than I remembered, but I also remembered Mom's advice and stifled my urge to turn and run. We went to the dance, she in a square dancing twirly-skirt, and I in one of my better shirts and slacks. The school cafeteria had been decorated by the members of the Girls' Club that afternoon, and the band and square dance caller were warming up and adjusting the sound system when we got there. Crepe paper streamers hung everywhere, with a scattering of colorful balloons fastened here and there. The chairs were arranged around the edges of the room and there were no lunch tables to be seen, so I couldn't hide under one of them.

There is a fortunate custom among square dance bands: The caller teaches everyone, step by step, how to square dance because no one ever knows how. Even those who had been to a square dance and learned all the moves have forgotten them. With all that detailed instruction to guide me, I managed to avoid alamanding left over into the next square, nor did I do-si-do into the rest room. When the caller said, "Swing your partner," my partner swung me. Another fortunate feature of square dances is that everyone, at one time or another, dances with everyone else, if only for a moment at a time. This let me believe that, amidst all the confusion, most of the time no one knew who my date was.

I survived the dance. My psyche suffered only minor damage and healed quickly, not because I enjoyed it, but because I was so relieved that it was over. When I walked Sondra to her door at the end of the evening, there was definitely no goodnight kiss. I avoided *that* humiliation with a quick "Thank you for inviting me. I enjoyed the evening," then hurried from the porch, jumped into the car, and escaped from the neighborhood.

Mom always said that every cloud has a silver lining, and there may have been one here, although I didn't see it at the time. Sondra may have had a good time at the dance, although if she did, I may not have contributed to it. At lease I tried to have a good time, and didn't act like too much of a jerk. And I learned not to swing my arms around too vigorously when standing next to a bedpost.

Chapter 19

Down a Lazy River

Our canoe floated down Big Bear Creek, a tributary of the Manistee River in Michigan, with only the slightest adjustment needed now and then by Jim Eaton in the stern to keep it on course. For the last few minutes the creek had been wide and deep, barely moving the canoe. Scenery floated by on both sides, arriving from ahead and disappearing behind us on its way to the headwaters we had left early in the morning.

While several families of Purdue professors were vacationing at Bear Lake, Michigan, some of the males in the party took a pair of canoes farther north for some wilderness adventure. Jim Eaton and I practiced our Boy Scout canoeing skills in one canoe, and both of our fathers were in the other canoe with Don Deer, a shop teacher in the West Lafayette schools and son-in-law of Professor Roscoe George.

Since putting in where the stream was smaller and faster moving, we had been joined by the water of four or five other streams. Now the rapids were farther apart and there was more time to watch the scenery and look for wildlife.

Kneeling in the bow I saw the other canoe disappear around the bend a hundred yards ahead. For a few minutes we were alone in the wilderness, Jim and I, no others within a thousand miles. It was a nice respite after getting through the last rapids where a couple of hidden rocks had jumped up from the bottom to attack us. The only hits sustained by the canoe were two bumps and scrapes, the third and fourth of the day. Not too bad, considering that we did this only two or three times a year, and never before on this stream. The other canoe had sprung a leak after a collision with a rock earlier in the day. We all had pulled out on the side while a canvas patch was applied and both crews waited for the glue to dry.

Now we approached the bend where our companions had disappeared. In the stern Jim said softly, "I hear fast water." Then I heard it too. It started as a faint whisper, like a soft breeze in the treetops, and grew louder as we approached the bend. Still no signs on the calm water ahead, but the banks were closer together now, and the water moved along a bit faster.

I stood up in the bow to get a better view of the surface ahead. As a general rule, standing up in a canoe is a very bad idea unless the canoeist wants to go swimming. When shooting rapids, however, the odds of taking an inadvertent swim are lower if the canoeist gets a really good look at the hazards ahead. Hence, an experienced canoeist, with the careful help of his teammate at the other end of the canoe, takes a small risk to avoid the larger dangers in the rapids.

The telltale sign of a solitary hidden rock is a series of ripples that start from where the rock is. In rapids, with the water boiling across the entire stream, the water pattern made by two rocks with enough room between them for a canoe forms a V pointing downstream. These features can be seen much better from higher above the water. An experienced canoeist will stand in the bow to get a photo in his mind of the rough water ahead. He does this while still in calm water. The stern man knows to stay perfectly still, not paddling, to stabilize the canoe. From his high vantage point, the bow man plans the route through the rapids, memorizing a map of his path between the Vs to the bottom of the rapids, if he can see that far. The bow man now becomes the captain of the ship and points out the entry path for the stern man. He also does most of the steering while in the rapids, with the stern man paddling to provide horsepower for speed. As the bow man kneels again, both of the crew pull together, paddling to go faster than the water, making steering easier. It also makes the rocks harder if you hit one.

Once into the rapids, the bow man can make sudden changes of direction much more efficiently than his partner. When a rock comes at him from dead ahead, the bow man sees it first. His paddle becomes a bow rudder, the upper part of the paddle clamped between upper arm and ribs, both hands gripping the shaft above the blade. Held this way, the paddle can quickly be put into the water on either side to avoid catastrophe. If a quick bow maneuver turns the boat so the side would hit the rock, the stern man must reverse the turn, pulling the stern to the side and around the rock. More moments of panic… a zig or a zag… paddle like crazy to gain speed again… look for the next V.

As I stood in the bow scanning the water ahead, there were no signs of rough water before the turn. Only the crescendo of the rushing water from around the bend hinted at trouble to come. As we approached, I knelt once more and quickly looked for a place to land where we could scout the menace beyond the bend before proceeding. No such luck. The banks were steep and by now the stream was narrow and moving fast. We aimed for the outside of the turn, where the faster, larger volume of water gave us a smaller chance of hitting rocks.

The water swept us into the turn where it had scoured out a bowl at the bottom of the cliff beside the stream. We found ourselves again in calm water, the roar of the rapids still fifty yards ahead. The other canoe was waiting for us by the shore after the inside of the turn where the water was shallow. As we approached, one of them grinned and yelled, "Did your heart go pitty-pat as you came into that turn? I'll bet you thought it was a waterfall!"

We pulled over to their side of the stream, beached the canoe next to them, and got out to stretch our legs. Obeying the old salesman's imperative, "Never pass a restroom," we each took solitary walks into the woods. It was nearly noon, so we broke out the bag lunches and sat on a log eating them. Jim's dad finished eating first and walked downstream to inspect the rapids. Don used the time to inspect the new patch on the bottom of their canoe. He proudly reported that no water had yet leaked in.

Returning from his recon mission, Jim's dad said, "Looks like it's not as bad as it sounds. Let's get started." We shoved off with the other canoe again in the lead. Waiting in the still water above the rapids, Jim and I watched the path of the other canoe, as they hit only one rock. "There's one to avoid," Jim said. "We can go just to the left of that spot where there's another V." I stood in the bow to take one last look, kneeled again, and said, "OKAAAY, readysetgo!" We both pulled hard toward the first V, straining every muscle, trying to stop the water from moving downstream while we charged ahead of it.

Then we were into it. We hit the first V dead center, shot through it toward a large boulder twenty feet beyond. As our stern cleared the V, I shoved my paddle onto the water on my left in a bow rudder maneuver just in time to prevent a head-on collision. Jim deftly did a stern rudder on the right side, avoiding the boulder and pointing the canoe downstream again, directly at another boulder. This time the channel with the most water was on the right, and I bow-ruddered in that direction. Again Jim pulled the stern around the rock, but not without tilting the canoe enough to take in some foamy water before we righted. We found ourselves aimed at the proper channel, where there was a two-foot drop in one length of the canoe. A plume of water was flying up where it hit the rock on the right, and as we shot through the opening we both got a shower.

With 30 feet of calm water before the next V, we both pulled straight ahead to gain speed. The opening was slightly to the left and Jim headed us toward it. Because we entered at an angle, I did another right bow rudder to straighten us out and Jim pulled the stern to the left as we shot into the breach and down another two-foot drop. Then it was over. Calm water and no rapids ahead.

As the noise of the water receded behind us, we took stock of our canoe while we caught our breath and relaxed. There was less than two inches of water in the bottom, not even worth stopping to bail out. Our kneeling pads would stay wet for a while, but we could live with that. And we hadn't hit a single rock, a claim that the old guys in the other canoe couldn't make. They had watched to see how we got through the white water, and were waiting for us below. "Whooie! We didn't hit a single rock," I hollered as we got within yelling distance.

"Yeah, that's 'cause we showed you the way," Don shouted.

"If we'd followed your path, we'd be swimming right now," Jim grinned.

"How much water did you take in?" asked Jim's dad.

"No more than a foot or two. How about you?"

"None, but one of my teeth fell out when we hit that rock," said Don. He had once lost the end of his finger at the middle joint in a shop accident at school. He held up that hand so we could see his short finger and said, "Look, the shock knocked off my fingernail, too."

We continued down the now peaceful stream. The sun was out and our clothes began to dry. Birds chirped and fluttered beside the creek, and a couple of cows stared at us from their pasture, chewing their cuds in bovine solitude, wondering why we were there. Our conversation continued as we drifted through the lazy afternoon, the two canoes only twenty feet apart now.

A soft popping noise from far beyond the right bank caught our attention. "Someone shooting?" asked Jim.

"Sounds like it, but I'm not sure," I answered. The men in the other canoe heard it too, and Don held up his hand and pointed with the other in the direction of the noise. Jim's dad stood up in his canoe to see over the bank, but it was too high. He shrugged his shoulders at us. The popping continued sporadically, but didn't get louder, so we relaxed.

A few minutes later the stream took a sharp right turn, and the popping got louder. Now it definitely sounded like shooting. The noise grew still louder, until we realized that the shooting was coming in our direction. We heard bullets zing over the bank above our heads, hitting the higher opposite bank.

"Get down!" Don yelled as he and Dad dove into the bottom of their canoe. Jim and I scrunched down as low as we could get, shoving aside the supplies that were in our way. Jim's dad stood up in his canoe, and waved his paddle back and forth high in the air.

"Stop the shooting!" he yelled at the top of his voice. The shooting continued, shots spaced three or four seconds apart, though we still couldn't see the person doing it.

"Stop the shooting! Stop the shooting!" Jim's dad still shouted and waved the paddle, assuming that whoever was shooting didn't know we were there.

We were just drifting now, not in the mood to paddle. The bank was getting lower, and Jim's dad sat down as it got low enough to see over. A house appeared, about a hundred yards from the stream, and the shooting stopped as it came into view. We saw a man bend over to pick up a satchel with his left hand, a rifle held in his right. He straightened up, turned, and walked quickly behind the corner of the house.

Then we were downstream, further from the shooter's house, which by now was out of sight again. Our two canoes had remained close together in the calm water, and we slowly lifted our heads above the gunwales and looked at each other with big eyes. The danger over, we relaxed and started paddling again. Don's face broke into a big grin as he looked at Jim and me. "You guys were so scared you were only about this thick on the bottom of that canoe," he said, holding his short finger and thumb about an inch apart.

"I hope you didn't hurt yourself diving into the bottom of your boat," I said.

"My only injury was this finger that got shot off." He held up the entire hand with all four fingers extended so we could see that one was too short. "What do you think that guy was doing?"

"Probably just target shooting or cleaning out his rifle," Jim said. "But maybe he just doesn't like canoeists. Should we go back and tell him he almost killed us?"

I demurred. "Not today, I'm not dressed for making new friends."

We dipped our paddles in unison, pulling further away from the shooting gallery toward the next rapids; then home for some dry clothes.

Chapter 20

The Wonder Years

I was channel flipping on an evening in early 2007, after watching C-Span, where Steve Forbes and T. Boone Pickens debated the prospects for world energy supply and demand. I flipped into the middle of a rerun of a "Wonder Years" episode where Kevin Arnold and his friend were fighting in Kevin's bedroom over a book that he had found in his mother's dresser drawer. The trouble with channel flipping is that you jump into the middle of a lot of stories without knowing what's going on, but this time it took me about three seconds to figure it out. The reason for the fight wasn't important. It might have been over who got to decide when to turn the page of the book, or which pictures they were going to look at the longest, or even who got to hold the book (and thus to decide what to look at in it). The subject of the book was obvious from the moment I saw it on the floor where it had fallen when the fight began. I couldn't read its title, but from a secret location deep in my memory where a similar situation was buried, I recognized that book.

Then disaster struck. Kevin's mother, responding to the ruckus, appeared in the doorway, asking, "What's going on in here?"

The fight stopped in less time than it had taken me to change the channel. "Whoops," the boys seemed to think, "We're in for it now."

The Wonder Years

I was a little older than Kevin Arnold was when I found a book, deep in the back of my mother's dresser drawer, under some sweaters and scarves. Copyrighted in 1926, seven years before my parents' marriage, it was called *Ideal Marriage: It's Physiology and Technique.* Sounding like the somniferous title of someone's PhD thesis, it virtually guaranteed the reader a good nap. But I wasn't convinced. If we had perfectly good knotty pine bookcases built into an entire wall of our new living room, why bury this one book in the back of a drawer in the bedroom?

I quickly thumbed through the pages and spotted some drawings that explained the mystery. This book with its ponderous title would require serious study.

I have since learned that the author was a Dutch gynecologist, Theodoor Hendrik van de Velde, who was apparently the Alfred Kinsey of the 1920s. Lacking Dr. Kinsey's scientific approach to taboo subjects, Dr. van de Velde got the information for his book from his own love life, from his patients, and from his personal observations of women engaged in, um, intimate activities.

I had found a goldmine of secret adult information. My motivation to study it increased by cosmic proportions as I realized that I could augment my education in a way previously unavailable. But when to study? As a high school sophomore I was still pretty naive, but I knew enough to be certain that I wasn't supposed to know of the book's existence.

There are rare times in our lives when the stars are in perfect alignment. The timing of events in the fall of 1950 can only be blamed on such an alignment. That summer my family had moved into our first home that was not a rental house. After saving and scrimping for years, my parents were finally able to buy their own home. The American dream was happening. To help make the mortgage payments each month, Mom had gone back to work as a fourth grade teacher, leaving a lonely gap of an hour after I got home, and before she got home from school; a perfect time for studying the newfound textbook.

Prior to my fateful discovery of that book, my sex education had come from three sources: My mother's discussion with me when I was eight about "germination" after I had laughed at two dogs behaving in a strange way; a small book given to me by my mother when I was twelve that covered some things that boys want to know; and some discussions with other boys in locker rooms, on street corners, and on Boy Scout campouts, where I learned about Eight-Page Thrillers.

I finally saw Eight-Page Thrillers when my friend Dave Franzen found a few dozen of them secreted in a shoe box under the stairs in his house. Eight-Page Thrillers were at the forefront of the pornography industry, a genre of tiny comic books with pages barely larger than a playing card, but thinner, drawn in pen and ink by highly talented artists with obviously extensive backgrounds of experience that I could only guess at. Each booklet featured a well-known comic character, and in eight comic panels illustrated in excruciating detail an encounter between the hero and a friend or acquaintance of the opposite sex: Moon Mullins in the back room of the grocery store where he worked, with a very attractive customer; Popeye on the deck of his ship with his girlfriend, Olive Oyle. Some of the panels illustrated anatomical impossibilities, but this merely increased their comic nature as well as their titillation factor.

I knew that Eight-Page Thrillers were sold in "The Hole," a downstairs pool hall in downtown West Lafayette with a disreputable standing in the community that my father had issued orders for me to stay out of. The price of one dollar each was ten times the price of a normal comic book, which was printed in color and had dozens of pages with multiple panels per page. My friend Dave had stumbled upon a treasure trove of these eight-page, awe-inspiring comics. Someone had spent a lot of money to buy them. Unfortunately, I only got a quick peek at two or three because Dave was so nervous about being caught looking at them. Thus my education remained incomplete and distorted until my discovery of *Ideal Marriage*. The book in Mom's drawer was about to expand my knowledge with more specificity than I had ever dared to hope for.

Most of my free time after school was devoted to other activities: Tennis practice, piano lessons, miscellaneous meetings associated with Scouts and school clubs, and once-a-week after-school serial movies, such as "The Iron Claw" and "The Invisible Man," designed to keep us off the streets, during which I was responsible, as a member of the high school's Technical Equipment Crew, for running the film projector. But now and then there were days when nothing was going on and I could study my newfound textbook.

The first two-thirds of the book was as boring as the title promised: personal health and hygiene, cooperating with each other, sharing the work, and other compatibility issues that didn't interest me at all. I whizzed through these parts, inventing speed-reading two years before the concept reached my school, so I could get to the good parts.

In later pages the narrative slowed me down and I found anatomical drawings (not new to me, but in more detail than I had seen before), how-to instructions (the really good stuff was here) that emphasized tenderness, caring, and a lot of other mushy stuff, and graphs of arousal level vs. time for both male and female when conjugally engaged. The male graph was a series of small stair-steps going up, followed by a quick drop from the peak. The superimposed female graph showed a slower, smoother rising curve, with a long, gradual drop back to normal. The major objective, according to the author, was to make the peaks of the two curves coincide in time, which would, presumably, be conducive to an ideal marriage. Tenderness and timing, it seemed, were everything.

By the time Mom got home from school, I was locked in the bathroom, tending to personal business, and the Book was safely back at the bottom of its drawer. I never did get caught reading it, but, as with all such novelties, the novelty eventually wore off, leaving me with more time to study my own books, play tennis, and hang out with my friends.

Seeing the episode of "The Wonder Years" decades later, I relived some of my own wonder years. They resonated as I watched a televised illustration of how mortified both Mom and I would have been if she had caught me reading her book.

Chapter 21

An Experiment with the Needle

As I progressed through puberty, I never had much of a problem with date rejection because I was usually too shy to ask for dates.

I had plenty of bad hair days, so if I could improve the way I looked, maybe the girls would give me hints that they wanted me to ask them out. I spent time in front of the bathroom mirror with a comb and a tube of Brylcreme. I searched for a new look, parting my hair on the wrong side, but with no noticeable improvement. I combed it straight back like my dad's, but it wouldn't stay and made me look like a porcupine. Dad had somehow trained his hair to stay in place that way, but mine wouldn't cooperate. I combed it straight back in front, but two inches back from the hairline, combed it sharply to the side, the way one of the handsomest guys in my class did. I tried every possible combination and permutation of how to comb each hair on my head, but never found a way that was good enough.

My acne problems were minor, but when they did occur I was treated with x-rays during weekly visits to a clinic. Little lead eye covers were put on me before the x-rays were turned on and aimed at my face.

Instead of serious acne, I got serious boils. Not many of them, and only one at a time, but those ugly, red, pus-filled sores were the scourge of my life for a year or two. The one on my right forefinger at the side of the middle joint burned with stabbing pain every time I bent my finger or bumped it on the edge of my desk at school. The one over the edge of my left kneecap hurt like crazy when I bent my knee or bumped it on the side of my chair. If I forgot and kneeled on the floor, I rolled on the floor in pain. The one on my abdomen hurt when I bumped a book against it and gave me a second belly button as it finally healed. The one on my chest was not only an ugly third nipple, but a painful one. We took the first two to Dr. Frasch to lance when they had "come to a head." My father lanced the others. He was just as handy with a needle and an X-Acto knife as with his woodworking tools and figured he could do it just as well as the doctor. If I ever need to be identified by the police, even today those scars will be helpful.

Weight problems, though, were a more serious matter: I was the skinniest kid in my school. The doctor said to forget about it; someday I would be happy to be slender. I didn't care about someday. I wanted to gain weight *now*. How could girls ever like a skinny guy?

The Charles Atlas ads in *Boy's Life* magazine told me that someone bigger than I was could kick sand in my face if I stayed skinny. If I gained weight, they wouldn't dare. Mom told me that those ads were misleading and that the spring-loaded exercise device they promoted wasn't worth the price.

I insisted that there must be a way to gain weight. Maybe my metabolism was abnormal. Could it be tested? Dr. Frasch was asked, and we made an appointment for the test. Lying on a special examination bed at the hospital, I breathed into the mouthpiece of a flexible tube connected to a fancy machine the size of the overstuffed easy chair in our living room. The machine, presumably, analyzed each molecule of exhaled air and somehow divined the efficiency with which my body turned food into muscles and fat. As I lay in my bed, visions of weight gain danced through my head. Surely these measurements would uncover the means by which pounds would accumulate and attract desirous glances from deserving females in my vicinity. In a few days the answer came back: My metabolism was normal. Impossible. Another path to popularity had been closed off.

"How about vitamin B?" I asked. Pills were purchased and swallowed each day for months, but to no avail. I would be an old man before I became normal.

Maybe *shots* of vitamin B would get it into my system more efficiently. Dr. Frasch gave me the first shot and showed my mother how to do it. At the drug store we purchased the syringe, a couple of needles, and a little brown bottle of liquid vitamin B with a red rubber membrane in the center of the bottle cap. On the way home we stopped at the grocery store to buy some oranges for Mom to practice on. Dad would supervise. He was handy enough to lance boils like a surgeon, but nurses gave shots. It was women's work.

After a few tries, the needle went into the orange to just the right depth, and we were ready. I could already feel the extra weight on my bones and sense, without even looking, the admiring glances of girls, the same way detectives in the stories in *The Saint Detective Magazine* always knew when they were being followed because of the tingles they felt on the back of their neck. The English language hadn't yet evolved to the point where the word "hunk" was used in this context, but whatever the word's predecessor was would surely apply to me. My persistence was about to pay off.

We boiled water in a pan on the stove and dropped the needle into it, eliminating all those tetanus and other scrofulous microbes lurking inside. Mom attached the needle to the syringe and poked it through the rubber in the bottle cap. Pulling the plunger back, she filled the syringe to the prescribed mark, pulled the needle from the bottle, held the needle upward, and plunged the air out of the syringe. Perfect. She swabbed my upper arm with alcohol, and the big moment was at hand.

I turned my head away, closed my eyes, and felt the familiar sting of the needle. It had barely punctured my skin. "You gotta push *harder*, Mom," I said. Several tries later, the needle went far enough into my pock-marked flesh that the vitamins could be injected. I felt them adjusting my metabolism as they surged through my system, adding large muscle cells as they went.

We repeated the ordeal for several days. After receiving multiple stabbings each time, I got mad at my mother because she was so timid. I learned that if I got *visibly* mad and yelled at her, she would reciprocate. I wanted her angry. When she was angry her fear of hurting me abated, and she drove the needle home with sufficient gusto.

After a few days of this warfare, the needle became more painful and more difficult to insert no matter how angry she was. "Is the needle getting dull?" Dad asked, as if my skin was made of chain mail. A magnifying glass revealed a microscopic hook on the very tip, caused either by the tough skin of an orange, my own tough skin, or by carelessly dropping the needle into the pan of boiling water. We didn't know how long the tip had been bent, but a new needle made the shots less onerous.

Actual weight gain was another matter. Nothing changed, and the daily emotional strain on Mom, accompanied by tissue damage in my upper arm, was too much for us. Whatever my weight was, I had to live with it.

When I graduated from high school three years later, I weighed 118 pounds, and when Marianne and I got married seven years after that, I was up to 125 pounds. The doctor was right. I had figured out how to be happy *and* skinny. What he didn't tell me was that decades later, when my weight was in the one hundred sixties, I would search for ways to lower it.

Chapter 22

Spelunking

The southern part of Indiana is riddled with dangerous holes in its underground limestone. Some are horizontal underground streams. Some are caves, ranging in size from tiny cubbyholes to huge caverns, formed by thousands of years of erosion. And some are vertical sink holes caused by the collapse of land into those streams and caves.

All of these holes provide fertile ground for explorers, and opportunities for adventurers to escape from otherwise boring weekends.

When my friend, Sonny Dunham, suggested that we go caving in southern Indiana during our freshman year Thanksgiving vacation, several of us said, "Tell me more."

As a member of the Purdue Spelunking Club, Sonny had made a few weekend trips with others to explore wild caves in southern Indiana, during which he had learned the basic equipment requirements and safety principles: Always carry three kinds of light, flashlight, carbide lamp, matches, or candles. Never go alone. Take extra clothing in case you get wet. He told us enough about these rules to convince us that it was safe, and we went home to tell our parents about the proposed camping trip.

After persuading our reluctant parents to not object, that we were adults now and could take care of ourselves, the next chore was to buy some equipment. Most of us were already well supplied with basic camping equipment. Tents, sleeping bags, cook kits, and methods of starting fires and keeping matches dry had been part of our Boy Scout assemblage for several years. My major purchase for this trip was a canvas hat with an attached carbide lamp, similar to that which we knew coal miners wore from seeing news reports of mining accidents and strikes led by union boss John L. Lewis.

Our trip was planned for Friday, the day after Thanksgiving. Six people and all our gear required two cars, and our base camp would be Turkey Run State Park, less than 100 miles from home. From there we would take side trips to explore caves on private farm property, but Sonny already had permission, via the Purdue Spelunking Club, to explore them.

Our morning stop, on the way to the park, was at a small dry cave, no bigger than the average bedroom but half as high, in which you might expect a bear to hibernate. The only sign of life in it was one solitary bat, hanging from the ceiling with a band on its leg. The temperature was in the thirties, and the bat didn't stir while we lit it with flashlights and peered. Nearby on the floor was a lunchbox-sized wire cage, apparently left there by the bat banders. Boring. I hoped the other two caves we would visit had more to offer.

The next exploration was an underground stream that we entered via a large sinkhole near some woods at the back edge of a farm. The sinkhole was fifty feet across at the rim, and twenty feet below the rim it narrowed, like a funnel, to an opening just large enough for a person to drop down through. We tied a long rope to a nearby tree and dropped it into the hole to use as a climbing aid when we wanted to exit from the stream that ran below. The stream was another ten or twenty feet below the bottom of the sinkhole, but fortunately the dirt and gravel that had fallen through the hole now formed a mound tall enough to reach with our feet as we dropped through the hole. We climbed and slid down the mound to the water below.

Donning our carbide lamp hats after lighting them, we left our supplies (towels, fresh clothes, etc.) at the base of the mound near the bottom end of the rope, and began walking downstream. The passage soon narrowed until there was no room to walk beside the water. We had no choice but to walk in the center of the stream. Passing occasional small stalactites and stalagmites at the sides of the stream, we plodded along as the passage narrowed and the water rose to mid-thigh. We could now extend our arms to touch both sides of the tunnel at once. The ceiling dropped so low at times that we had to lean over with our face nearly in the water to pass by.

After continuing in this fashion for perhaps a mile, the passage opened into a large cavern a hundred feet across and three stories high, with a huge mound of dirt in the middle. Five other tunnels similar to the one we had come through could be seen at differing levels, four of them 10 to 20 feet above us and spaced around the periphery of the cavern. The fifth tunnel was at our level on the other side of the mound, obviously the continuation of the stream we were following. The four tunnels above us had been made by two other streams that had crossed our stream, like an underground, three-level overpass on the freeway. With three streams crossing at the same location, erosion had weakened the earth at that spot and the whole thing had caved in sometime in its dim history, leaving the mound in the middle of the cavern. We were able to climb up into one of the other tunnels to explore for a short distance, but found nothing of interest and decided to head back to our sinkhole entrance.

We arrived there tired and cold, dried ourselves as best we could, changed to dry clothes, and climbed up and out into daylight We arrived at the park in time to set up our tents, dig a crude trench latrine, build a fire, and cook some supper before we leapt into our freezing sleeping bags and. shivered ourselves to sleep.

The next morning, sparkles of frozen moisture floated in the air, adding to the dusting of snow on the ground, as we struggled in mittens and gloves to cook breakfast and keep warm at the same time. Today's cave, according to Sonny, was a "wet" one, unlike the others we had visited the day before where only our legs were under water. No simple wading in the water this time; to pass under the lowest ceilings, we would crawl on our stomachs in water and mud.

Second thoughts about this level of adventure and stimulation bubbled through my brain. Just how uncomfortable did I want to get? Thinking fast, I volunteered to stay in camp and cook dinner for my more adventurous friends. One other camper stayed with me while the four valiant ones drove off in their car.

While the others were gone, our day in camp consisted, first and foremost, of keeping the fire going and staying warm. Between explorations of the local woods around our campsite, we collected dead branches to feed to our fire, washed the breakfast dishes, ate our noontime sandwiches, and got ready to prepare a feast for the hungry subterranean explorers when they returned.

In late afternoon they returned and parked out by the road. Anxious to impress the chicken patrol that had stayed behind, they told tales of bravery and heroism, of lurking danger, and of mud and wetness. Crawling on their bellies in mud that was several inches deep to traverse the tight spots, they had survived the ordeal and returned to the sinkhole entrance. Emerging from beneath the earth like creatures from the brown lagoon, they had removed all their clothes, cleaned themselves as best they could in the frigid outside air, and put on dry clothes. They then dragged their pile of mud-impregnated exploratory garments to the car at the end of a rope.

Dinner that evening was no ordinary serving of gruel shared by six hoboes gathered around the fire. It was a feast for heroes: four Odyssean wanderers and two Penelopes celebrating heroic deeds and their reunited clan. We topped off the meal with a cake baked in my folding reflector oven that, years ago for a merit badge, I had fashioned from sheet aluminum and wire coat hangers when those commodities became available after World War II.

Before our last Siberian night in sleeping bags, the four wanderers removed from the trunk of their car the sodden clothes that by now were frozen into a single, solid lump of muddy ice. They dragged it by its rope to a nearby tree, leaned it against the trunk, and went to bed.

Two Shakes of a Lamb's Tail

III

Learning To Fly

Time is the most indefinable yet paradoxical
of things; the past is gone, the future is not
come, and the present becomes the past, even
while we attempt to define it, and, like the flash
of the lightning, at once exists and expires.

Charles Caleb Colton

Time flies. It's up to you to be the navigator.

Robert Orben

Chapter 23

Sleeping in Class

Professor Charlie Siskind was the Purdue Electrical Engineering Department's designated curmudgeon. I never saw him smile. He either didn't know how or didn't have a sense of humor and therefore wasn't required to smile. He was, however, a superb teacher. In the hallways he perambulated from office to classroom and back, aimed straight ahead with papers tucked under his arm against his vest. No visible signs of personality escaped the bubble that surrounded him. But in the classroom he was one of the best teachers of my entire college experience. In front of the class and at the blackboard he oozed clarity. He made complicated formulas seem simple, and he reduced impenetrable concepts to something that even I could understand when I stayed awake in class.

And he flunked me.

Professor Siskind's specialty was AC and DC machinery. That field consisted of three kinds of electrical devices: motors, generators, and transformers. Charlie Siskind knew everything there was to know about those devices, and what he didn't know, he invented. My classmates and I could have believed that he had educated Edison and Steinmetz. Magnetic flux and the permeability of steel were child's play to him. He was unmarried, had no family or friends that anyone knew about, and thus had plenty of time after work to write textbooks about his specialty. His many textbooks were used in universities all over the country, making him the biggest money earner in McGraw-Hill's stable of authors.

He flunked me, and I deserved it. My list of transgressions, other than low quiz scores and missing homework assignments, included falling asleep in his class a few times, most importantly during an exam. When he called me into his office, I knew a storm was imminent.

I sat down in front of his desk as the thunder started, precursor to tornado-force winds that would shred my shirt and muss my hair. The climax of his tirade was something I would remember the rest of my life:

"Some of your classmates will graduate and do some good things," he said. "But you won't."

And there it was. The facts of my performance laid out for us to see, and the obvious conclusion. As I left his office in tatters, I worried... *What will Dad think?*

Attending Purdue University was preordained. I was qualified, and it was cheaper than finding an out-of-state engineering school. I had graduated from high school near the top of my class, a member of the National Honor Society, with math and science proclivities. As a junior, I had cooked up a new tool to trisect an angle, and the resulting paper explaining it was a winner in the Indiana Westinghouse Science Talent Search, with a special citation for math topics. My dad's position on the Electrical Engineering faculty got my already low in-state tuition cut in half to about $100 per semester, and I could save a bundle by living at home. Textbooks were all under ten dollars, half that if I bought used ones. I was a licensed radio amateur (call sign W9UOX) and had built my own "ham radio" transmitter. As a hobby experiment, I had built a motor out of a magnet, steel nails, and copper wire that was powered by a dry cell, and I had taken apart or put together countless circuits, erector set projects, old radios, and miscellaneous doodads. It was natural that I would take electrical engineering like my dad.

Before registering for freshman courses, I took tests that either got me into advanced-placement courses, or established credits without taking the course. By the end of the first semester of my freshman year I had established 32 hours of credit, but my grades were all over the place. I got D in advanced math, D in advanced chemistry, A in English composition, and some Bs and Cs. My qualifications for entry into Purdue may have been excellent, but I was deficient in the most important area and I didn't even know it: I hadn't learned to study. High school had been too easy for me, and I was on track to flunk out in my freshman year if things didn't change. The second semester I dropped the advanced math program and took the basic analytic geometry course that most new freshman engineers took. I got an A, but my study habits didn't improve, and I proceeded to load up on extra-curricular activities as I had done in high school.

I went out for the tennis team, wrote articles for the campus newspaper, and entered the fraternity rush program. In my sophomore year I pledged the Pi Kappa Phi fraternity. My grades again started to slide, but my activities kept me too busy to notice. Walking around campus with my pledge box held beside the slide rule hanging from my belt made me feel accepted, important. During hell week, I slept at the fraternity so I could be woken in the middle of the night by the pledge master who always had a variety of interesting tasks for me and my pledge brothers to accomplish. We lined up nude in the great hall (curtains over the windows), divided into two teams to compete in a relay race. Each of us in turn had to sit on a block of ice to pick up a chocolate-covered cherry between the cheeks of his ass and crab walk on all fours, facing up, to the other end of the room and back without dropping the candy. When my turn came, my skinny butt wasn't sufficiently prehensile for picking up candy. I spent the rest of my turn sitting on the block of ice, vainly trying to grab that little brown mound of sweetness while the upper classmen laughed themselves sick. As penalty for losing the race, we each got to eat a semi-crushed chocolate-covered cherry served up on a fraternity paddle by the pledge master so that he didn't have to touch them. One night we ran a gauntlet of various abuses, and on another night were led blindfolded through a series of stations reminiscent of a haunted house tour. At one station, I was made to swallow a large pill that was said to be a pig's testicle, and for the entire next day and a half my urine was brilliant orange. On another night we went on a scavenger hunt that began at 2:00 a.m. The list of things we were to bring back to the house included a black brassiere, a Tavern Beer can with a cone top, and a computation of the area, in circular mils, of the traffic circle on the mall in front of the Purdue administration building. A circular mil is a measure of the cross-sectional area of electrical wire.

We divided into teams to find our treasures and scattered hither and yon around the Purdue campus and among the nooks and crannies of Tippecanoe County. Since I was an electrical engineering student—still with a moderately untarnished academic reputation—who happened to know what a circular mil was, I volunteered to find the area of the traffic circle. My partner and I made a beeline for the campus mall where I paced off the diameter of the traffic circle. On paper, I converted the resulting diameter in yards to inches, then to thousandths of an inch, squared the result, and we had met our goal. Back at the fraternity house, we woke the pledge master to present him with the result of our labor. In his sleep-induced fog, he stuffed the paper containing our magic number into his pocket and said, "Fine, go to bed."

The next day we heard about the adventures of the other teams. Tavern Beer was no longer brewed by the Lafayette Brewery, which had been closed two years before. To find their beer can, that team broke into the abandoned brewery, found an empty cone-topped can, and brought it back to the house without getting caught by the police. The team looking for the black brassiere wasn't so fortunate. To find the object of their search they woke the girlfriend of a team member by rattling the window of her dorm room with stones thrown from the lawn below. The resulting ruckus attracted the attention of the campus police, who took the brothers into custody, resulting in the eventual placement of our entire pledge class on social probation.

In my junior year I moved from home into the fraternity for a semester, fomenting a major academic disaster. That year my studying for quizzes and tests began the night before the event, and stretched through the night. When I had trouble staying awake all night, I did what other stupid students did: I went to the Student Health Service, told them I needed help staying awake to study, and was given a bottle of Dexedrine (dextroamphetamine) pills by Doc Miller, who was very liberal in his medical treatment policies. Dexedrine was used as a diet pill at the time, but one of its side effects was to get the user hopped up so that staying awake all night was easy. Nobody told me that the pills didn't enhance learning ability. The net effect was exhaustion, which made sleep much easier during class the next day.

After one semester of living in the fraternity house, I moved back home, where there were fewer distractions.

Inability to concentrate infested my other studies that year. The new head of the Electrical Engineering Department had decreed that all faculty members must teach courses. Specializing in research alone was no longer allowed, and Roscoe George, the head of the EE Experiment Station, who had never taught classes, became a teaching professor against his will. I took his magnetic circuits class, in which he faced the blackboard, covered it with mathematical symbols and equations without ever turning around, then began again, erasing his prior scribbles as he went, to make room for fresh ones as he mumbled cryptic explanations. I learned nothing in that class, due more to my incompetence as a student than to Professor George's lack of teaching ability. He was generous and gave me a D. I never learned why the department head didn't grandfather the one or two existing full-time researchers and allow the passage of time to flush them out when they retired. My father never overtly criticized the department head, but I could tell from his attitude that he thought the head was as poor at leading teachers as those he forced to teach were at teaching.

The ultimate mortification came when I was flunking the course for which my father wrote the book. My face-saving maneuver of dropping the course prevented me from collecting another F. I took the course again later, and by then had my head straightened out enough that I got reasonable grades.

To make up for the dropped course and the F in Professor Siskind's course, I went to school in the summer following my senior year and graduated with an overall average of C and an ROTC commission as a second lieutenant in the Army Signal Corps.

1957 was a good year to graduate from college. Jobs were plentiful, and the recent end of the Korean War took away the concerns of facing combat when I went on active duty to fulfill my ROTC commission commitment. During my senior year I had several job interviews at the Purdue Placement Office, and was invited to fly to visit six companies, located in Dallas, Minneapolis, Cedar Rapids, Cincinnati, Long Island, and Rochester, NY.

The commercial flights on a Lake Central Airline's DC3 from the Purdue airport began with an uphill climb to find my seat in the sloping passenger cabin of the "tail dragger" plane. The stewardess then came down the aisle offering little packets of Chiclets gum to the passengers to chew to avoid painful pressure-induced ear pops as we climbed to altitude. The vibration during takeoff was so intense that the copilot had to hold the throttle levers to keep them in place where the pilot set them.

Of the six companies I visited, three offered me jobs, and I chose Stromberg-Carlson in Rochester, where I was offered $100 per week. By the time I got to Rochester in the fall, the company had been absorbed by General Dynamics, and I was assigned to work on a government development contract at the General Dynamics Electronics Division.

The agonies of school and the humiliations of facing my parents when I got low grades were over. Now I was really on my own, ready for a new start, and determined to succeed.

Chapter 24

Making Out

For every female student at Purdue University in the 1950s, there were four males, which tells you something about my odds of getting a date during my college years. If you account for all the males who were assured of a date if they wanted one—the athletes, the editors of the school paper and the yearbook, the fraternity presidents, the cheerleaders, the glee club singers, and assorted other Big Men On Campus who had no problems finding female friends, my odds of finding any overlooked ones were between zero and nil.

There was a fundamental reason for this imbalance in the population: A large majority of the students were majoring in either engineering or agriculture. In the mid-twentieth century, women didn't major in those subjects. In all of my engineering and other technical classes during my four years in college, there were only two women. Most of the time, the only women in the Electrical Engineering building were two or three department secretaries who were either senior citizens or were already married to graduate students. The female twenty percent of the student population, mostly liberal arts or home economics majors, were said to be there seeking their MRS degree. The odds were in their favor.

The perceived peer pressure weighed on me. Throughout my first two years of college, my Muse sat on my shoulder, giving me knuckle raps on the head while whispering questions in my ear: *Why were all the other guys dating as though it was the most natural thing in the world? What did they have that I didn't? Why was I such a verbal klutz who couldn't start a conversation with a female other than my mother unless I had known her since kindergarten?*

Getting a date to go to a Saturday night movie, or to a fraternity dance required careful planning, an aggressive temperament, and opportunities to meet women, none of which were part of my repertoire.

On my very short list of possibly datable women was Jeanne, a classmate with whom I had gone out a few times in high school, and who was now a Purdue student. We had dated a few times in our junior year at college, and since I already knew and liked her, starting a conversation wasn't difficult.

We weren't going steady, so I asked her for a date to the Junior Prom well before any of the other fifty guys who might have known her even thought of doing so. She said yes and we went to the prom. I wore my tux that was left over from my high school prom. Yes, it still fit me.

I borrowed my parents' car for the evening and picked her up at her parents' home where she still lived. Coming down the stairs in her strapless formal gown with my orchid corsage fastened firmly right where a strap might have been attached, she was beautiful, and I was falling in love. Since we would be out late, I was to return her to her sorority house where she would spend the night.

The huge ballroom in the student union building was a crowded picture of romance. Balloons and crepe paper streamers hung everywhere. Blue lighting thickened the atmosphere, a scrim between us and all the others in the room. Orchestra music wafted across the dance floor from the instruments of the Benny Goodman big band while we and a thousand other couples danced.

Then the prom was over and her sorority curfew approached. We hurried to her sorority house with less than five minutes to spare, where we faced a crowd of another kind. A crush of conglutinated couples, jammed into the large entrance hall, were all desperately saying goodnight to each other, unaware of us as we pushed our way through, trying not to look at anyone. Privacy was clearly not their primary concern. The couples were rooted in place like a forest of tree trunks with two backs, each having achieved motionless carnal lip-lock.

This was something for which my college education had not prepared me. My only experiences with goodnight kisses had taken place in the relative privacy of a date's front porch or, perhaps a more energetic version in the front seat of my dad's car at the end of a date. Going out with a town girl who lived at home had shielded me from sorority front foyers where making out in throngs was apparently the order of the evening. The athletes and the other Big Men On Campus had become immune to discomfiture at the end of their evenings. Their big egos and self-confidence protected them from caring what the surrounding crowd thought, an attitude bolstered by the fact that the rest of the swarm was engaged in exactly the same activity.

Virginally embarrassed by this mass make-out display, we searched for a non-existent private corner, but the deadline arrived. The sorority's designated curfew Nazi pushed her way through the crowd, tapped each tuxedo-clad back, and shouted, "Goodnight, gentlemen! Good*night* gentlemen!" to expel the males from the house.

No one moved.

Fervently hoping that no one saw me do it, I gave my date a chaste kiss, thanked her for a wonderful evening, and vacated the premises. "Good*night* gentlemen!" followed me out the door and echoed in my head as I drove home.

Jeanne and I dated for a while after the prom, but eventually one of those fifty other guys captured her attention, and I was once again dateless. My Muse returned to my shoulder and resumed those annoying, ego-destroying questions. On the positive side, however, my grades improved during my senior year. I graduated and moved to my new job in Rochester, New York. Three years later, Marianne Knox repaired my ego when we fell in love and married, unencumbered by platoons of other make-outs in her front foyer.

Chapter 25

Learning to Fly

After working at General Dynamics for a few months, I was called to active duty to fulfill my Army ROTC obligation. I had no clue that, just for fun, I would soon be practicing forced landings in a light plane.

My first army duty station in 1958 was in the 586th Signal Company at Fort Sheridan, Illinois. I had no close friends there to occupy my spare time. Hanging around the bar at the officers' club wasn't my style, and, in my part of the world, singles bars hadn't yet been invented. My roommate in the Bachelor Officers' Quarters, also a second lieutenant, liked to read the Bible in the evenings, which wasn't my style either.

I was bored and time crept. I bought a turntable that would play both 33 and 45 rpm records, a kit of parts for a high fidelity FM receiver and amplifier, and a speaker cabinet kit that, when built, housed a ten-pound speaker with flat audio response from 20 to 20,000 cycles per second. When all the vacuum tubes lit up, I could turn up the volume to shake the walls and annoy everyone else in the BOQ. I soon got bored again and needed a new hobby.

The Ft. Sheridan Flying Club kept a Piper Super Cub and two Navions at the Chicagoland Airport a few miles west of the post, and I considered joining. I hesitated because during my first and only flight in a private plane a couple of years earlier, my fraternity brother had looked sideways at me from the pilot's seat and said, "Wanna do a stall?"

I had never heard of a stall, so how bad could it be? My other two fraternity brothers in the back seat said, "Sure." Not to be outdone, I agreed. Peer pressure was at work here, providing both bravado and boundless trust in our brother the pilot.

An airplane "stall" occurs whenever the plane goes so slowly that the wings don't provide enough lift to keep it aloft. It stops flying and plummets, nose down, toward the earth. All pilots learn to do stalls as a training maneuver so they can learn how to prevent them, and, should one inadvertently occur, how to get out of it so the plane doesn't fall all the way to the ground. But I didn't know that.

The pilot pulled back on the stick, pointing us at the sky to slow the plane. When the plane stopped flying, the horizon whizzed up past the windshield as the nose pointed at the earth, and we went into free-fall. About to make a splat mark on the Indiana landscape, I stretched my feet out to soften the crash and clawed at the cockpit door to escape, even though we were still a half mile above the ground. My terror turned to embarrassment as the plane gained speed and resumed horizontal flight, and my fraternity brothers got a belly laugh at my reaction.

At Ft. Sheridan, I told 1st Lt. Pete Miller, our company training officer and my boss, of my wish to join the flying club and of my panic reaction during my only flight in a light plane. Pete was also the company pilot, in charge of flying and supervising the maintenance of an L-19 two-seat reconnaissance plane.

"No problem," he said. "I'll take you up on one of my training flights in the company plane to get you used to it."

It didn't bother him that the pantywaist in the back seat might climb onto his shoulders and wrap himself around his head as soon as the plane left the ground.

At the airfield Pete briefed me on the airplane's features and showed me how to climb into the rear cockpit seat and put on the headphones so we could talk to each other. We strapped ourselves in, using shoulder and waist straps that were part of the packed parachutes that did double duty as the seat cushions. *Parachutes? Was that a good sign or a bad sign?*

In the air he gave me the works. The pull and direction of gravity became variables as he did stalls, spins, chandelles, wingovers, and every other aerobatic maneuver for which the plane was rated. When gravity became zero during free-fall and my stomach tried to remain up where we had been a moment before, I felt the same old panic, but now that I knew what to expect, the imperative to leave claw marks on the inside of the cockpit was less intense. I soon got over even that. For a while I enjoyed the wild ride, but then began to feel queasy as my last meal threatened to decorate the back of Pete's seat.

"Uh...Pete?" I asked into my microphone, like I was talking to my mother about something I knew she didn't want me to do. Pete looked at my green pallor and decided to land. I was grateful, not only for the turbulence training, but for the consideration he showed in ending it. In retrospect, I think he landed only because he didn't want his subordinate to barf all over the expensive government property we rode in. After all, he was responsible for protecting it.

The next weekend in West Lafayette, my friend Don Katter and I took dates to the Tippecanoe County fair. To get further acclimated to turbulence and unnatural positions, I took all the wild rides I could find. Then I was ready. On Monday I joined the Fort Sheridan Flying Club.

My lessons began in "ground school," comprising classroom courses in rules of the sky, navigation, how airplanes work, and the requirements for getting a pilot's license. My first flight with an instructor was preceded by his showing me the parts of the airplane, including the "stick" that emerged from somewhere below the cockpit floor, its movement confined laterally by my two knees and longitudinally by the dashboard and my crotch. He explained the use of the stick, the pedals, the five panel instruments, and how to inspect the plane before climbing in to make sure there were no flat tires or holes in the wings.

The Piper Super Cub was a very basic airplane. Because there was no automatic starter, someone had to "prop" the plane—a process roughly equivalent to hand-cranking the engine of a Model T automobile. This brave person stood in front of the propeller using all his weight to start it spinning by hand while the pilot choked the carburetor, managed the throttle, and, most importantly, held the brakes on so the person pulling the prop didn't become hamburger when the engine started. Trust is a big part of flying.

The gas gauge was a piece of what looked like coat-hanger wire that stuck up through the gas cap in front of the windshield and was moved up and down by a cork that floated inside the tank. A half-inch from the top end of the wire a right-angle bend kept it from disappearing into the tank when the gas cap was removed or when the tank was empty.

After twenty minutes of explanations on the ground, we climbed into the plane, my instructor into the front seat and I in the rear. The rear seat was where a solo pilot would sit to keep the plane properly balanced. A duplicate set of controls and instruments in the front seat allowed the instructor to fly the plane until he signaled me to take over the controls.

More modern planes than ours had tricycle landing gears with a nose wheel that kept the plane level when resting on the ground. Our Super Cub's tail wheel, when resting on the ground, caused the plane's nose to tilt upward, and prevented the pilot (in either seat) from seeing what was directly ahead. He had to taxi using wide sweeping "S" turns so he could view the path ahead by alternately looking out first one side window then the other until he got to where he was going.

A non-pilot observing a taxiing, tail-dragging Piper Cub might think the pilot was drunk. Once airborne, the plane was level, and visibility was good.

My instructor gave me six one-hour lessons in the air over the course of six weeks, letting me fly the plane most of that time. I practiced take-offs, landings, turns, spins, and stalls, all the while learning to navigate until I convinced the instructor that I wouldn't get lost when I finally got to fly the plane by myself. From the air, everything on the ground looks alike to an untrained pilot. Finding my way back to the airport was not a simple matter. The only road signs were rivers, creeks, railroads, towns, distinctive farm buildings and other landmarks hundreds or thousands of feet below. With only a compass in the plane, I had to pay close attention to the direction of flight so I could reverse it to find my way home.

Forced landings were rehearsed when the instructor, during any maneuver, suddenly pulled the throttle back to simulate a failed engine, and yelled, "Forced Landing!" I was expected to already have a landing field picked out, usually on a farm. I had to immediately push the stick forward to avoid a stall and then demonstrate that I could land safely. When we got to within a few feet of the ground, the instructor took the controls and aborted the landing.

During my seventh hour of lessons I practiced take-offs and landings for a while, and then the instructor told me to pull over and stop on the runway. He got out of the plane and said, "You take it around and land it by yourself this time." I gulped and did as he said.

I had soloed.

✧

Two Shakes of a Lamb's Tail

Back at the Army base, my job changed. The Signal Company to which I was assigned didn't really need my services, so when the Signal Officer of the Fifth Region Nike Missile Command on the post needed extra help, I was loaned to him for the duration of a missile system test. The test was called "Weapons System Evaluation Group" or WSEG (pronounced "wesseg"). My job was to help the signal staff pull together the equipment that was needed in the communications center during the test. Much of my effort was focused on running around the post scrounging surplus equipment and parts for the comm center at the behest of my boss, Captain G. G. Kent.

The actual test, when it ran, simulated Russian bombers attacking the US from over the North Pole. By then, my scavenger activities were finished, and Captain Kent and I got to sit in the gloom of the control center's observation balcony at Nike missile headquarters, watching the action as it was plotted on a side-lit transparent map of the northern hemisphere that covered an entire wall of the regional command center. Below us on the main floor officers and technicians wearing headphones sat at dimly lit desks and mumbled softly into microphones, making decisions to prevent Chicago and Detroit from being vaporized in mushroom clouds. Behind the map in the murky shadows, soldiers wearing headphones erased letters and symbols and drew new ones of new colors, writing backward so we could read them from in front of the display. At the top of the map a soldier on a ladder drew some new symbols near the North Pole: Soviet bombers. One by one, he erased them and drew new ones farther south, extending the lines behind them like contrails in the sky. Missile crews at Nike sites near potential target cities in the US were put on alert and the missiles came up from their underground hideouts into firing position, someone's finger on each trigger like sharpshooters waiting for their prey. By now our own SAC fighters and bombers, based along an arc that stretched from

Greenland to North Africa, were presumably in the air, going toward Russia, each with its own sets of trigger fingers and plans for retaliatory death and destruction.

The Soviet bombers crossed the US border and the Great Lakes, arrived at their targets, and then the test was over, the results never revealed to those of us without a need to know and a high enough security clearance. It was enough that I had glimpsed Armageddon, and I hoped that, as a deterrent, the leaders of our country had demonstrated something similar for the Soviets: *Make my day. My gun is bigger than your gun, and if you fire yours, you will wish you hadn't.*

Meanwhile, in my off hours, the preparation for my pilot's license proceeded. To accumulate flying hours and to practice my navigation skills, I planned a solo cross-country trip south into central Illinois. My destination was Peoria, where I had spent two summers while in college, working as an engineering intern in the R&D Department of the Caterpillar Tractor Company. The 140-mile trip would take about two hours in each direction. I could fly there, have lunch with friends, then return.

I fueled the plane and went over my check list: sunglasses in my shirt pocket, maps in the airplane's map pocket, along with my Jeppeson navigation slide rule/computer. Ever mindful of the Boy Scout motto, "Be Prepared," I made a final visit to the restroom, and after some tire kicks and an inspection walk-around I was ready to go.

The summer weather was perfect as I climbed to 3,000 feet, leveled off, trimmed the controls, and made a slight correction for the winds aloft. On my left was Lake Michigan, and farther south on its shore the skyline of Chicago which we had recently saved from nuclear destruction during our WSEG test. Below me in the sparkling sunlight lay small towns and farm fields bordered by roads, railroads, trees, and streams, and above me, only blue sky. My plane and I were suspended by an invisible cord extending beyond the blue ceiling above, while the earth ahead crawled toward me at earthworm speed and disappeared under the plane to the rear. Without nearby landscape whizzing by as in a car, I could sense the airplane's movement only through the vibration of the engine or occasional bumps of turbulent air, as though a cosmic fisherman high above jerked our suspension cord, jiggling his bait to tempt another airborne fish to bite.

A private pilot, while aloft in a small plane, must focus on three primary tasks: collision avoidance (Are there other planes in my vicinity?), navigation (Am I going toward my destination?), and identification of potential fields for forced landings (If the engine quits right now, where would I land?). As I scanned the area around me, I spotted movements below, near a large airport. Military fighter jets were landing and taking off at O'Hare Field, which had not yet been opened to commercial traffic. Not wanting to upset any fighter pilots or the control tower operators, I climbed another thousand feet and made sure not to fly directly over their airport.

During the recent evenings when I planned this trip, it hadn't occurred to me to consider other familiar places that might be near my route. O'Hare Field was, of course, on my map, so I already knew about it. As I traveled further downstate and away from the heavier traffic around Chicago and O'Hare, I checked my map periodically for landmarks that would verify that I wasn't lost. As I passed Aurora, an exotic-sounding town named Romeoville was twenty miles to my left. Then came Sugar Grove and Plano, and then Sheridan, probably named for the same general as Fort Sheridan, my current home. Next was Ottawa, the site of one of the famous Lincoln-Douglas debates. *Ottawa? Wasn't my Uncle Albert's farm somewhere near Ottawa? I* checked my map and found nearby Minonk, where my dad and his siblings, Aunt Sue and Uncle Albert, had grown up. Nearby were Dana and Long Point ten or fifteen miles from my path, tiny places where my cousins and I had once traveled when we wanted to "go into town" from their farms to see the free Saturday night movie or to buy a loaf of Wonderbread.

I still had plenty of time to get to my lunch appointment in Peoria, so I turned left and took a little side trip to find Uncle Albert's farm.

A quick look at my map showed a railroad going from Minonk, where my grandparents had lived, to Dana, near Uncle Albert's and Aunt Zora's farm. When I stayed at their farm for some summer weeks as a boy, we went south less than a mile from the farm to the hard road, and then turned east for a couple of miles to Dana. The view from 3000 feet in the air let me see Minonk and the railroad running northeast out of town about four miles to another, much smaller town that had to be Dana. So far, so good. Then I worked backward from Dana to find the farm. All the roads in that part of Illinois were on a one-mile grid, so it was easy to judge distances. Two miles west, turn right, and there was the farm, just before the next road to the north, right where the creek crossed.

I was tempted to land in what looked like a cow pasture on the opposite side of the barn from the house, but it looked shorter than the grass runways that I had used at small airports, so I checked it out from up close. I "swept the field" by pretending I was going to land, but just flew the length of it at an altitude of about 50 feet. Still uncertain, I did it again at 25 feet. After four of these sweeps, I landed and had to use the brakes to keep from hitting the fence at the end of the field.

On the other side of the barn Uncle Albert and some of my cousins were busy shelling corn and hadn't seen me land. I walked up to Albert and tapped him on the shoulder.

"Hi," I said.

He looked at me in surprise and said, "Where did you come from?" It was easy to read his lips over the deafening noise of the shelling machine.

I pointed up at the sky, and he gave me a look that said, "Sure you did. And I just arrived by ocean liner."

Albert and my dad were always big teasers, so it was normal for him to think his leg was being pulled. He wouldn't believe me until I took him around the barn and out to the pasture to show him the plane I had just parked there. After a quick trip to the house to say hi to Aunt Zora, where I had to turn down a lunch invitation, the whole family followed me back to the pasture to watch my takeoff. As I pulled the prop myself from behind the propeller and jumped quickly into the cockpit to hold on the brakes and run up the engine to keep it from stalling, I considered the short length of the field. I had never taken off from a field this short.

I had used the plane's wing flaps only once before, and then only when the instructor showed me how. Flaps are extensions along the rear edges of the wings that are retracted when not needed. When extended by the pilot, they increase the lift provided by the wings, allowing slower takeoffs and landings. With the flaps extended, I would increase the possibility that I could get the plane off the ground before hitting the fence at the other end of the pasture. I stared at the fence. It was very close. My mouth was too dry to swallow, so I took a deep breath and told myself to get on with it.

Brakes on, with plane aimed at the far fence, I pulled the flap control lever all the way up. I wanted the engine revved up before the plane began moving to get maximum acceleration before I got halfway down the field, so I shoved the throttle forward all the way and released the brakes. The process worked almost too well. The plane moved about 50 feet, leapt off the ground, and climbed for the wild blue yonder. I had to push the stick forward with all my might to keep from climbing too fast and to gain airspeed so I could retract the flaps. Then a quick look at my map gave me a new compass heading and I was on my way to Peoria again.

My friends picked me up at the Peoria airport, took me to lunch, and had me back at the airport to gas up the plane before 2:00 PM. The weather was still nearly perfect as I climbed to 3,000 feet, leveled off, and set my course for home. This time I was more comfortable flying over strange towns and unfamiliar landscapes as their eccentric shapes and convolutions diverted my attention from the boredom generated by the vibrations of the engine. As the starboard landing gear floated into my field of view between my eyes and a farmer's windmill that I examined, I noticed a clump of weeds caught between the wheel and the strut that supported it. Weeds don't normally grow that tall on airport runways, nor do they float around in the air at 3,000 feet. I must have picked them up in that unauthorized field on Albert's farm. I hoped that no one would notice them when I landed.

At Chicagoland I tied the plane down in its usual parking space, surreptitiously removed the downstate weeds from the landing gear, and went on my way to dinner at Fort Sheridan. If my instructor were to know about my intentional landing in a strange farm field at my level of experience, I would have received an embarrassing lecture on how dumb that stunt was. I didn't need that lecture. I already knew it was dumb, so I somehow forgot to mention my side trip to Uncle Albert's cow pasture.

My six-month army tour ended in August of 1959, and I returned to Rochester, moved back into the Squire's Club (my boarding house), and at General Dynamics was assigned to a new engineering development program, designing a single-sideband radio transmitter for shipboard use by the U.S. Navy. I also joined the Lakeside Flying Club to continue my effort to qualify for a private pilot's license.

Two Shakes of a Lamb's Tail

The Lakeside Flying Club had about a dozen members and owned a Piper J-3 Cub airplane that was flown out of a 1200-foot grass airstrip at Hilton, New York, twenty miles west of Rochester. The plane was nearly identical to the Piper Super Cub that I had flown in Illinois, but without its souped-up features: No wing flaps, a less powerful engine, and a cruising speed of only 60 knots (69 miles per hour) instead of whizzing along at the 85-knot speed that I was accustomed to. As a practical matter, flying the J-3 was exactly like flying the Super Cub, except that it didn't go as fast and would need a longer cow pasture if I expected to take off from Uncle Albert's farm again.

Just prior to my joining the flying club, they had become embroiled in a legal problem. The plane had not passed its annual inspection and needed new fabric coverings on the wings. The work was to be done by an FAA-approved company at a small airport near Lockport, New York, about 70 miles west of Rochester. The club president decided that, rather than have the plane disassembled and trucked to Lockport, he would just fly it over there and save the club a lot of money. He did so, but his transgression in flying the unlicensed plane without a ferry permit was discovered by the FAA, who refused to renew the license, even after the fabric covering was replaced and successfully inspected. Only by firing the president and finding a new, untainted one could the sin be forgiven and the plane licensed and flown once again.

And so, at my very first monthly flying club meeting, during which I joined up, I, a virginal, uncorrupted novitiate, was unanimously elected president of the organization, having previously met only one member.

My lessons resumed, this time in the newly re-licensed Piper Cub and with a new instructor. Soon I was nearly qualified to take the flight exam for a pilot's license, lacking only one more long solo cross-country trip. A trip to Indiana and back to visit my parents would more than fill that requirement.

I planned the 1200-mile roundtrip flight for weeks. I reserved the flying club plane weeks in advance, bought the necessary flight maps, and laid out the route in detail, planning four refueling stops on the way to the Purdue University Airport in West Lafayette, the very same airport used by Amelia Earhart when she was on the Purdue faculty. The cruising airspeed of my Piper Cub was 65 knots, making the entire one-way flying time ten hours. During one of my lessons, my instructor went over my flight plans and some basic facts about the plane, including the fact that the gas tank held enough for three hours of flying time with a fifteen-minute reserve. My refueling stops were all about two hours apart.

As the date for my flight approached, I knew that my weakest piloting ability was performing forced landings. I just didn't feel confident when the instructor pulled back on the throttle and yelled, "Forced landing!" so during my last weekly lesson before the trip, I asked him to help me practice them. He agreed and gave me several surprise opportunities to demonstrate that I could land in a strange farm field successfully. When the yell came and the engine appeared to stop, in the space of about one second I pushed the stick forward to maintain air speed (We don't want to do a stall here...) and decided on an approach to the field that I had already selected, hoping that it was longer than Uncle Albert's cow pasture. As I got within a few feet of the ground, the instructor took over the controls, aborted the landing, and took the plane up to where he let me have the controls again. After several of these exercises I stopped worrying about forced landings.

I was ready to go to Indiana.

On Friday evening I moved the plane to the Hylan Airport (now the site of Marketplace Mall shopping center just outside the southern Rochester border) to have it near my home so I could get an early start. I went home after filling the gas tank and spent a partially sleepless night waiting for dawn.

At the airport on Saturday I loaded my overnight bag into the tiny luggage compartment, arranged my maps and other miscellany where they were handy, and took off. Climbing out from the airport I could see ground fog obscuring part of the surface below me, so I stayed in the landing pattern and came back down to wait for the patches of fog to burn off. None of the fog covered the airport, so I couldn't see it from the ground, but from the air, I could see the patches of it that covered over 20 per cent of the countryside. A half-hour later I took off again, but the fog was still there, so I landed again.

Clouds are frightening if you're a pilot who is not trained for instrument flying. If the ground is invisible, navigation is impossible unless you know how to fly using only the instruments in the plane. I didn't. I might as well have tried to fly with my eyes closed. The partial fog coverage was enough to make visual navigation, at least at my experience level, difficult and really scary. I could easily get lost. I had no choice but to wait until the sun cleared away the fog.

By nine o'clock, when I took off a third time, the fog was gone and I was on my way to my first stop for gas at a small grass strip just before the Pennsylvania border. But when I got there, I couldn't find the airport. It looked as though it should have been right where they were building the extension of the New York Thruway that was eventually to hook up with the Ohio Turnpike and become Interstate 90. After a few minutes of searching I decided that I had just enough gas to get me to my next stop in eastern Ohio, so I flew on.

Flying past Cleveland, I could see Cleveland Hopkins Airport on the horizon to my right, an area that I wanted very much to avoid. Flying where the traffic consisted of big commercial airliners, DC-3s and Constellations, was the last thing I wanted to do. My fuel gage now showed empty, which meant that I was flying on my 15-minute reserve as I began to look for my destination airport. As I approached its location I dropped down to 1500 feet, then to 1000 feet, but I still hadn't spotted it when the engine stopped.

I was out of gas.

Unlike the practice sessions when my instructor had simulated engine failure by idling the engine, the real thing was much quieter. The only noise was made by the air rushing past the cockpit, and the propeller stood still in front of my face. I later realized that in calculating the gas usage to get to my second intended stop, I hadn't included the fuel used to take off and land twice in Rochester when the ground fog had delayed me, nor the extra gas used as I had circled what would someday become I-90 near the Pennsylvania border.

But when the engine quit, I wasn't thinking about the absence of engine noise, nor was I calculating gasoline consumption errors. Thanks to my practice session with the instructor the prior weekend, I already had a farm pasture picked out and focused all my attention on softly settling the plane down into it. A few sharp S-turns let me keep the field in sight while losing altitude without overshooting the field, during which I spotted the power lines running alongside the railroad track over which I must land. I side-slipped over the power lines, rapidly losing more altitude and straightened my glide path just in time to stall and land. As the plane stopped I spotted the house and barnyard of the farmer in whose field I had landed. At the barnyard, the farmer looked doubtful when I pointed at the plane sitting all alone in the middle of his field and asked if I could buy some tractor gas from him for it. When I explained to him that little airplanes used 80-octane gas just like tractors did, he relented and helped me carry a few gallons out to the plane.

We had just gotten the gas into the tank when three men came across the field toward us from the direction of the road.

They explained that they had watched me come down from across the road at the airport and wanted to make sure I was ok.

They helped me get the plane started, and I took off and flew across the road to land at the airport to fill up on gas. The airport owner gave me a ride down the road to a restaurant where I got lunch. As I walked into the restaurant, my knees finally started to shake as I had time to think about what had just happened. I had filed a flight plan with the FAA, telling them my estimated time of arrival at the Purdue airport. Since my dad was also expecting me there, I called him from the restaurant to say I was running late, and would he please call the airport and tell them about my delayed arrival time? I didn't mention that I had run out of gas, as he still harbored the belief that I had in my head a modicum of brains, and I didn't want to disabuse him of that impression. I did mention something about a headwind, which was true, as the prevailing wind in that part of the world is usually westerly, and the cars on the roads below crept along faster than my plane.

After lunch, the walk back to the airport cured my shakes, and I was able to take off and fly to my next stop in western Ohio. While at that airport I had to make another phone call to delay my ETA. It seemed that every stop I made took longer than I expected, and I made still another such call from my fourth stop in eastern Indiana. I arrived at the Purdue airport while it was still barely light enough to land, and, after tying down the plane in a guest parking place, had a pleasant dinner with my parents and spent two nights in my own bed at their house.

As I left to return to Rochester on Monday, I was glad I hadn't mentioned my forced landing, because Mom got all weepy anyway as I hugged her and climbed into the plane. If she had any more information about my adventures, she would have flooded the airport runway with tears, and I wouldn't have been able to take off.

My return to Rochester was uneventful; the wind was at my back, and there were no more unplanned events.

A few weeks later, after learning how to use a radio to talk to the Rochester control tower, a brand new requirement that fall, I took the flight test, passed it, and got my private pilot's license. During the flight test the FAA inspector made me do a forced landing.

I aced it.

Chapter 26

More Boy Scout Training

Six months after Marianne and I were married and settled in our small third-floor walk-up apartment on Bobrich Drive in Rochester, Julius, a co-worker and casual friend, asked me to be an usher in his wedding. It was unusual for a casual friend to honor me this way, but Julius was a little different. My first impression upon meeting him at work was of an arrogant man who was very smart and knowledgeable, but who thought he knew more than everyone else and didn't try to keep it a secret. He was nearly twice my age and divorced. I couldn't imagine becoming close friends with him. Except that we both worked for the same company and were both engineers, we had little in common.

Marianne's and my good friend Helen had been introduced to Julius by a mutual friend. They began dating and eventually were engaged to be married. Except for both being seriously overweight, they were as different as could be. I had never seen Julius laugh, although an alert observer might have noticed the beginning of a smile on a couple of occasions. Helen, on the other hand, was jolly and outgoing, always looking on the bright side of things. At Halloween she put on an orange pullover smock that might have been worn by a pregnant lady and said she was going to a party as The Great Pumpkin.

✧

As the wedding date approached, Julius, who was paying for the ushers' and best man's tuxedo rentals, took us after work to get fitted. We were duly measured, pinned up, chalk marked, and recorded as we tried on our finery. Julius then took all of his attendants out to a fancy restaurant for shrimp cocktails and drinks. We sat at the bar and I ordered a Manhattan.

We teased Julius about his approaching doom, and he teased us back about our newlywed status. I ordered a second Manhattan to drink with my shrimp cocktail. The evening wore on, and I don't think I ordered any more drinks, but with at least two serious cocktails in my 125-pound body and with no substantial food underneath them, who knows? As I went out of the restaurant into the parking lot, a drunk (not I) banged his car into the one next to it. I felt a little woozy myself, so I headed for home without reporting the incident to the police.

I managed to find our apartment, a mere two miles from the restaurant, and began to climb the stairs, which got steeper with each step I took. When I reached the third floor and let myself into the apartment, Marianne was already in bed and asleep. By the time I got ready for bed and went into the bathroom, the room was rotating, and I felt faint.

Then my Boy Scout first aid training kicked in. If the patient feels faint, it's because he's in shock, which causes the blood to leave his head, and you should make him lie down and elevate his feet. As former Boy Scouts, my friends and I had had this rule and many others drilled into our heads repeatedly. At the annual "First Aid-O-Ree" we had competed against other scout troops to see which one could best analyze an emergency injury situation, apply appropriate first aid treatment, and call for the ambulance. Adults, who were Scout leaders from other troops, Red Cross officials, or even doctors, stood over us with clipboards, pencils, and stopwatches as we reacted to the emergency.

We had learned to treat bad injuries and symptoms in order of their priority: Bleeding, Breathing, Shock. If the injured person was bleeding, that took priority over all other problems. A close second priority was a non-breathing person. Get him breathing with artificial respiration before treating him for shock. Only after those three major items were treated were we to worry about little things like burns or broken bones.[1]

Not having a bleeding or breathing problem, my faintness could mean only one thing: I was in shock and should lie down. I immediately did so right there on the bathroom floor and put my feet up on the rim of the bathtub to elevate them.

Liquor has different effects on different people. Some people lose their inhibitions and get silly or overly expressive when they are drunk. Some get belligerent and start fights, and still others just get sleepy. I am one of the latter. So, having satisfactorily treated myself for shock, I immediately fell fast asleep. A more experienced observer of the nature and behavior of tipplers might think that I passed out, but I'm not convinced. Hadn't I calmly and logically treated my ailment before drifting off to dreamland, albeit very swiftly and without so much as a "Goodnight Sweetheart" to my wife?

Later that night at an unknown hour, Marianne awoke and wondered why I wasn't yet in bed. Searching the apartment, she discovered me lying on the floor of the bathroom, dead to the world, so to speak. When she shook me and got no response, her concern deepened. She finally got me awake.

"What happened?" she asked.

---

[1] While I was in Scouts a new edict came down from the powers that be: Burns were no longer to be treated by applying butter to the wound. The newer, more effective treatment was to apply a paste made of baking soda and water.

"I just fell asleep," I said.

"On the floor of the bathroom?" she said.

By the time I explained and crawled into bed, her side of the conversation was decidedly chillier than it had been the prior morning when we had both left for work.

At breakfast the following morning we discussed the matter as I held my head in both hands and stared into my cereal bowl to keep from looking at the bright light coming in the window. The chilly atmosphere in the apartment had not improved, and I couldn't understand why. What could be better treatment for a shock patient than sleep, having already received proper first aid?

Forgiveness came slowly, but come it did. After all, weren't we still newlyweds? How could she stay mad at me? Nonetheless, that was the last time I ever came home in a state of shock, and at Julius' and Helen's wedding I was completely sober and performed my duties admirably.

Chapter 27

The Second Time Around

"To the scores who have been killed while trying to scale it, the thousands wounded and dragged away before they could reach it, the millions who have been spiritually maimed by its erection in August 1961."

Curtis Cate, in the dedication of his book, *The Ides of August*, a history of the Berlin Wall Crisis of 1961

Life was good in early 1961. Marianne and I had been married in June the previous year after a year of courtship and a six-month engagement, she being the only woman I had ever dated with whom I was completely comfortable. Her sense of humor was similar to mine, although a little more subdued. We enjoyed many of the same activities except for flying, which made her nervous. And neither of us was overly talkative or quirky, unlike some of our previous dating acquaintances. We both had good jobs that we liked; she as an underwriter for Travelers Insurance Company, and I as an electronic engineer at General Dynamics Electronics, developing two-way radio equipment for the military. We were firmly and permanently in love.

The Cold War simmered in the background as we enjoyed an idyllic life in our third-floor walk-up apartment. My active duty military service was behind me, and in March we learned that we were expecting a baby. As spring blossomed into summer our biggest worry was deciding when Marianne should tell her boss and start wearing a pregnancy smock, her badge of impending motherhood. Travelers had a rule that a woman's employment ended at six months of pregnancy (although a co-worker had been allowed to bring home files and continue part-time work). This was a mild, completely acceptable requirement compared to the experience of Marianne's mother in 1930: As a kindergarten teacher in Rochester during the Great Depression, her salary had been cut in half by the school system on the day she got married. Furthermore, her condition of eventual pregnancy was not allowed to be visible, as it might sully the sensitivities of the school children for whom she was expected to set an example of purity and immaculacy. Mothers were acceptable; after all, didn't each student have one? But the process of *becoming* one was inappropriate.

At work, when Marianne couldn't hide it any more, she overcame her shyness, told her boss, and began wearing her smock. We still didn't know that I would be going back in the army at about the same time the baby was due.

The term "Cold War" wasn't coined until 1947 in a speech given by Bernard Baruch, although historians refer to its birth at the end of World War II in 1945 when Stalin began taking over eastern Europe. In 1948 Stalin blocked the allies' (Britain, France, US) ground access to Berlin. The allied response was to mount a massive airlift of food, coal, and other supplies into West Berlin. Over two million tons were moved this way by an average of several hundred cargo flights per day until the Russians canceled their blockade in 1949.

The Cold War continued to heat up, and nuclear war with the Russians seemed more and more possible. School children were taught to react to a bright flash in the sky by falling face-down on the floor under their desks with a hand over the back of the neck to protect it from radiation. Communities established emergency fallout shelters, and some families stocked their basements with food and water to prepare for atomic attack. Nike air defense missile sites were installed around the largest US cities. The free world learned to live with the fear of what the communist thugs might do next.

After the Russians lifted their blockade in 1949, they again tried to kick the allies out of Berlin in 1961. By then, 3.5 million East Germans had escaped to the west, or about 20 percent of the entire East German population. The East German government, with the approval of Khrushchev, who had finally won the Soviet power struggles following the death of Stalin, put up the Wall in August of 1961 to keep East Germans from escaping through Berlin, where it was difficult to control border crossings in the divided city.

When the order was given that the allies would no longer have access to West Berlin, President Kennedy said, in effect, "We're staying in Berlin, period," and announced a recall of American military reservists to emphasize his determination. He was speaking to me.

My membership in the 411th Signal Company had begun well after my 1958 discharge from six months of active duty at Ft. Sheridan, Illinois. I still needed to serve out my remaining 7-1/2 year active reserve obligation, so when a position in the 411th for a 2nd lieutenant opened up in early 1960, I was there to fill the slot. When the unit went to Fort Devens, Massachusetts in June for its two-week summer camp, I was getting married and got permission to go a few weeks later with another unit to Fort Dix, New Jersey. The following year I went with the 411th to summer camp in August 1961, during which we heard the announcement of the Berlin Crisis reserve call-up. We were Signal Corps communicators, so even in the midst of a field exercise in the boondocks of Fort Drum, New York, we could listen to our expensive, government-issued radios to hear the news. The list of recalled units did not include the 411th, and we all breathed a sigh of relief. Our baby was due in mid-September, and Marianne was rapidly approaching the size and shape of a Volkswagen. My recall into the service would have been a major disaster.

Soon after the 411th got home from summer camp, Chet Curtis, who lived across the hall from our apartment with his wife Lennie, received his draft notice. We were invited to share a drink in their apartment while we commiserated with them and watched the late news on TV. The news was not good: My reserve unit had been added to the list of those recalled to active duty. Chet was a radio news announcer on station WHAM in Rochester. Later that same night, he took me downtown to the studios where he worked and made for me an audio tape of the news program announcing the recall of the 411th Signal Company.

A few days later we got our orders putting us on active duty on October 1. The 411th was to report to Ft. Monmouth, New Jersey two weeks after we were activated, the delay giving us time to prepare for the move. Our next meeting at the reserve armory took on a new intensity. We were no longer trying to stay busy with marching drills and uniform inspections, weapon disassembly and cleaning, and classes taught from the Army field manuals. We were preparing to go to war.

Meanwhile Lennie Curtis became pregnant, thus exempting Chet from the draft. As President Kennedy told the nation after announcing the recall, "Life is unfair. Some people have to go to war, and others get to stay home." For me, that speech and my situation were both saturated with irony.

First, the unit had to figure out who would be activated and stay with the unit and who wouldn't. Our commanding officer, a Major, got his employer to ask that he be exempt from the recall by virtue of the essential nature of the job he did there. His executive officer, a Captain, was eager for still more glory and took over command of the unit. One of the enlisted men had a heart problem with occasional angina pain and was exempted from the recall. Several others were exempt for a variety of reasons, including one who faked mental problems and bragged about it to some of his buddies. My supervisor's boss in the engineering department of General Dynamics Electronics offered to write an exemption request for me, but I declined. I had an obligation and I would fulfill it.

Our preparations included physical exams for everyone, conducted assembly line style. We were heart-checked, hernia checked, weighed, and measured. I donated a blood sample via a needle attached to the rim of an open test tube. We all lined up, standing in our skivvies. A medical corpsman from another unit came down the line sticking a needle into a vein in each man's forearm and left the test tube hanging on its needle while blood ran slowly into the test tube. When my dangling test tube was filled, someone came by, removed its needle from my arm, and corked and labeled the test tube. I never saw the results of these tests but assumed that I had passed when I was sworn in to active duty right on schedule. I suspected that if I had substituted saliva or some other bodily fluid for the blood in the test tube, I still would have passed.

Our baby was due just before I was to begin active duty. When the predicted delivery date came and went with no sign of the baby except for frequent kicks on the roof of Marianne's passenger compartment, her doctor said it would be ok to encourage it a little. We wanted the birth well before I left town, so at bedtime Marianne drank a concoction of ginger ale and castor oil, suggested by the doctor, to encourage the beginning of labor. It must have worked. She went into labor at 3:00 AM, and we headed for the hospital after notifying the doctor.

Her labor was not easy on her or me. My 18 hours in the labor room with her was followed by more waiting while she was in the delivery room where fathers were forbidden. When I finally got to see her and the baby, she looked like she had been kept awake for a week and tumbled inside a cement mixer, but she and the baby were fine. The sudden relief from all that tension was too much for me. I found a stall in an unoccupied rest room to use as a wailing wall and broke down and bawled for several minutes.

We named the baby David Lee; David because we liked the name, and Lee after Marianne's favorite (and only) uncle who had died in his early fifties before I had a chance to meet him. The doctor said that when David was six weeks old, he and his mother could move to New Jersey. In the meantime, I moved into the Bachelor Officer Quarters (BOQ) at Fort Monmouth, and traveled back home to visit the family every other weekend. We broke the lease on our apartment, which federal law allowed for those called into the military, and Marianne and the baby moved temporarily into the spare bedroom at her parents' house in Rochester.

Life in the BOQ was relatively uneventful, although one night we returned there at about 1:00 a.m. after an evening of partying at the Officers' Club to find the community latrine at the end of the building looking like it had been visited by an angry King Kong. The stall doors were broken, pulled off, or hanging by one hinge. The urinals and sinks were pulled from the wall, pipes disconnected, and a general confusion of paper tissue and towels scattered everywhere. We marveled at the mess, but being unable to clean it up at that hour we shrugged and went to bed.

We got up the next morning at 6:00 p.m. to find the latrine completely rehabilitated. Broken stall doors had been replaced, pipes and fixtures remounted and connected, and the mess cleaned up. It was as though Dorothy had returned home from Oz to find that her experience was all a dream. The latrine was not only repaired, it was pristine. Had we come home drunk and imagined the whole thing? No, too many of us had seen the decimation for that to be true. One wag explained the miracle as a case of immaculate restitution.

We later heard that visiting officers from the Corps of Engineers at another base were staying there. One of them had come home drunk, went berserk, and wrecked the latrine. His buddies, who probably knew people at the base facilities maintenance department with access to their door and toilet supply depot, had quietly fixed up the place during the five hours that we slept.

One of our officers, Dick Ashcroft, found an apartment on the base in a cluster of converted barracks buildings affectionately known as Splinterville. He was high on the priority list because he already had three children. I wasn't yet that lucky, so I initially spent much of my off-duty time searching for an off-base apartment.

Rental property was scarce in the resort towns of Red Bank and Long Branch, just outside the gates of Ft. Monmouth, so when I found a two-bedroom apartment in West Long Branch, I grabbed it. The property was an old converted carriage house with four apartments that looked like it had been recently renovated. The landlord lived in one of the apartments, usually a good sign. There was no yard as the property had not yet been landscaped after the renovation, but there was a gravel driveway between the weeds and piles of dirt and an outdoor parking space next to the building.

Until our furniture arrived, Marianne stayed with the baby for a few days in a spare room in the house that Andy Koppenhaver had rented for his family, where she and Joan Koppenhaver took turns sterilizing baby bottles. As the most senior lieutenant in our unit, Andy had been named executive officer, a fortuitous move by the CO. Besides being an excellent administrator, Andy was the most even-tempered of our officers and thus the best suited for working closely with the Captain, whose loopy decisions and pronouncements frequently elicited hoots of derision from those of us who didn't work in the same office with him.

Learning to Fly

Soon after we arrived at Ft. Monmouth, the word came down from headquarters that a reception for our officers and their ladies was to be held in our honor by the base commander, and we were all expected to show up in our dress blues. It was, in Army parlance, a command performance to welcome us to Ft. Monmouth. It didn't seem to matter to the command hierarchy that most of us didn't own the snazzy blue dress uniforms. It wasn't a reserve requirement and those who had once owned them had sold them after their prior active duty tour. A set of dress blues would cost $300, about what a 411th officer received in his monthly army paycheck.

We asked our Captain to petition the authorities for relief from the dress code. He said he tried, but was unsuccessful. Some officers thought that he really liked the idea of getting all gussied up to meet the general and hadn't put his heart into it. He had received the answer, and that was the end of the matter.

General William Alger, the reserve corps commander under whom we had served in Rochester, concerned about the welfare of the good citizens under his command who had been called to active duty, planned to pay us a visit. The company officers, without our Captain's knowledge, decided to petition the general directly about the reception dress code. We asked Lt. Goldman to speak for us, knowing that in civilian life as an attorney he had been accustomed to speaking to important people. Lt. Goldman, the lowest ranking officer of all of us had, in effect, willingly drawn the short straw.

The company area was policed. This was military jargon for lovingly picking up every scrap of paper, every cigarette butt, every out-of-place bit of effluence and chaff that might deflect a general's eye from the brilliance of the brass on our uniforms and the blinding reflections from the polish on our shoes. Fresh uniforms were donned and the men lined up on the company parade ground as the General trooped the line and made brief comments to the assemblage acknowledging the sacrifice the men were making.

Afterward, during a less formal gathering of the unit's officers in our mess hall, he asked whether we had any problems that he could help us with. Here was Lt. Goldman's cue. In respectful tones he explained the officers' plight and asked for relief from the stern dress blues decree. The General assured Lt. Goldman that he would look into the matter.

Soon after the General left the company area, Lt. Goldman was told that the colonel who was the CO of the brigade to which the 411th was assigned was embarrassed and outraged. He had been blindsided by a second lieutenant and wanted to see him in his office the next morning.

The visit went badly, according to Lt. Goldman. He was lectured about military protocol and the Army way of doing things. He was sternly warned that his military career was in serious jeopardy. (We visualized the utter dejection on Lt. Goldman's face as he was given this ominous warning… or was it just that he was suppressing a grin because he didn't want to be there in the first place?) He was ordered to write an apology for ignoring the chain of command and to provide a written plan for how such unmilitary conduct would never again happen. The visit lasted about half an hour, but seemed longer.

The lieutenant did as ordered. A few days later, tailors from downtown New Jersey came to the company area and measured the officers. The dress blue uniforms were delivered and paid for. Then General Alger did as he promised. He looked into the matter and the Army decided that dress uniform would be optional for all recalled reserve officers serving during the Berlin call-up. The optional directive was issued after the dress blues had been paid for and before the General's reception. The 411th officers chose to wear our dress blues to the reception, where we were duly welcomed by the general and where we basked in the admiring glances of our ladies.

After moving into our apartment in West Long Branch, our home life had settled back to as "normal" as could be expected with a two-month-old baby living there with us. We gradually noticed a strange smell in the apartment that was somehow...not right. It may have been a sewer smell, but the landlord said he didn't know its origin. It was hard for us to believe that the smell didn't seep into his apartment also, but he seemed to think it came from loaded baby diapers, several of which were generated daily by our son. One day, while poking around the back of the building, I found a stairway into the building's basement. At the bottom, there was only a wet dirt floor that smelled exactly like a sewer. Either a toilet in the building was emptying into the basement, or there was a bad leak in a pipe or septic tank.

The landlord and his family, who turned out to be complete slobs in other ways also, didn't seem to care about such sanitation problems, and we were too young and naive to call the health department, thinking that if we did, they might condemn the property and kick us out. We just lived with the smell for the rest of our time in New Jersey and recognized that there was probably a reason that the apartment had been vacant when we found it.

When the order came to prepare to go to France, the word was that we were to take the place of a similar unit that was moving from France into Germany to back up the President's determination to maintain the allies' presence in Berlin. The announcement late in 1961 shocked the officers and men of the 411th. We had just settled our families into new homes in New Jersey after being uprooted from jobs and homes in Rochester, and now they were going to transfer us again, this time to France? This time *all* of the families would be split apart, more mortgages would be defaulted, more leases broken, and husbands exposed to battle... all because Nikita Khrushchev and his henchmen wanted to make trouble.

It was a false alarm. The President never decided to send recalled reservists overseas, and a few weeks later the pending order was cancelled.

Our mission was to provide long-range radio communications, primarily digital message traffic, between an army area in the field and the Starcom command and control network back in the United States. To perform these duties, our 300-man company was divided into teams: a radio team for each truck-mounted two-way radio system, a microwave team, a message center team, and two wireline teams, in addition to administrative and support groups that included the Supply Room, the Mess Hall, the Orderly room (company Headquarters), the Motor Pool, and the Training Office.

The captain had named me as the company Training Officer, a position that soon outran me. I got behind in my work and wasn't able to keep my head above the waves in an ocean of details. Fortunately, my very capable Assistant Training Officer, Lt. Dick Ashcroft, helped me avoid disasters in producing and managing a weekly training schedule that included arranging all the activities of each of the communications teams. It became apparent to me that Dick would be the better Training Officer, and I should be his assistant, so I went to the captain to suggest that our jobs be reversed. Dick had levels of leadership maturity and organizational ability that I hadn't yet developed. The captain agreed, and I was soon much more comfortable working for Dick than I was in the previous relationship.

After we were settled at Ft. Monmouth several more individually recalled officers were assigned to our unit. Most of them were from east coast locations, so they left wives and families home, commuting on weekends to see them. The Rochester officers didn't have much social interaction with these "filler officers" but our social lives were full anyway. There were two officers' clubs: One was on-base, and was primarily a restaurant and bar, and the other was off-base and was an elegant country club with golf course, swimming pool, rathskeller, a ballroom, and a very fine restaurant with reasonable prices where we could run up our credit card bills until the next payday. The club also owned a beach at Sandy Hook. Our use of these facilities made the recall at least tolerable and a social success, although the army rules against officer fraternization with enlisted men limited our contact with a few friends from Rochester.

Too many filler officers, all first lieutenants, were assigned to our unit. We didn't have jobs for most of them, so some were loaned to other Ft. Monmouth units, and several were sent home early. One such person was assigned to an investigative unit in the base Judge Advocate General's office. It was rumored that he had been assigned to investigate something about a nest of lesbians in the female barracks on post, and our lascivious imaginations were crushed when we didn't hear any details.

Another filler officer was a first lieutenant who had served in the army in WWII, parachuted behind enemy lines, and served with Tito's partisans. He had then been recalled in 1951 during the Korean "conflict" and served there. Then, ten years later in 1961 he was again recalled to serve with us during the Berlin Wall Crisis. At 52 years of age when he joined the 411th, we guessed that he was the oldest 1st lieutenant in the entire army.

A notable filler lieutenant from northern New Jersey had been a truck dispatcher in civilian life. In the 411th he was friendly with the mess hall staff, where his entrepreneurial skills allowed him to build a clandestine business bartering or selling steaks and other food to his friends until the Criminal Investigation Division put a stop to it. The investigation was conducted very quietly, but we knew that some of the mess hall crew were given lie detector tests, after which the lieutenant wasn't with us. His storytelling at the Officers' Club bar had convinced us that in civilian life he had had mafia connections.

The mess hall food was generally well-prepared, but it was, after all, army food. Complaints about it were to be expected. Most of the mess hall cooks were from Rochester's Italian community, and their fine dining seasonings drew frequent protests about too much garlic in the food. When the complaints reached a fever pitch, rebellion was threatened, a petition was circulated, and the joke around the company was that the men didn't like garlic in their corn flakes. A compromise was negotiated, truce was declared, and the proliferation of mess hall garlic subsided.

Another mess hall delectability was chipped beef and gravy served over toast, and dubbed throughout the service as "shit on a shingle." In polite society, it was known more simply as "SOS," and because of its worldwide status as a military staple, complaints and petitions had no effect on its frequent appearance on mess hall menus. Lt. Goldman actually liked it, but then, he was the most junior officer in the company and wasn't expected to have sophisticated tastes. He also liked Spam.

At the end of each two-week pay period, the enlisted men had to line up to report to the lieutenant who was that pay period's designated pay officer to get their stipend. A snappy salute would earn them an envelope of cash, which was counted out for them on the spot. The captain apparently liked this show of respect for the pay officer and wanted in on it. When the officers' monthly paychecks arrived in their mail slots in the company area, the captain nabbed them, put them in his office safe, and ordered each officer under him to perform his report the next morning, snappy salute and all, in order to receive his paycheck.

When the captain opened the safe to pay the first officer who reported, a mouse jumped out, ran across the orderly room floor, and disappeared behind some furniture. Because access to the combination was closely controlled and none of those who knew it would admit to perpetrating a mouse caper, it was decided that the little rodent must have crawled into the safe unassisted on the previous day before the safe was closed for the night. It was clearly a case of immaculate incarceration.

Lt. Frangos strenuously objected to this interference with paychecks in the US Mail, and warned of repercussions if the captain didn't stop this violation of federal law. The CO apparently saw the logic in this argument, and from then on we officers were allowed to retrieve our own checks from our own mail slots without help from the captain.

We had to relearn several military practices and customs that we had learned during our first time around, but had forgotten as civilians: An officer's wife or girlfriend was referred to as his "lady." Fraternization between officers and enlisted men was taboo. When walking outdoors, stay alert for passing officers, whether on foot or in a vehicle, and salute as they go by. The lower-ranking person salutes first, and the higher rank returns it. If passed by a jeep or sedan marked by a general officer's silver stars on an orange background (Orange was the official color of the Signal Corp.) in the license plate holder, be especially attentive and formal when you salute.

Lt. Donaher was in charge of the motor pool, where several trucks and jeeps were maintained. A jeep and a driver were always kept ready for our captain in case he needed transportation. After noticing general's stars on the base commander's jeep, the captain suggested to Lt. Donaher that he put captain's bars on the jeep in which he rode, and furthermore, it would be nice to have carpet on the floor of the jeep as well as an air conditioner on the vehicle. Donaher tried to ignore these suggestions, but the captain was more insistent each time he asked about the progress of his chariot upgrades.

Finally, Donaher relented and explained the captain's requests to the Motor Pool Sergeant.

A few days later the jeep sported a sparkling six-inch image of captain's bars on a bright orange background, framed by the license plate holder on the front of the jeep. Air conditioning and carpets on the floor soon followed, as well as a canvas cover for the captain's bars to keep them out of sight when the passenger was someone other than the captain, just like the canvas cover for the stars on the general's vehicles. After garnering snappy salutes accompanied by bright smiles while being driven around the post, the captain was delighted with his luxurious jeep. Then the master sergeant at post headquarters spotted the insignia, and the captain received a curt order to "Get that insignia off that jeep." It was a privilege reserved for generals. Lt. Donaher vehemently denied having had any intent to make the captain look like a jackass but had trouble keeping a grin from his face when he said it.

In the training office, we arranged for most of our men to attend various Signal Corps schools on base. Because Ft. Monmouth had no school for message center personnel, wiremen, or switchboard operators, arrangements were made for that training at Ft. Gordon, Georgia. Each Monday morning until the course was completed those men were bussed to McGuire Air Force Base, New Jersey, where they got on scheduled Air Force MATS flights to Georgia, and returned on Friday evening.

Lt. Donaher, being an engineer with a master's degree who was more valuable in technical assignments than as a supervisor of grease monkeys and jeep jockeys, was sent to Microwave School. There, he was trained in the use of various microwave communications equipment, including a portable 100-foot antenna tower kit that a skilled team could remove from its 2-1/2-ton truck and put up and take down in less than a half day. When the instructor came into the classroom to begin that segment of the training, he said, "Men, today we are going to teach you how to have a proper erection."

After the school ended, Lt. Donaher was put in charge of our Microwave Team, and provided microwave links from one end of the post to the other, as well as for our field exercises at the officers' club beach on Sandy Hook, and in the war-torn central New Jersey boondocks at Ft. Dix. After much practice putting up the antenna tower, Donaher's team was able to brag that they could have *two* erections per day.

In the Training Office, we felt that the company needed some field experience before an upcoming mandatory field test of our effectiveness. This Army Training Test (ATT) was to be conducted at Ft. Dix, New Jersey during a two-week bivouac, where evaluators from other units would observe our performance under stressful combat conditions and score us on various aspects of our effectiveness. One major problem persisted. We couldn't get the equipment that a unit such as ours required for the teams to carry out their missions. In Rochester, and at summer camp, we had made do with a few handheld and backpack radios, some field telephones and rolls of wire, and two AN/GRC-26 one-kilowatt two-way radio systems mounted in huts on the backs of 2-1/2-ton trucks. At Ft. Monmouth, much of the equipment that we should have had for training was being sent to Vietnam as the situation heated up there.

Finally we managed to get more equipment, including one AN/GRC-98 high-powered radio system mounted in a semi tractor-trailer similar to a moving van, and two huts, each on a 2-1/2-ton truck. Our company headquarters and barracks area wasn't big enough to hold all of this, so we found space for it next to an old WWII barracks building that had been converted to offices on the other side of the post. Now we could really communicate around the world. This "Angry 98" was known as a tape relay system and included crypto equipment, transmitters, receivers, tape readers and generators, antennas, as well as motor-generator trailers to produce the power to run the entire rig.

We planned a few days of bivouac and rifle range practice prior to our ATT. Getting some planning help from a "friend of a friend" in a supply unit at Ft. Dix, Lt. Ashcroft ordered rifle ammunition, cherry bombs (large firecrackers) to simulate hand grenades, and other supplies for the events. The other supplies included an atomic bomb simulator which came in a 55-gallon drum. When set off, it produced an earth-shaking concussion and an awe-inspiring mushroom cloud. This device added some stress to enliven our training exercise and gave the men an opportunity to practice their prescribed procedures when threatened with nuclear annihilation.

Although Signal Corps personnel were not, strictly speaking, combat troops like the infantry or the artillery, we were expected to engage in combat when necessary. We had rifles, although most of them were not the nine-pound M-1 rifles that the real combat troops used. Our primary weapons were .30 caliber M1 *carbines* that were lighter than the M-1 rifle, and used smaller bullets.

Ft. Monmouth didn't have a firing range on base, but arrangements were made to use, during our practice bivouac in the middle of January, a range shared with the National Guard on the seashore at Sea Girt, New Jersey. The target pits and shooting pads were positioned so that we fired our weapons toward the ocean, where a Ft. Monmouth "Q-Boat" patrolled the area to keep other boats away from danger. In groups of perhaps 20 men, we each fired our weapons in prone, sitting, kneeling, and standing positions, at distances of 50, 100, and 150 yards. Scores were kept by other soldiers in the target pits who showed us where each shot hit the target using a marker on a pole. If we missed the target completely, the scorer waved over the target a red flag called "Maggie's Drawers."

Learning to Fly

In the middle of December, even New Jersey was bone-numbing cold, especially on the seashore. The sounds of the weapons firing and the smell of gunpowder assaulted us as we stamped our feet to stay warm, awaiting our turn. When my turn to shoot came, I chose a rifle that had been used by a high-scoring fellow soldier, so I knew that I at least had a weapon that was consistently precise. After my firing was finished, I had seen not a glimpse of Maggie's Drawers, and the pole marker had indicated near the center of the target for each shot.

When we received our scores from the pits, I learned that I had shot a perfect score, something that the range sergeant had never seen before. Lt. Goldman, who was taking his turn in the pits, stood and looked up at my target. Although he didn't know at the time who was shooting, he reported that whoever it was hit not just the bulls-eye with each shot, but the *center* of the bulls-eye with each shot.

This feat apparently was the equivalent of bowling several 300 games in succession, or of hitting three successive holes-in-one on the golf course. Not only did I get a marksmanship medal that said "Expert," but the Ft. Monmouth Public Information Officer asked that I be sent to his office for an interview in an appropriate field uniform and helmet with my weapon for a photograph.

The Army at the time was anxious (desperate?) for some positive publicity for the reserve call-up after enduring negative publicity caused by complaining soldiers. News releases were sent out to the media, and my photo appeared in the *Army Times*, the Ft. Monmouth newspaper, the *Rochester Democrat & Chronicle*, and the Lafayette (Indiana) *Journal & Courier*, accompanied by news articles generated from the press release. Earning my Boy Scout marksmanship merit badge had paid off. I got my 15 minutes of fame early in my career.

As a consequence of my perfect score I was invited to try out for the Ft. Monmouth target-shooting team that entered competitions with teams from other bases. At the post's indoor target-shooting range I met a few team members who showed me how to use one of their competition target rifles. Lying prone on the firing pad, I couldn't hold the rifle still, even with the sling so tight that the circulation in my arm stopped. It was heavier than a foot locker full of bricks, and the muzzle moved around the bulls-eye like a bee looking for a flower. I was five feet ten inches in height, and weighed only 125 pounds, so scrawny that I wasn't strong enough to hold the rifle steady. If I hit the target, it was an accident.

I didn't pursue the idea of making the team.

After returning from our Ft. Dix bivouac and firing range session, Lt. Ashcroft was asked to visit the Ft. Monmouth supply officer, who wondered what the $9,000 expense item for ammunition was all about. $4,000 of it was for an atomic bomb simulator, which puzzled the supply officer even more. After Lt. Ashcroft explained that it was all for our recent training exercise, he was ordered to buy no more such items, as there was not now and never had been money in the Ft. Monmouth budget for them. We were becoming a thorn in the side of the Ft. Monmouth establishment.

During our ATT, the judges who scored our performance occasionally declared a soldier or an officer to be a casualty, causing that person to retire to the sideline for the remainder of the test. Eventually, our company commander was sidelined this way. The judges, in their final report on our performance declared that the unit performed better after the captain left the battlefield.

When the recall happened, nobody in the unit except our captain was happy about it. There were men in the unit who would have avoided their "second time around" if they could figure out how, without ending up in jail. One young enlisted man went home on a weekend pass to Rochester and just didn't come back until he was arrested and court marshaled for going

AWOL. He then spent 30 days in the Ft. Monmouth prison, a maximum security facility where the government later held mobster Joe Valachi while he was testifying before congress in the fall of 1963 about the "Cosa Nostra." When our soldier got out of the hoosegow, he became a model of good behavior, and declared, "I hated it in there, sir. I am never going back." He must have been impressed by the criminal justice system, because after his release from active duty, he went back to school and became a Rochester police officer, and later was the Chief of Police in one of the Rochester suburbs. It appears that prison does, occasionally, rehabilitate.

Some recalled reservists were getting bad press for the rest of us by complaining to their congressmen and to the newspapers that although the Berlin Wall Crisis was over in a few weeks, President Kennedy was keeping us on active duty far longer than necessary. Most of us agreed with that view, but we considered it unpatriotic (and risky) to go over the Army's head to publicly complain about it.

Secretary of the Army Elias J. Stahr, Jr. was reported to have referred to the recalled reservists as "bitching freeloaders," willing to take their reservist paychecks, but whining when their services were needed on active duty. Into the midst of this publicity and low morale firestorm came our CO, determined to do his part to solve it.

Our mess hall was allowed only two gallons of peanut butter per month, but got five gallons of jelly each month. The peanut butter was always depleted before the end of the month, and there was a surplus of jelly. Our captain would kill two birds with one stone: He would resolve this entanglement of morale-lowering problems and save money for the Army's food budget at the same time. The morale would be as easy to adjust as the volume control on a radio.

Our mess sergeant was a resourceful fellow who, upon arrival at Ft. Monmouth, quickly tuned in to the network of other mess sergeants on the base. When he found out that the WAAC company on base had a surplus of peanut butter but was short of jelly, he arranged a trade with the WAACs: two gallons of our jelly for one gallon of their peanut butter, which made the two commodities come out even for us—three gallons of each. The captain, who knew that peanut butter was a healthy source of protein, most people liked it, and the men would appreciate it, was delighted that this morale-raising trade had occurred, and ordered that it continue. For another morale booster, he added potted plants to the decor of our mess hall. The men would rather have seen their cost put toward a ping-pong table or pool table for their day room, but nobody asked them what they thought.

Possible insubordination reared its ugly head when the potted plants slowly withered and died, giving rise to various theories. Were the mess hall cooks watering the plants with vinegar? Or perhaps they were urinating into the pots. Like any good leader, Lt. Frangos mounted a vigorous defense of his men in response to these allegations. He was said to have declared, "My men have more brains and self-control than that. They would use a receptacle where nobody would notice, like the coffee pot." The mystery of the wilting plants was never solved.

John Goldman was the company's only second lieutenant, but he had enough time in grade for a promotion to first lieutenant while we were still at Ft. Monmouth. After the promotion, he threw the mother of all parties at his rented home. All the unit's officers were there, the liquor flowed profusely, and many of us had headaches the next morning that were retroactively admired and compared for many years.

Somehow the country survived the Berlin Wall Crisis, and the men of the 411th survived the recall. Months before we returned home in the summer of 1962, Khrushchev had dropped his demand that the allies abandon Berlin. The Soviet premier lost interest and began an even bigger project: He fomented the Cuban Missile Crisis. The Berlin Wall, having stemmed the hemorrhage of Germans escaping to freedom in the west, stayed in place until 1989, when the Wall came down and Berliners were once again allowed to walk across their city without interference by government thugs.

The 411th Signal Company moved back to Rochester and was de-activated on August 11, 1962 after ten months of active duty. A parade was held, celebrations proliferated, and grateful speeches were made at a ceremony in Highland Park Bowl by the mayor of Rochester, the lieutenant governor of New York, and a couple of reserve generals and other dignitaries, all of whom were anxious to publicly welcome us back and to thank us for saving the world for democracy.

It was good to be home.

On a visit to Berlin in 1990, Marianne and I were forced to book a room at the Palast Hotel in what had been East Berlin. West Berlin was a thriving, vibrant city where the hotels were full. In comparison, East Berlin, where we arrived three days after official reunification of East and West Germany, was nearly deserted. There was still bomb damage that had not been repaired since WWII ended, and the citizens suffered from the culture shock of sudden exposure to the west.

On a visit to what was left of the Wall, we broke off pieces of it to bring home to some of my fellow 411th officers. The largest piece, six or eight inches in its longest dimension, now sits on the fireplace mantel in our living room as a reminder of how sick and disgusting power-hungry politicians can get without checks and balances.

Two Shakes of a Lamb's Tail

IV

The Spectracom Saga

O I will walk with you, my lad, whichever way you fare,
You'll have me, too, the side o' you, with heart as light as air;
No care for where the road you take's a-leadin' anywhere,--
It can but be a joyful ja'nt whilst you journey there.
The road you take's the path o' love, an' that's the bridth o' two--
An' I will walk with you, my lad -- O I will walk with you.

James Whitcomb Riley
A Song of the Road – v. 1

"The time has come," the Walrus said,
"To talk of many things:
Of shoes – and ships – and sealing wax –
Of cabbages – and kings –
Of why the sea is boiling hot –
And whether pigs have wings…"

Lewis Carroll
Through The Looking Glass, Ch. 4,
The Walrus and The Carpenter

Chapter 28

In Search of Success

My desire to have my own company probably had germinated in a conversation with my dad when I was a young teenager. We were discussing his early employment at small companies during the Depression, soon after he got his master's degree, when he couldn't find a job with a company that didn't soon go broke.

"Why didn't those companies succeed?" I asked.

"Well, they wanted to make a million dollars and weren't careful enough about how they spent their money," he said.

A million dollars. A person could do that?

As a child I exhibited what today might be viewed as minor obsessive-compulsive behavior, not stepping on cracks in the sidewalk, making my own bed with hospital corners, and striving for perfection in other ways. Jim Eaton and I, as Boy Scouts, won tent pitching contests, first aid contests, and knot-tying contests. Advancement became a standard goal as I earned badges in Cub Scouts and Boy Scouts, a good citizenship medal in sixth grade, and was elected president of the Hi-Y Club in high school.

In my late teens, unable to find a summer job, I mowed lawns and tended shrub beds to make spending money for college. Dad let me drop him off at work and keep the family car for the day to move our lawn mower and a few other garden tools from house to house as each property needed attention. Word got around that I was reliable, and I found enough work to stay busy for the summer. I liked running my own little service business.

My high school career was topped off by election to the National Honor Society by my high school teachers and as "the most likely to succeed" by my classmates. This recognition imposed on me an even more lofty set of standards to live up to.

While in college at Purdue I could make five dollars at the football stadium on Saturday afternoons by ignoring the game and selling bottled Coca Cola up and down the aisles to the fans.

When I graduated from Purdue in 1957 with a BSEE degree and a commission as an Army Signal Corps second lieutenant, I was hired as an electronic engineer at General Dynamics in Rochester, New York, and helped develop communications equipment for the FAA and for the US Navy.

In the army reserves in Rochester, I flexed my newly discovered entrepreneurial muscle, tiny as it was, and filled a need for name tags for the troops to wear on their uniforms. I bought plastic laminate, cut it up in my basement, cut each name into the plastic using a pantograph engraving machine that belonged to my employer, and epoxied thumbtacks onto the back sides to stick through the uniform material. The name tags were held in place by standard little metal "grabbers" (now called "frogs" I'm told) that I bought and furnished with each name tag. Getting paid was a problem. The commanding officer had told me the reserve unit would buy the nametags from me, but it turned out that he wasn't authorized to spend the money. Lesson learned: When doing contract work, always get an order in writing before spending time or money to fill it.

When the project engineer that I reported to at General

Dynamics Electronics Division was about 28 years old and I was about 25, he told me that by the time he was 30, he would have his own company. It was a bold declaration, and it sounded very much like he meant it. Our Chief Engineer, Elmer Schwittek, and his sidekick, Roger Bettin, had recently left General Dynamics with Bill Stolze to start RF Communications, a two-way radio manufacturer that had found a niche market selling wireless communications equipment to third-world countries that didn't have good phone systems. They financed their start-up in 1961 with a stock offering to the public of 200,000 shares at one dollar a share. It sold out immediately. In our lab, my boss and I and a hundred other co-workers salivated. The romance and excitement of starting a company tickled our nerves and generated fantasies.

Two years later, when their company had about 50 employees and was growing rapidly, I was invited to lunch by the three founders to discuss the possibility of going to work at RF Communications. We picked a restaurant some distance away from where I worked and met at noon on the appointed day. After some discussion, Elmer Schwittek, with a flourish, pulled an envelope out of his inside jacket pocket and handed it to me. It was an offer of a 25 per cent higher salary of $10,000 a year and an option to buy 1500 shares of RF Communications at $2.00 per share.

In the game of poker, on those rare occasions when the stars line up just so and a tingle runs up your spine, you know that this hand will be a winner. Like several years before, when I realized that I should marry my girlfriend, Marianne, before she got away, knowing she was a winner. As Elmer handed me that letter, I knew I should do it. The move would be a winner. Of course, I tried to keep a poker face and be a little coy.

"Can I have a couple of days to think about it?"

"Yes, but we need to find someone pretty soon."

The next day, after talking it over with Marianne, I phoned

Elmer to accept the offer.

While I worked at RF Communications in the mid-1960s, one of the young lab technicians started a part-time business in his basement, making and selling small, simple electronic products. Entrepreneurs were everywhere. The prospect of following suit intrigued me, but in a conversation about it with our company purchasing agent, he scornfully referred to the basement operation as "Peachfuzz Electronics" and I lost interest for a while.

After returning from army active duty during the Berlin Wall Crisis in 1962, I enrolled in the MBA program in night school at the University of Rochester. I had no specific goal in mind but knew that I wanted to do more than be a product development engineer for the rest of my career. I really liked the course material, and after a rocky start in the first course (I got a D in Marketing), I managed to earn top grades in the rest of my classes.

Nearly flunking Marketing wasn't a new experience. My academic history had been spotty ever since graduating from high school. At Purdue, bad semesters were followed by good semesters and vice versa. I hadn't yet learned to set priorities and concentrate on the top ones. In my first two jobs after graduation, five years at General Dynamics Electronics followed by seven of my ten years at Harris RF Communications, where I designed two-way single sideband radio equipment for the Navy, I settled down and did some good work. At GD I was awarded a patent, and at RF Communications I was the first person to use a computer. I wrote programs in the Fortran language, using punch cards and rented IBM computer time to do thousands of calculations as I designed impedance matching networks for servo-controlled automatic antenna couplers.

I had a fuzzy view of Marketing, equating it with the sale of used cars by men wearing checkered sport coats and loud neckties. I definitely did not want to be a salesman. Engineers were detail people; salesmen were not. Engineers used their brains to solve problems; salesmen used their mouths to create problems.

At RF Communications, by then a division of Harris Corporation, marketing sneaked up on me. As a project engineer, I found myself actually talking to customers and helping them decide what they needed as I wrote bid proposals and design plans for them. In concert with Navy personnel on the roof of the Pentagon, I tested and demonstrated a prototype automatic antenna coupler that I had designed and built, leading to a follow-on contract for the design and production of the next generation. At Quantico, Virginia, the Marine Corps customer and I went to a supermarket to find a variety of empty shipping cartons which we placed here and there on a Jeep, simulating the locations and sizes of two-way radio transceiver, antenna coupler, and control units. By including the customer in this process, we paved the way for the ultimate success of our bid proposal, leading to tens of millions of dollars in future business. Without realizing it, I was in both sales and marketing, helping the customer to figure out what he needed.

The fire in my belly continued to burn. I occasionally went out of my way to drive down Linden Avenue in East Rochester to admire the row of buildings that housed small companies there. Small buildings, medium-sized buildings, one story, two stories, some with fancy entrances, some not so fancy, some with company names on signs too small to read from the road, and some with large signs that you couldn't miss. What was it about them that attracted me? It wasn't the possibility of money that those companies represented; it was the smell of *success* that leaked into the car as I drove by.

Along the way, three co-workers and I started our own part-time basement company. We named it Paramatron Corporation, and decided to keep it secret from our co-workers, thereby avoiding derisive nicknames like Peachfuzz Electronics. Secrecy would also avoid upsetting our employer. Each of us contributed $100 to the startup and worked for free. Because there wasn't one on the market, we developed a simple oscilloscope calibrator for use with low-cost oscilloscopes. We bought ten sets of parts for it and offered it for sale for $200. We soon learned something I had missed in my marketing class: There were no other such calibrators on the market because there was no real need for them. We sold six units by submitting new product news releases for publication in trade journals, but the experience provided a valuable lesson about what *not* to do in starting a company.

In 1968, I finished my MBA program after six years of continuous night school, where I got good grades in accounting, finance, behavioral science, and production management courses. It was hard work, but I loved it. At Purdue, I had never had any similar course work, not even a psychology course. The engineering curriculum didn't leave room for accounting, finance, and production.

My MBA schooling changed me. I began to really understand what a CEO was and to believe that I could do the job. Maybe not run a division of Harris like Bill Stolze did, but managing a smaller company was very similar to managing a project. Many of the tasks were the same. In positions as project engineer, program manager, and engineering section head at RF Communications, I had responsibility for budgets and schedules; I had hired engineers and technicians; I had purchased parts and supplies; I had dealt with customers over contract details and contract specifications; and I had overseen small manufacturing runs of new products.

The last class in the MBA program was a case study course called Business Policy. It put us vicariously in corporate CEOs' chairs as we wrote reviews of actual company problems and recommended solutions after listening to the real CEOs talk about them. The course was taught by a retired vice president of General Electric, who was assisted by Bill Stolze, the founding CEO of Harris RF Communications. I worked extra hard and got an A in the course.

Upon getting my diploma, I went to Stolze to ask him what effect my MBA degree would have on my career at RF Communications. He made two observations: First, that I was still the same person the day after getting my degree as I was the day before getting it, so I shouldn't expect automatic changes or promotions just because of the degree. Advancement would come because of who I was and what I could do for the company. Secondly, the people who run high-tech companies generally have either engineering or marketing backgrounds, with experience in both areas being important.

This news was a bit of a letdown, but it made perfect sense, and I was glad that Bill was so forthright with me. At least he now knew of my advancement goals, and I had a more realistic view of the path to accomplish them.

The following year Bill came around to my office to suggest that I go to work in the new Electronic Instrument Operation (EIO) that the company had started the prior year. Their first products were about to go into production, and a national sales manager was needed to introduce them to the market. I jumped at the opportunity to organize and manage a national distribution network of manufacturers' sales representatives who sold commercial electronic instruments to industrial customers. There was no requirement for checkered sport coats or loud neckties.

I loved the job, like a breath of fresh air after working for twelve years in the government contracting business where customer and vendor behaved like adversaries much of the time. Selling commercial customers a standard product that advanced the state of the art was much more pleasant than fighting with the federal bureaucracy over interpretation of military specifications, documentation requirements, acceptance testing, and product features that would seldom be used.

Three years later the RF Communications Division of Harris "sold" EIO to another division of the corporation. The products had been badly designed and were failing in the field faster than we could repair them. The engineers had designed the product with the cheapest parts available and had packaged too many features in too small an enclosure, causing overheating and rapid failure. In one transmitter application on the missile range at Vandenberg Air Force Base in California, the click made by a switch adjustment caused a modulation transient that activated the destruct signal that would blow up an ICBM as though it had flown off course during the launch.

The product concept and market research had been brilliant but the execution had failed. I knew that, given the chance, I could do better. With a market like that, anyone could see that product reliability was far more important than using dirt-cheap parts to have the lowest price. The fire was burning brighter in my belly.

When the sale of EIO was announced, I and five other second-tier managers and engineers were offered transfers to the other division. Those who refused the transfer would be let go from the company with a $5,000 separation payment. The five others all accepted their transfer to Florida. Sales and marketing was to take place in Long Island and since the new owner already had a sales manager, I was offered the job of product manager.

The transfer of EIO to the new owner took about six months. I fired each of my sales reps and merged my product line into the new owner's distribution network. I spent the six months traveling around the country to train the new sales team and to make sales calls with them.

Meanwhile, I had decided that I did not want the transfer to Long Island, nor did I want to work for the new boss, who had a much more authoritative management style than Bill Stolze and his management team, whom I had been very happy working under. What I really wanted was to start my own business.

I hooked up with two engineers who had more circuit design talent than I did, and we began working nights and weekends to develop our product. They did the electronic design, and I did the mechanical design and the purchasing, wrote the business plan, and incorporated the company.

Spectracom Corporation was born.

Then the bombshell went off. Someone had reported my activities to Stolze after promising me that he wouldn't. Stolze and I had our little discussion in his office and I was out of a job.

"We're going to have to let you go," he said. "Go back to your office and clear out your desk, and then see the personnel manager before you leave."

My two partners were terrified that the same thing would happen to them, and they withdrew from our little enterprise. With the product prototype half built and poorly documented, it was far too complex for me to finish on my own.

It was time to start over and to concentrate on paying the mortgage and grocery bills.

Chapter 29

Legal Training for a Beginner

My legal adventures began at the same time I started Spectracom. Before the end of the work day when Bill Stolze fired me, I had my exit interview by the personnel manager and was out on the street headed for home in a daze. In the fifteen years since graduating from Purdue, I had not been unemployed for one minute, nor had I ever been fired. I could understand their point of view: I was not only a potential competitor, but even worse, I had committed the cardinal sin of disloyalty. Never mind that Stolze and his co-founders had done exactly the same thing twelve years earlier when they had left General Dynamics. There was one key difference: *They* had kept their plans secret until they were ready to resign.

When I told my wife what had transpired, she held her thumb and forefinger a quarter-inch apart, saying, "Well, you were this far from being let go anyway."

She was right. I had decided not to take the transfer with my division's move to Long Island and Florida, and there was no other job for me in RF Communications at that time. We would just have to accept the loss of $5,000 separation pay. Unemployment insurance would offset part of it for a while.

In my search for investors in my new company, I had written a business plan and was shopping it around town, showing it to various people who occasionally invested in start-ups. When I explained to one of them that someone had "ratted me out" to my bosses, he said, "Well, you can't make an omelet unless you break some eggs."

Applying for New York State unemployment insurance benefits was degrading and discouraging, but I decided that if the state had forced me to pay for this insurance for the past fifteen years, only death or disability would stop me from collecting on it. I would do whatever it took, including applying for jobs, standing in long lines, and suffering abuse by civil servants whose demeanor told me they disliked their jobs and didn't think much of their clients, either.

After a few weeks of receiving checks, I was notified by mail that I would no longer be eligible for benefits because I had "provoked my own discharge." I could appeal the decision by appearing at a hearing before an examiner who would review the case. At the hearing, I explained that instead of my having provoked my own discharge, my employer had, by telling me of my impending termination, provoked me into trying to find new employment, which was exactly what the unemployment office wanted me to do. One of the ways I was trying to stay employed was by starting a company.

It didn't wash. My appeal was denied. At that point I consulted my attorney, John Goldman, with whom I had been recalled into active duty in the army and who had written our wills and helped us buy our house. My next step was to appeal my case to the New York State Supreme Court where it would be reviewed. John pointed out that my odds of winning at that level were low, even with an attorney's help. Furthermore, the amount of money I might collect if I won was less than his fees would be, so it didn't make economic sense to pursue the case. I said if that was the case, I would pursue the appeal on my own if he would just point me in the right direction. After all, my own labor was free.

By this time, Marianne had gone back to work part-time in

an insurance office to help pay our bills, and I had found a part-time consulting job to help. On top of applying for jobs and standing in line at the Unemployment Insurance Office to protect my claim if I should win my case, I continued looking for venture capital as I developed product in my basement laboratory and wrote my appeal brief for the court. John Goldman had told me how to find the law library in the county court building, and he said I could use the copying machine in his law office for free. I submitted what I'm sure was the most amateurish brief ever seen by the court, asking that my claim be paid with interest. My claim was again denied.

By then I had learned more about researching cases in the law library and was treating the case like a hobby in my spare time. Nearly two years had gone by when I decided to appeal one more time. The New York State Court of Appeals is the state's highest court. They hear appeals from decisions of the State Supreme Court. This time in my filing of intent to appeal, I reserved the right to appear before the court in Albany to personally argue my case. I wanted them to know that I was serious about my case and wasn't about to give up without a good fight.

At the law library, I had been treated like a leper. The people behind the desk were used to dealing with licensed attorneys, not pesky untrained interloping neophytes like me, so they tried to be as minimally helpful as possible. When I finally found an assistant who truly wanted to help, things went more smoothly.

My "Eureka" moment came when I found a case that had been decided just the previous year, where the court had stated that denial of an unemployment claim on that grounds that claimant had "provoked his own discharge" had no basis in law. In other words, there was nothing in the law to justify those grounds for denial of a claim. If the reason for discharge didn't meet the legal definition of misconduct (e.g., slugging the boss or stealing office supplies) the insurance claim must be paid.

Eureka!

I rewrote my brief and included a citation and summary of the case I had found, and submitted it to the court, still expecting to be given a court date to appear in Albany.

Weeks later, when the phone rang, it was an attorney in the state prosecutor's office in New York City. He sounded tentative as he told me that no court date would be set.

"We don't like this case," was all he would say about its merits.

Don't like the case? What did that mean?

"We're sending it back to the State Supreme Court," he said.

"Will I still have to go to Albany?" I asked.

"Wait until you hear from the court," he said.

Was I about to win my case?

I waited. And waited.

My answer finally arrived in the mail in the form of a written decision that allowed my claim but denied my request for interest on the money. I was incensed. They had withheld for a couple of years the $1200 they owed me based on a bogus conclusion of "self-provoked discharge" and on top of it had put me through a wringer of standing in lines at the unemployment office, hours and hours of library research, and besmirchment of my name and reputation, and they weren't even going to pay me interest? Baloney!

I didn't even bother to research any legal requirements for the state to pay the interest. I wasn't too rational at this point, but I had been wronged and wanted to get everything I could out of them. I also wanted my case, and especially my brief, filed in the archives of the Appeals Court so the world would know how I had been treated. One way to ensure this, I thought, was to file another appeal with the Appeals Court asking for the interest payment, which would force them to render a decision.

I lost that one. There was no provision in the New York

labor law for payment of interest penalties when a state agency erroneously denies a legitimate claim. My appeal was denied, but by then I had calmed down and it didn't matter much. I had won my case-in-chief and was solving other problems—feeding my family and getting Spectracom off the ground.

—◆—

Ten years later, well after Spectracom was a going concern, paying our salaries and making a profit, we had a dispute with a supplier.

During Spectracom's startup, we had done everything ourselves to save money. When you're not able to pay your own salary, your labor is cheap, so I painted Spectracom's front panels with baking enamel myself. I dried the paint by baking the parts in our kitchen oven. The resulting perfume that permeated the house made our eyes water and would have driven away any guests, but hosting dinner parties wasn't on our agenda during those years. I made the printed circuit boards myself, using the crude methods of a hobbyist.

I also designed the product literature myself, but because I'm neither a graphic designer nor an artist of any kind, it looked pretty amateurish, like maybe an engineer had designed it. Later, when the company could afford it, we took the product data sheets to a commercial artist and told him to fix it so it looked like a professional designed it. We then used the same printer that had produced our earlier product literature. The product photographs were sharp and clear and the halftone screening looked good. The brochures clearly had been designed by someone who knew what they were doing. It was one more step toward becoming an excellent company.

Then a minor disaster struck. We bought the second printing from the lowest bidder, who did a terrible job. We had specified a 20% screen of the second color that overlaid part of the large product photograph on the front side of the data sheet. When the printing job was delivered, there was far too much of that color. The result was that it looked like it had been printed with mud instead of ink. I asked the printer to do the job over, this time using a 20% screen instead of what looked to me like at least a 50% screen. He declined and said that he *had* used a 20% screen. When I refused to accept the printing job and said that we would pay them when the job was done right, they took us to arbitration. The fine print on the order I had signed said that any disputes would be solved by arbitration, which would take place in Olean, New York, a two-hour drive away from our plant.

When I called John Goldman to see what I should do, he again said, "Well, you can't hire me because my bill will be more than you'll collect. Why don't you write it off to experience?"

My stubborn streak had reappeared because I knew I was right, and I decided to pursue the case without a lawyer, just for the experience, if nothing else. John must have rolled his eyes and thought, "There he goes again!"

By then, we were purchasing our circuit boards from a professional supplier, but we still had the negatives made by a specialty photographer. I had them take high-resolution photos of the screened area of the data sheet, from which enlarged prints were made that showed the screening dots blown up to two inches in diameter. I was then able to measure, using normal drafting tools, the percentage of the area covered by the dots. It was just over 50%. *Aha!* I thought. *I've got them.* I could now prove that their print job didn't meet our specification of 20%.

On the appointed day, armed with my rolled-up ten-square-foot photograph of dots, I drove the two hours to the arbitration hearing that was held in a conference room at the upstairs offices of the printer's attorney. With everyone sitting around the large conference table, I unrolled my dots and explained what it all meant. The printer then pulled out a little hand-held instrument that he said measured screening percentages, put it on a data sheet that he had printed, and reported that the instrument confirmed that the screening was 20%. We had a "He said, She said" standoff.

When it was all over, the arbitrator announced his decision in favor of the printer because the printer was an "expert" in printing technology and I wasn't. I now had to pay for the printing job, coincidentally the same $1200 amount that I had collected in my unemployment case a few years earlier, and I couldn't even use the product I had to buy because it looked so bad.

On the way out the door of the hearing room, the printer said to me, "Now that this is settled, we would like to continue doing business with you, and I hope we can get a chance to bid on your work in the future."

I said something non-committal, like, "We'll see," or "Maybe," while I thought to myself, "Mister, there isn't a snowball's chance in Hell that you'll get more of our business."

To judge the wisdom of pursuing such a case, the economics must be considered. It was clearly uneconomical to hire an attorney. Pursuing it on my own, the out-of-pocket costs to Spectracom were only for gasoline and photographically enlarged dots—probably less than $100. That expenditure had a good chance, so I thought, of saving us $1200. The costs of my time and my diversions from more important matters are harder to evaluate, but a rational decision maker probably would say that pursuit of the case wasn't worth it. But when all was said and done, I was glad I had pursued it because I learned some important lessons: Make sure your expert witness not only knows his stuff, but he also must appear to be more qualified and smarter than the opponent's expert. I was a sorry example of an expert witness. I didn't know that a measuring device like the opposition had demonstrated even existed. Properly prepared, I would have found my own version of such an instrument and used it before I decided to pursue the case. Secondly, at the arbitration hearing, I couldn't think fast enough to question the calibration of his instrument, which I now believe was faulty; perhaps intentionally so. And we were manufacturers of calibration equipment! Our products were in a very different field, but I should have known that such an instrument would need calibration and that I might need to question the opposition about its accuracy.

I had gone hunting with defective ammunition in my weapon, but the lessons I learned were inexpensive compared with the much higher stakes in some later legal adventures.

Chapter 30

Committed

After I left my Harris employment, I continued the unsuccessful search for outside financing for Spectracom. I visited several wealthy people who were known to dabble in start-ups. I showed them my business plan and, in some cases, a mockup of our product. It was the beginning of an emotional roller-coaster that continued until Spectracom's first product was firmly on the market. When a potential investor said, "I'll call you," after listening to my story, I was elated, floating on a cloud. When he didn't call, I was back down in the dumps again.

A few such episodes taught me that the words "I'll call you" were not a commitment; they were only the first part of the sentence. The unspoken clause was "if I ever get interested enough in your proposal to bet real money on your success." None of them called.

I never did find investors that were willing to take that chance with me. Why would they? One of the more forthright of them told me, "You have no product, no sales, no employees, no assets, and no money." And for all practical purposes, I had no company. All I had was my own commitment to success and the belief that, one way or the other, I would make it happen. They, on the other hand, didn't share my optimism.

A few facts of life were now clear. The product that was half-developed would never be finished now that my design engineers were gone. Without at least a half million dollars, I needed to start over with a much simpler product and another engineer for a business partner, and if we wanted to keep our house and put bread on the table, we had to earn some money. Since I had no other choice, I would do all of this with no outside investors.

Earning some money was our first priority. Marianne went to work in an insurance agency office, where her experience as an underwriter before we started having children eased her transition from full-time mother. I told friends that to put bread on the table I had to rent her out. More than a few of our meals included Hamburger Helper and milk that was cut by 50 percent with water and powdered milk. I cut our kids' hair myself, and Marianne stopped spending money on permanents and hair-dos. She tried cutting my hair, but we worried that the resulting mess would frighten my business contacts. More importantly, the friction created during the haircutting process threatened to move us toward divorce, so I resumed paying a few dollars every two or three months for a professional cut, and did some minor trimming myself with a "trim-comb" in between cuts. We also reduced *all* our expenses to the bare necessities. Marianne never complained. She just kept on taking care of our three children, now aged six to eleven, watering the milk, and working at her new job when the kids were in school.

Meanwhile, Spectracom continued struggling, its headquarters a desk and a workbench in our basement, where the primary goal was to bring the first product to market. I found part-time consulting jobs, operating as Spectracom. I helped Radionics and Scientific Radio Systems write bid proposals to the government and developed a new printed-circuit transformer product line for Coil-ler Manufacturing, a company founded and managed by Gene Dorland. Spectracom also operated as a quick-turnaround printed-circuit prototype supplier to several companies in the Rochester area. In three days after providing Spectracom with a schematic diagram, a drawing of the part and its interfaces, and an example of each part, a client received one or two completed prototype circuit boards ready to stuff with circuit components. This service was an extension of capabilities already available in our basement, since I was building Spectracom's own circuit boards there, not having the money to buy them from outside suppliers. I made "tape-ups" of the circuit board patterns on a home-made light box and the RA Ellis Company made photographic negatives of the pattern, a service that had to be paid for. Photoresist from a spray can sensitized the boards, and an infrared lamp quickly dried the photoresist without exposing it. I then taped the negative to the board, exposed it under an ultraviolet lamp, and etched the pattern into it with a ferric chloride bath in a Pyrex baking dish pilfered from Marianne's kitchen. An old Erector Set motor that I had kept since my junior high school days tilted the dish back and forth to accelerate the etching.

An hour or so of etching removed the unwanted copper laminate from the board, and solvent removed the resist from the remaining copper traces. Holes for component leads were drilled using carbide bits in a Dremel Tool held in a miniature drill press fixture, and the board was scrubbed with steel wool. Solder plating was not available, but if the customer wanted nickel plating over the copper to protect it from corrosion, I did it in an old electric frying pan, also confiscated from Marianne's kitchen, using electroless nickel plating solution. Both the ferric chloride and the nickel solution were purchased a gallon or two at a time, and the spent chemicals were disposed of down the storm sewer drain in front of our house during rainstorms in the middle of the night. Over three years, I put a total of less than five gallons of each spent chemical into the subterranean environment. Unless there were copper pipes in the sewer system, it was unlikely that any damage occurred. If there were copper pipes, maybe the nickel solution would plate the surfaces before the now weakened ferric chloride could etch them.

Spectracom had no facility for providing plated-through holes, but I made double-sided boards by visually aligning the top and bottom negatives, taped them together in place, and inserted the board between them prior to exposure. Negatives were held tight against the board using clear window glass weighted down with rolls of solder or whatever heavy tools were lying around on the workbench. Since these were only prototype boards, the customer didn't mind making his own through-hole connections by soldering component leads on both the top and bottom of the board.

Circuit boards for the first Spectracom products were made this same way, always nickel plated, with Spectracom doing the top-and-bottom soldering to connect conductors on both sides of the board. A few of those early products with homemade circuit boards came back from customers for repair ten or twenty years later, showing corrosion of the nickel plating. In the opinion of Jim Rall, the Production Test Supervisor who repaired them, the circuit boards were not of the highest quality.

During the three years spent developing the first product, I viewed Spectracom as a separate entity. It wasn't just Bob Hesselberth in his basement, it was a *Corporation*. That was how I wanted my customers and suppliers to view it, so that was how I viewed it. I continued, now and then, to drive slowly down Linden Avenue in East Rochester past the companies that resided there, nurturing my commitment, focusing it with envy. Then, my batteries recharged with inspiration, I went back to my basement to donate more perspiration.

Our savings soon disappeared, but we were helped by a $6,000 loan from my parents. For two years running, we owed no income taxes and actually got a small amount of money *from* the federal government in their first experiments with a negative income tax as an alternative to welfare payments. When I was ticketed for speeding, I pleaded unemployment and a list of other extenuating circumstances. The judge took mercy on me and fined me only ten dollars.

During our family's third year of poverty we started missing mortgage payments. When I asked the bank if we could have a little time off from making payments, they refused. We were mortified that we couldn't pay our bills but were too proud to ask parents for another loan. We crossed our fingers.

We had managed to hold onto the Harris stock that I had purchased by exercising the options given me when I was hired. While I was employed, I had paid for the stock with a loan from the bank, using the stock as collateral. When I left my employment the stock market was in decline, drying up the supply of venture capital and eventually decreasing the market value of my Harris stock to a level near the value of my loan. The bank asked me to pay off the loan or put up more collateral to avoid their having to sell the stock to protect themselves. We had neither money nor more collateral, so we crossed a few more of our fingers and hoped that because it was a different bank than the one that held our mortgage, we might have some time before the two banks put their heads together and figured out that we were deadbeats.

I remained convinced that Spectracom would succeed.

Chapter 31

Sexing Gerbils

The Spectracom startup years weren't all work and no play. Even though I worked a lot of 14-hour days, I tried, as best I could, to stay involved in family activities. I was active with our son, David, in Cub Scouts, and later, in Boy Scouts, but left to Marianne the Girl Scout duty with David's younger sisters, Mary Jo and Susan. We both went to the kids' schools for parent-teacher conferences and to church, where the kids went to Sunday school and where I had to resign my position as a ruling elder due to the time commitment required.

The subject of pets was sometimes a sore point in the family. When the kids wanted a dog or a cat, we had to say no because of Marianne's allergies. We tried tropical fish and kept tanks of them for a few years, but they were difficult to snuggle with and weren't pettable. The kids' involvement quickly faded, Marianne hadn't been interested in the first place, and Dad was left with the maintenance responsibilities.

When David was nine, he was offered a gift from a friend's gerbil menagerie. We assumed that gerbils were non-allergenic and gave our approval. During the time of our household gerbil infestation we never had allergy problems that we could trace to the furry little beasts, but there were other problems. We should have made some inquiries regarding their reproductive talents.

David chose two males and brought them home in a shoe box. While we wanted to avoid inflicting on a single gerbil the life of a reclusive hermit, we did not want the responsibility of finding new homes for an exponentially expanding battalion of the little critters. Two months later, one of those males gave birth to eight babies.

I began to regret the hours we had spent preparing a home for the animals in a converted 20-gallon fish tank in David's bedroom. The container that had once housed guppies and angel fish, and later a spotted salamander that we found in the woods, would now encage mammals. We fabricated a cover for the aquarium from wire mesh "hardware cloth" that fit tightly over the top. We acquired a water bottle and an exercise wheel, donated by another family that had already learned their lessons regarding small animal husbandry. We bought a bag of cedar shavings for nesting material, and inserted all of the above, along with the gerbils, into the aquarium, and then sat back to watch their charming antics while, unbeknownst to us, they began their clandestine assignations under cover of darkness and piles of cedar shavings.

They cuddled together at times, presumably to keep warm as they napped. Once, when David called me into his room to see them, he said, "Look, Dad."

I looked. They were behaving like two bumper cars, one behind the other. When the one in the rear collided with the one in front, the one in front immediately ran several steps ahead. When it stopped, the one in the rear ran ahead until another collision occurred. After a few of these puzzling collisions, I asked, "What are they doing?"

"They're mating, Dad," David said.

"Oh," I said, and left the room. A ten-year-old was telling me about the birds and the bees. It didn't resemble any mating activity I had ever seen, but what did I know? I was only the dad.

Their public antics included the continual use of the noisy exercise wheel, frequently at 3:00 AM. David put a stick through the spokes of the wheel at night so he could sleep.

But every action has a reaction, and with less to do to amuse themselves, the gerbils found substitute pastimes and more babies appeared. One escaped while its cage was being cleaned and disappeared for two weeks until it was nabbed while darting across the living room toward shelter under the La-Z-Boy. Months later, preparing for the arrival of house guests, we opened the Hide-A-Bed to find large holes chewed in the top side of the mattress where the fugitive gerbil had used the stuffing as nesting material. Why hadn't we borrowed a neighbor's cat as soon as the rotten little rodent escaped? To help our guests sleep, we turned over the mattress.

As we watched the babies grow, we contemplated the scary prospect of eight babies becoming four couples, each producing eight more babies. Were we committing moral turpitude by enabling gerbil incest? More importantly, would our entire disposable income be consumed by the purchase of geometrically increasing numbers of fish aquaria and bags of cedar shavings? The gerbils would proliferate like zucchini and be difficult to give away. We had to somehow separate the sexes or be inundated, but how to tell the difference?

I researched the library's literature and found that the gerbil gestation period was 25 days, their native land was Mongolia, and the organs of interest were completely interior. The only way to tell the boys from the girls was to detect subtle differences in exterior curvatures of the lower abdomen when comparing two or more animals. At least it wasn't as difficult or as risky as sexing alligators, where, I'm told, you must reach inside and feel around to figure out who is a boy and who is a girl. And an alligator would get much more annoyed than a gerbil, who is merely being looked at.

There were enormous problems in getting the squirmy fur balls to submit to the indignity of holding still while lying on their backs with rear legs splayed so I could inspect their invisible privates. I developed new proprietary techniques for holding them on their backs in my palm, thumb and pinkie finger suppressing rear leg kicking and scratching, while I flagrantly invaded their privacy and peered shamelessly at them to divine their innermost secrets. After a few tries, and with some instruction from a friend more experienced than I, my technique was perfected. It was then that we discovered a basic truth of gerbil husbandry: By the time a baby has matured enough that we could find a difference in their, um, development, it was already too late to prevent a first litter.

We gave babies away, causing a neighborhood gerbil population explosion. As each pair of our gerbils had babies, we gave them away to more households, the result being an atom-splitting chain reaction, its fires fanned by the fad of all the neighboring ten-year-olds needing their own gerbils. After a couple of litters each human mother said "Enough!"

Calling me on the phone, they said, "I hear that you know how to tell the males from the females. Please tell me how."

"I can't explain it on the phone," I said. "I need to inspect your animals in person."

As my reputation spread, I became the neighborhood's de facto itinerant gerbil sexing expert, called by mothers far and wide to consult on these matters from up to three blocks away. This was before the human sexual revolution, and fathers, still the hunter-gatherers, tended not to be involved with their family gerbils' characteristics. I broke fresh ground for fatherhood in this highly subjective technology, and gave new meaning to the concept of being of service to my neighbors.

I cannot tell you for sure why the world is not, by now, overrun with and ruled by gerbils whose ancestry can be traced back to our son's pets, but I have a theory: The kids in the neighborhood got bored. How many weeks in a row can a ten-year-old sit still, staring into a cage, watching a Mongolian rodent sleep, eat, exercise; then sleep, eat, and exercise? And how many parents are willing to feed the animals, clean the cages, search for escapees, and figure out what to do with all those babies?

The precise reasons for the end of the gerbil era in the Hesselberth household are lost in the mists of time and memory, but the benefits of that end are clear. It eliminated the inventory expenses for cedar shavings; it ended the requests for gerbil sexing; and it allowed me to focus on inventing new products for Spectracom without the need to invent gerbil contraceptives.

Chapter 32

Turnaround

In 1975, the stock market nosedive stopped just before the bank would have sold our collateral and kept most of the proceeds. More importantly, after three years of designing mistakes and finding moonlighters to help with the difficult challenges, Spectracom put its first product on the market in the fall of 1975. The Model 8160 WWVB Receiver-Comparator was about the size of two thick, stacked phone books, and was aimed at the calibration lab market. We knew there was a market because Hewlett Packard had a similar instrument that they had sold for decades, but the design was obsolete and its niche market too small for HP to invest in an upgrade. At least, that's what we gambled on. The model number was chosen with impeccable logic: It rolled off the tongue easily and was not similar to any model numbers used by my previous employer.

The Spectracom unit sold for $1200 and allowed the customer to use the signal broadcast from the government radio station WWVB in Colorado as a comparison standard to keep frequency counters, signal generators, and communications equipment accurately on frequency to within one part per billion. It was first exhibited at a regional test and measurement trade show in Washington, DC in a corner of the booth of another company whose sales manager was a friend of mine. In return for setup help and booth duty, Spectracom wasn't charged for its three feet of table space. At that first trade show, I met the man who was to become our mid-Atlantic sales rep, Jim Ewing of the Gawler-Knoop Company.

During the next few months I was embroiled in a flurry of activity. I wrote letters and made phone calls to recruit sales reps in other parts of the country. I traveled to their territory to train them and made sales calls with them to demonstrate the equipment. I wrote product data sheets and published them. I wrote the technical manuals for the first products and placed advertising and sent new product announcements to technical magazines and newspapers. I loved it. I didn't have time to drive down Linden Avenue to admire the companies there anymore, but it didn't matter. We had our own company. We began to generate our own smell of success.

When Spectracom moved out of our home basement, production began behind a bowling alley in Penfield, in the 1200-square-foot rented basement of a small kitchen cabinet manufacturer. First employees were either part-timers or moonlighters. Our first production worker's day job was on the order desk of Rochester Radio Supply. He had prior production experience and moonlighted to build cable harnesses and complete the first products. Bob Cole, who years later was to become our mechanical designer and all-round technician, moonlighted as the first test technician. Linda Dodd, our super-secretary who had left Harris before I did to raise her three small stepchildren and help her husband in his sales rep business, joined us part-time as the first secretary, buyer, bookkeeper, and order entry and shipping department head. My wife, Marianne, moonlighted as part-time bookkeeper when needed, but it wasn't until 1980 that she was promoted from volunteer to a salaried position and gave up her outside employment.

During Spectracom's rented basement phase, we introduced the rest of the product family: Model 8161 WWVB Receiver-

Comparator with built-in Frequency Standard, chart recorder, and optional frequency distribution amplifier; Model 8140 Frequency Distribution Amplifier; and the Model 8130 Frequency Standard.

In 1977, a friendly Tektronix salesman suggested that a WWVB Receiver-Comparator configured as a plug-in for the Tektronix TM-500 mainframe would have a significant market.

A few months later Spectracom began introducing a family of such products for the TM-500: Model 8163 Receiver-Comparator; the Model 8130 Frequency Standard; the Model 8150 Precision Phase Comparator; and the Model 8212 Strip Chart Recorder. AT&T Bell Labs and Motorola purchased several of these frequency calibration systems for $5,000 each during their collaboration to build the first cellular phone system in Chicago.

Another significant competitor was the True Time Instrument Company, who had started in business about the same time as Spectracom, but had brought a WWVB product to market sooner. Spectracom's advantages included the option of getting a high-stability frequency standard built into the unit and a built-in frequency distribution amplifier as well. Spectracom's chart recorder was a better design, more rugged, easier to use, more reliable, and it provided better measurement resolution. Further, Spectracom's receiver design had better reception sensitivity and noise rejection.

In the beginning, Spectracom didn't have its own WWVB antenna design, so we purchased antennas from True Time and resold them for use with Spectracom's receivers. When True Time decided not to continue this arrangement, Spectracom designed its own antenna with more gain and better temperature stability than the True Time unit.

In early 1978, the next logical step for Spectracom was to develop a WWVB clock. HP had no such product, and True Time was the only significant competition. Here, the company was helped by another design advantage. The Spectracom receivers included, for the price of a very few extra parts, a *synchronous* time code demodulator that could more reliably set a digital clock in a shorter time than the competition. However, such a clock required a microprocessor chip at its heart. Although I could design TTL logic circuitry for the existing Spectracom products, I didn't have the knowledge or experience to design a microprocessor.

Tom Donaher and I had served together in the army during the Berlin Wall Crisis in 1961. We had both worked as engineers at the General Dynamics Electronics Division in Rochester before and after our recall, Donaher in the Digital Communications Laboratory and I in the Radio Communications Laboratory. By coincidence, my father had been Donaher's faculty advisor when Donaher went to Purdue for his master's degree in 1958. Tom and I had become friends when serving in the same army reserve unit prior to the Berlin Wall recall. We had worked together at Fort Monmouth for ten months during our army service, and remained friends after our discharge and return to General Dynamics. In 1978 we began discussing a business partnership, and decided to work together during our nights and weekends to develop the new Spectracom WWVB clock. Donaher would develop the microprocessor hardware and software as well as the necessary peripherals such as digital display and serial ports, and I would design the mechanical packaging and the more mundane portions of the electronics, such as the power supply. If the product went to market, Donaher would be paid for his efforts with a partial ownership of Spectracom and would come on board as Engineering Vice President if we could afford to pay him.

Eighteen months later, the Model 8170 WWVB Clock was ready for market, and Donaher joined the company as a salaried officer and part owner.

In 1979 Spectracom outgrew its basement facility in Penfield and moved to 3000 square feet of rented space at 320 North Washington Street in East Rochester. As sales and production rates grew, Gene Dorland joined us as Manufacturing VP in 1980, adding professional management experience to the production efforts, and a third owner to the list of stockholders.

We established a profit-sharing plan that, over the years, paid into every employee's retirement trust fund account a significant addition to their annual earnings. Company success depended as much on the loyalty and enthusiasm of our employees as it did on that of its management team, and we did our best to make them aware of that fact. Everyone needed to know the importance of their role in the business, so we had monthly all-company meetings in the lunch room where we reviewed new policies, changes in procedures, and how each person's work related to what was going on in the other departments. We explained how the customer used our products and why it was important to service repair orders quickly. Large new orders were trumpeted and the customer's application was described. At those meetings, we even announced whether the Sales Department's new orders for the month had exceeded the Production Department's shipments, or vice versa. A little friendly competition between departments added spice to the meetings.

In 1984, we again outgrew our space and built a 10,000 square-foot facility two blocks down the road in a new industrial park at 101 Despatch Drive in East Rochester. Facilities Manager was one of Dorland's job assignments from the time he joined the company, and as such he was the program manager for the new construction. The building was built and owned in equal shares by a partnership of Donaher, Hesselberth, and Dorland (DHD Associates), who leased it to Spectracom for almost 20 years before selling it.

Now that we were in a larger facility with more employees, I wasn't as personally close to all the employees as I had been. I started trying to apply Bill Hewlett's practice of "management by walking around" as he built HP into a large, excellent company. Each day when I could, I walked through the office, the engineering lab, and the factory to say hello to as many employees as I could. There wasn't time for long conversations, but at least it kept me in touch. I didn't go as far as Bill Hewlett, but perhaps I should have. When walking through his engineering and R&D labs, he would ask an engineer, "What are you doing today?" After he got an answer, he would ask, "Why is that important to the company?"

There was now a well-rounded management team in place: Dorland as Manufacturing VP, Donaher as Engineering VP, and Hesselberth as CEO, CFO, and Sales and Marketing Manager. In 1988 Ed O'Connor came on board as National Sales Manager, working his way up to Sales VP and then to President until he resigned to start his own sales company in 1996 with Spectracom's frequency control products for simulcast two-way radio as his major product line.

For a while, there was a weight loss contest between all four of the company officers, with each of us posting our goal at the beginning for everyone in the building to see. Graphs of our public weekly weigh-ins were posted on the factory wall, right next to the scales. At the end of the contest, the person who was closest to his goal got to name a charity that all four of us contributed to.

In the early 1980s, the Model 8164 WWVB-disciplined oscillator was developed and patented. The unit was also sold as a master oscillator for public safety simulcast two-way radio transmitter sites, automatically keeping all the transmitters at each location accurately on their assigned channel frequency. A precise automatic frequency offset capability was included, as covered in the patent, making the product unique in its field, and leading to the establishment of simulcast frequency control as a significant market for Spectracom.

The Spectracom Saga

The word "simulcast" is used in two ways. The broadcast industry uses it when they simultaneously broadcast the same program on both radio and TV. Paging and radio communications systems are said to be simulcasting when multiple transmitters scattered around a county or a large area all send the same signal *on the same frequency channel*. They do this to get better geographical coverage, but if the transmitters aren't precisely controlled to within a part per billion or better, the signals can interfere with each other and cause pages to be missed or radio conversations to be garbled.

Spectracom continued selling WWVB disciplined oscillators to the simulcast two-way market. The military's Global Positioning System (GPS) was coming into common civilian use, and its signals were a better frequency standard reference than WWVB. Because precise navigation requires accurate clocks, the GPS satellites transmit their super-precise signals, derived from atomic clocks, using techniques that are less susceptible to noise interference.

Bowing to the inevitable, we added GPS receivers to our frequency standard product line, giving Spectracom another product that True Time didn't have. The closest competition was HP with a general-purpose product, sold primarily with their test equipment products. When digital television was about to appear on the market in the late 1990s, Spectracom used its GPS product to carve out a niche in the digital TV transmitter market, offering accuracy of one part per ten billion, and later, when rubidium oscillators were included, one part in 100 billion. This enabled the new digital transmitters to stay more precisely on their assigned channel frequency, preventing interference with other TV stations.

Since the Global Positioning System (GPS) was also an accurate source of time-of-day, Spectracom added that capability to its products, giving customers a choice between WWVB and GPS. True Time had the first GPS clock on the market, but Spectracom's product succeeded because it provided a total solution to the public safety market.

Gene Dorland began to take a larger interest in the marketing of the time-of-day product line in 1990 and sensed a need for time synchronization in 9-1-1 dispatch centers around the country. Our involvement in that market began when the Dallas, Texas police department used one of our WWVB clocks to synchronize the record-keeping time stamps in computers and voice loggers in their 9-1-1 center. We were told that an emergency call had come in from a woman whose husband was having a heart attack. The man died, and his wife sued the city and the police department because she felt that their slow response had led to her husband's death. The city couldn't show how quickly they had responded to the call because each of the record-keeping clocks in the 9-1-1 center showed a different time for the events. What time had the call come in? When was the ambulance dispatched? Did the records show that the ambulance was dispatched *before or after* the call came in? These inconsistencies resulted in a large award to the woman, and a million dollars of it was charged against the 9-1-1 center's budget. The Dallas police concluded that a few thousand dollars spent on automated time synchronization would be good insurance against recurrences of that law suit, and would eliminate the need for technicians to run around every few days resetting every clock in their equipment.

Dorland proposed a new product that became the Spectracom NetClock, an updated and miniaturized version of the Model 8170 WWVB Clock that would be designed specifically for this market. It would provide legally traceable timekeeping to computer networks and all of the electronic equipment in the dispatch center. He was so enthusiastic and committed to this new market that he was made its product marketing and sales VP, and Donaher took over manufacturing management, running both that and the engineering department. Dorland built the public safety time-of-day (TOD) market from scratch, making Spectracom the first, and for many years, the only supplier to it. He guided the industry standards committee's efforts to define the TOD needs in 9-1-1 centers and made sure that Spectracom's products met that standard. He also set up a national dealer-installer-reseller network when our test and measurement sales reps were found unable to service the public safety TOD market. As the foremost authority on public safety timekeeping in the country, he met and courted virtually every product manager of every vendor that supplied this market with voice recorders, telephone systems, computer dispatch systems, and radio control consoles, convincing each of them to include in their designs an interface for the Spectracom NetClock. Dorland's development of this product line was a classic case of marketing excellence worthy of being a case study at major business schools, and it gave Spectracom almost exclusive ownership of the 9-1-1 market for many years. Thousands of Spectracom's NetClocks are now scattered throughout the US in nearly every modern emergency response system.

✧

In the late 1990s, as Tom Donaher and I approached retirement age, we faced a major dilemma: *How can we retire gracefully?*

We had achieved our goal of building an excellent company. Tom had announced that he would retire at 65, the same year that his wife retired from her grade school teaching job in 2000. It appeared to me that his heart problems had also influenced his decision. I was the same age as Tom, but I had no burning need to retire. If I kept working a few years more, how would I replace him? There was no one in the company with his breadth of knowledge about our product designs, nor his ability to manage development programs. And if I waited to retire, we would need to find a way to buy Tom's share of the business. Not an easy task with a company that had 33 employees and had grown its sales to $5 million per year.

Chapter 33

The Perils of Business Travel

Red lights flashed on the tops of a cluster of police cars in the lighted motel courtyard as our airport shuttle van drove in from the dark street. To avoid the police cars, the driver stopped just inside the courtyard, and I stepped out onto the blacktop. My breath turned to steam in the cold air while the driver removed my suitcase from the back of the van, set it on the ground, and pocketed his money before driving off to his next stop. I headed for the office to check in, stepping carefully around several large puddles of blood that decorated the blacktop. No one standing around the area seemed to care if I stepped in them, but I was careful anyway.

"What happened?" I asked the desk clerk.

"A guest was followed back from a bar and was shot," the clerk said.

"Where?"

"Right in the doorway of his room." He pointed across the corner of the courtyard to a unit where the door stood open.

"Do you know why?" I asked.

"Maybe robbery," he said.

His voice was subdued, and the only way I could get him to talk was to keep asking questions. He and two other employees were standing there in shock. The victim had died at the scene, but only after staggering around the parking lot while his blood drained onto the ground.

Had they heard the gunshots? Had they looked out and witnessed the murder or had they seen the victim as he did his bizarre dance around the parking lot creating puddles? I was in too much shock myself to ask, and the staff wasn't interested in more conversation. I took my key, picked up my suitcase, and headed for the outdoor stairs, just past the victim's room. To get to the stairs, I had to step around more colorful pools of blood, one right in front of the victim's open door.

Jim Ewing, Spectracom's sales rep in the Washington, DC area, had made my reservation at the Quality Court Motel in Silver Spring, Maryland because it was near his home. He could easily pick me up the next morning for some sales calls, then drop me at a Washington hotel where I would display my products at a small trade show for the next three days. He also chose that motel because I wanted something cheap. Spectracom's first products had been introduced the prior year in 1975, and I was enabling the company to break even by limiting travel expenses and by paying myself less than I had earned mowing lawns a couple of decades earlier. More years would pass before I felt secure enough to voluntarily pay for better hotels.

The clerk had given me a room on the second floor so the activity in the parking lot wouldn't bother me as much. I was glad my plane had been late.

In my room, I double-locked the door and fastened the chain. I wasn't about to leave the room again, so I got into my pajamas and went to bed. When I couldn't sleep, I got up to investigate noises below in the parking lot. A crew of street cleaners scrubbing the blacktop with noisy equipment reminded me of the grisly happenings there a couple of hours earlier. Back in bed I stayed awake for another hour listening to the blood being hosed and vacuumed out of sight. When I called the desk to ask for another room, they offered to move me to the far end of the complex, into an unheated part of the motel. I agreed, got dressed, and moved there, shivering through the night.

The next morning as I checked out, the motel was back to normal. The police cars with their flashing red lights were gone and the parking lot was pristine, as though new blacktop had been put down while I slept. Jim Ewing arrived as I checked out, and we went to breakfast on the way to our first sales call.

The next year, 1977, I went back to Washington during the week of the same trade show. Jim had agreed not to put me in the Quality Court Motel again. He reserved a room for me at the Georgian Court in downtown Silver Spring, another moderately priced hotel. As I walked up to the registration desk, the clerk didn't smile.

"Don't put your hands on the counter!" she said.

"Why not?" I asked.

"The police haven't fingerprinted it yet."

"Fingerprinted it?" I said and drew my hands back to my chest. "Why do they need to fingerprint it?

"We were just held up. The police are still investigating," she said.

She registered me at the other end of the counter, using a surface that no criminals had recently touched. As I went back out to my rented car to get my luggage, a police helicopter hovered overhead, shining a bright light down on me, but no one tried to arrest me, and I got to my room with no further problem.

In 1978, Jim reserved a room at the Sheraton in downtown

Silver Spring. The desk clerk said, "We can't put you in the room we had planned for you. I need to change you to another room."

"Why is that?" I asked.

"We just had a fire on the fourth and fifth floors, and we can't use them for a while," she said.

There were no further incidents on that trip.

The next year, Jim decided to get me away from downtown Silver Spring, which prevented me from jinxing any more hotels there, and gave additional consideration to my health and safety. The registration desk at the motel he chose was behind thick bulletproof glass, where I had to deal with the clerk through a narrow slot. Hunkered down in my room that night, I was kept awake by a noisy party in nearby rooms, with people coming and going into the wee hours of the morning. Was a business being run in those rooms? Perhaps with rentals by the hour? I never found out for sure, nor did I use that motel the following year. By then I could afford a better class of hostelry, and from then on Jim parked me at the Silver Spring exit from the Beltway in a very nice Holiday Inn.

Anyone who travels a lot on business is certain to have occasional problems. Many of them are almost routine: bad flying weather, plane delays, lost or damaged luggage, taxi drivers and bartenders working their short-change tricks. At the end of one trip I arrived back at the Rochester airport to find my suit bag soaked with hairspray. We guessed that a suitcase piled on top of mine in the plane had contained a pressurized can of the stuff that burst during the flight. Another time I went to Portland, Oregon while my luggage went to Hawaii. At least the airline *told* me it was in Hawaii. When I got it back there were no leis in it.

Trips to California were my favorites, especially after the DC-10s were put in service and could land in Rochester on a newly lengthened runway. There was a lounge in the back of the plane where I could stretch out, enjoy a drink, and read a book or chat with a stewardess or fellow passenger. I could leave Rochester on American Airlines right after breakfast, land in Chicago for an hour, and go on to San Francisco without the hassle of a plane change. I arrived about 11:00 a.m. west coast time, in time to do a half-day of sales calls or set up a trade show booth before dinner.

Once, as I relaxed in my recliner seat, the pilot began an announcement: "Good morning ladies and gentlemen, this is your captain speaking. If you look out the left side of the plane in a few moments, you can see the Grand Canyon as we pass near it on our way into the Los Angeles airport. We expect to arrive a little early."

I was on the left side in an aisle seat, so I leaned across my seat mate and looked out the window. As I admired the view, my mind wandered. *Grand Canyon? Los Angeles? I'm going to San Francisco. Isn't this a little out of the way, or did I hear him wrong?* I pushed the stewardess call button.

"I'm going to San Francisco," I said. "Am I on the right plane?"

"Let me see your ticket," she said.

I showed her my ticket. She frowned while she studied it, and then said, "I'll be right back." She went forward, into the pilot's cabin and came back ten minutes later and handed me my ticket.

"You're on the wrong plane," she said, speaking as though I was six years old. "You should have changed planes in Chicago. When we get to LA, you and two unaccompanied children on the plane will be met at the gate. You'll be escorted to a connecting flight that will take you to San Francisco."

She gave me a wry smile, patted me on the cheek, and went about her business. I thought back to our stop in Chicago. At the gate, I had stayed on board as always, along with a few others who didn't need to change planes. When all the other passengers had deplaned, the ground crew came through to clean out trash and restock the pantries. A supervisor came on board, stopped at my row, and asked to see my ticket. He took it out of its folder, studied it, put it back in its folder, handed it back to me, and went on his way down the aisle toward the rear of the plane. He should have paid more attention to what the ticket said, and I should have also.

So here I was, already past the Grand Canyon, on my way to LAX. I sat back and enjoyed the ride. Everything went as the stewardess had said, and I arrived at San Francisco only one hour late, with my luggage already waiting for me.

Now and then I was exposed to some of the seedier aspects of life, including, um... ladies of the evening trolling for business. In California, one of them was hanging around in my motel near the elevator as I returned from dinner. She was so skinny that the warm summer breeze coming into the door at the end of the hallway might have carried her out across Ventura Boulevard and up into the Hollywood hills.

"Hi," she said. "D'you want some company tonight?"

I sensed right away that she wasn't suggesting a game of bridge. I said, "No, I'm tired and going right to bed."

"I could help you get to sleep," she said in a seductive little girl voice. She was so emaciated that I wondered how she could remain standing. Was she ill, or just poorly fed because her money went for drugs?

Not wanting to hurt her feelings, I said in my most wistful voice, "I'll bet you could....... but no thanks anyway." I got onto the elevator and hit the door-closer button. Up in my room, I wrote a quick note to the hotel management complaining about being propositioned by their house hooker who was working the hallways.

Getting up at 4:00 a.m. to catch an early flight back east, I packed my suitcase and stopped at the front desk to check out. The lobby was full of firemen, some of whom were examining an electrical panel that had apparently caught fire. No one was behind the desk to help me check out, so I fastened my hooker complaint to my room key and dropped it over the counter onto the desk. They could sort out the charge and put it on my credit card without me.

In the parking lot, I couldn't drive to either of the two exits because fire engines were blocking them. Back in the lobby I found a fireman who moved one of the trucks enough to let me head out for the Burbank airport.

In a pizza restaurant on Ventura Boulevard in Studio City, a very attractive blonde young lady in the next booth started making eyes at me that said, "I could arrange for a mattress right here under the table if you're interested." Never having seen such expressive, shiny eyes before, I looked away, embarrassed, both for myself and for her male companion who didn't appear to notice her shenanigans as he concentrated on cutting his pizza and stuffing it in his mouth. Then I realized what their relationship was and took another look. She had switched off her Marilyn Monroe come-hither look and both were eating their pizza. She saw me looking and again switched on her professional male magnets. She was clearly high on something. Was she being treated to a meal to celebrate the exceptional earnings that she had recently brought home to him? If I had owned such a magnificent eighteen-year-old asset with eyes that when switched on could set men afire, I'd have furnished her with pizza, too.... not to mention whatever controlled substances were needed to optimize both her dependency and her earning potential.

I paid my bill and left the restaurant, ashamed that I was of the same species as the pimp in the next booth.

In New York City for a trade show, before I had left RF Communications in 1972, my co-worker Roy and I walked down Broadway from the Coliseum to see the sights one evening after our show closed. It was years before Mayor Giuliani's big cleanup, and the street-walkers were out in force, making kissing noises as they passed by, or asking in *sotto voce*, "Wanna date?" Roy was on the other side of me from these generous, ego-boosting offers, didn't hear what was going on, and didn't believe me when I told him.

We found some dinner near Times Square, and then started back up Broadway toward our hotel. A few blocks later, in a coffee shop where we stopped for dessert, several of these ladies came in to rest their feet in an adjacent booth. I could hear enough of their conversation to leave no doubt about their profession. Roy remained oblivious. Then a young man hurried in from the street and headed straight for their booth.

"The police are sweeping the street, picking up everyone they see," he said. "Don't go back out for a while." He left the restaurant, probably to warn others. Was he their pimp, or just a pimp-in-training, running errands and protecting the girls for a fee and occasional side benefits while the boss cruised the streets in a Cadillac, supervising?

Later, while Roy and I were paying our bill at the cash

register, the girls got the all clear signal. One of them was already outside on the curb when I exited. While I waited there for Roy to finish paying his bill, she said to me, "Hi. Wanna date?"

Here was a perfect opportunity to convince Roy that I wasn't just making up stories. I needed to clear my name, to convince him that I was telling the truth, and besides, in my judgment, it was as close to a real adventure as Roy would ever get. An offer from a black hooker in New York City? It was a story he could tell his grandchildren.

"How much?" I asked the girl.

"Five dollars, plus five dollars for the room," she said.

I considered the price. Not being familiar with the price schedules of such working girls, even as early as 1970 it seemed like quite a bargain if you didn't think too hard about her personal hygiene, or about the fleabag hotel she would take me to, or the legendary muggings that took place in such situations. I couldn't think about it too long, because it was time to dangle a hook of my own.

"No.... I guess not, but my buddy in there might be interested," I said.

A moment later, Roy came out of the coffee shop. I beckoned him over.

"Roy," I said, "She wants to ask you something."

Roy came over to the curb, his innocence oozing from every pore.

"You wanna date?" she said to him. Her conversational vocabulary was a little limited.

I couldn't resist embellishing the offer a little. "Tell him how much," I said.

"Five dollars plus five for the room," she said to him.

To his credit, he didn't take long to decide. "No, I guess not," he said.

I said to her, "Thanks anyway," and we left her there on the curb, crossed the street, and headed for our hotel.

I couldn't suppress a few giggles. "See? I told you they were all over the place," I said. "Do you believe me now?"

"Yeah, but don't tell my wife about this. She wouldn't understand," he said. Over the years since then, as other travel details and problems fade into the past, this episode remains bright and clear: The night I got Roy propositioned.

A few years later, during the same trade show, while staying in the same New York hotel as John O'Halloran, Spectracom's California sales rep, he asked me at breakfast if he could borrow twenty dollars. He told me that after he had gone to bed late the previous evening, two burly plain-clothes policemen had come to his room. One of them had John's wallet in his hand.

"We were staked out, driving a taxi for cover," one of the cops said. We saw the two hookers snuggling up to you, and knew right away that they were picking your pocket, but we were already beyond you and had to go around the block to bust them. By the time we got back, you were already gone, and they were getting into a car across the street. Is this your wallet? We found it in their car."

"Can't be," John said, "Mine is in my pants pocket in the closet."

He checked his pants pocket in the closet and didn't find his wallet.

"We had to question doormen and front desk attendants up and down the street until we found you registered here," the cop said as John identified his wallet for them. "We can't give the wallet back to you because we need it for evidence when we charge the girls."

I gave John the twenty dollars he had asked for. He missed the trade show that morning because he was busy signing affidavits and identifying his pickpocket perps at the precinct station. He told me that those girls were really friendly, but he finally "had to knee them out of the way" to escape to his hotel. Our opinion of the New York City police department climbed a few notches higher.

⟡

At a trade show in Las Vegas, a co-worker asked me if I felt all right.

"Yes," I said. "Why do you ask?"

"You don't look too good," he said. "Your face is all red. Take a look in a mirror."

I was reminded that, a few years earlier at RF Communications, my boss had told me the same thing, and it turned out to be measles brought home to me by my kids—my second case of it, which the doctor said couldn't happen. He said my first case, in grade school, was probably misdiagnosed, but when I later told my mother, she got indignant and said, "You had the *measles*!" The doctor had lost the debate. Could my Las Vegas red face be a third case?

The nearest mirror was up in my room, where Marianne awaited the end of the trade show so we could go to dinner and a show together.

"Do I look red in the face?" I asked her.

She peered at me, looked worried, and said "You'd better take a look in the bathroom mirror."

Red splotches decorated my face, but I felt fine. An inspection of the rest of my body found red spots everywhere. (Yes, *everywhere*.) The attendant at the front desk said, "We'll put you in touch with House Doctor," after I described my problem.

"What's his name?" I asked.

"It's not a person, it's a medical practice that makes house calls when hotel guests have problems," she explained.

When I called the number she gave me, the phone attendant said, "The doctor can come to your room tomorrow morning at nine. In the meantime take a Benedryl in case it's an allergic reaction."

"I don't need a house call," I said. "I can come to your office."

"We don't have an office," she said. "We only make house calls."

I took a Benedryl, and we went to dinner in a restaurant with a dark and gloomy atmosphere where Marianne could be free from worry about people thinking she was dating a leprosy carrier. By morning the spots were nearly gone. The doctor decided that the Ampicillin pills I had taken for a sinus infection had caused an allergic reaction. He told me to stop taking them and gave me a little envelope of three Prednisone pills. I took the first one, but never needed the rest. While he was in our room, I learned that his practice consisted of six doctors, mostly retired military, each serving on call for two days a week. They had an answering service and no office, working only out of their homes and their well-stocked black bags.

The doctor was with me for about ten minutes, for which the hotel added $210.00 to my bill.

Chapter 34

Side Trips in California

"Ray, now you cut that out!" Aunt Mildred shouted. We were on our way home from dinner in their Cadillac, and Uncle Ray had just breezed through an intersection where the light was red well before we got there. Mildred was always ready to let him know about his transgressions. Mildred was one of my mother's three younger sisters. She and Ray had moved from Trenton, Missouri to California after he was discharged from the Navy at the end of World War II. Ray got a job selling insurance for Metropolitan Life, and they settled in Pomona in a small two-bedroom house. In Missouri, Mildred had worked as a bank teller, and in California she got a similar job with Kaiser Steel, where she eventually became head cashier. Not ever having any children, she was free to concentrate on her career until she retired, unlike most women in that postwar era.

Before I started traveling to the west coast on business in the late 1960s, I had seen them rarely while growing up, most recently at my grandparents' funerals in Missouri. By the time I started visiting them in California, Ray had developed a full mane of pure white hair that gave him the look of a distinguished United States senator. He had a talent for pontificating on his favorite subjects and pet peeves in a voice that parodied a well-warmed-up Senator Bullhorn, or a sincere Deacon Andy Griffith. His Missouri accent and the sparkle in his eyes added to the effect, as did his penchant for vodka or gin on the rocks.

The Wescon electronics trade show was held annually in California during the electronics boom years after WWII and lasted a few decades. The location alternated between the Cow Palace in San Francisco and the convention center in Los Angeles. On alternate years, after the show closed in LA, I stayed with Mildred and Ray for the weekend, and made sales calls the next week in southern California, or flew to San Francisco to visit customers there before heading back to Rochester. When the show was in San Francisco, I reversed the process, flying to LA after the show to stay the weekend with Mildred and Ray before making sales calls in southern California. This arrangement worked well for several years. I got two weeks of doing business on the west coast for the price of one round-trip plane ticket and free room and board with my aunt and uncle on the middle weekend.

By a happy coincidence, those trips usually coincided with the final week of the Los Angeles County Fair. Uncle Ray, who was a passable amateur jazz drummer, belonged to the Los Angeles Jazz Club which provided entertainment at the fair on its last Sunday each year. For several years running, Ray and Mildred took me along to see Ray play occasional sets with others in the club, including various Hollywood and LA musicians who were also club members.

Ray and Mildred had grown up in Trenton, Missouri as classmates of Yank Lawson, who had become a nationally known trumpet player in the Tommy Dorsey orchestra and now had his own Dixieland group, modestly called "The World's Greatest Jazz Band." Mildred and Ray had collected all of Yank's many LP recordings, and they played them for me when I visited. I got to meet Yank once when he was in Rochester for a gig, but he was never in town when I visited Pomona.

My west coast visits were the beginning of my jazz education and laid the groundwork for my later-life enthusiastic enjoyment of jazz.

✧

In 1979, the summer after our oldest child, David, graduated from high school, Marianne and I felt that with the kids starting college careers, we might not get them all together again for a really big vacation. So we took all three of them on a ten-day tour of California starting in San Diego, and ending in San Francisco, visiting all the sights and attractions: The San Diego Zoo, Disneyland, Hollywood, the Hearst Castle, the Madonna Inn, Monterey, and Fisherman's Wharf.

We visited friends along the way, including Spectracom's west coast sales rep, John O'Halloran, who owned his office building on Ventura Boulevard in North Hollywood. One tenant of his building was a recording studio where Casey Kasem produced his "American Top 40" radio show each week. Casey wasn't in the studio when we visited, but the kids were given an LP record of one of his weekly shows, and they got to meet Robert W. Morgan, another radio personality who recorded there.

While we were in the Los Angeles area, we went to Pomona so our kids could meet their great aunt and uncle, Mildred and Ray.

During previous visits with the Hubbells, I had been introduced to their collection of land turtles that lived in their small walled-in back yard. They ranged in size from a coffee cup saucer up to a dinner serving platter. When a turtle showed up in the area, the neighbors brought it to the Hubbell's house to add to the herd. Ray described the annual party they had in the back yard, where friends and neighbors gathered with a bottle of gin, an empty fruit juice can, and a bottle of red nail polish.

When the assemblage was well-oiled with gin, they caught a turtle and placed it on its stomach on the upended juice can with its legs flailing away in the air. The appointed nail polish artist then painted or repainted a large red number on its shell before releasing it as the group cheered. After another swig or two of gin, another one was branded, and so on until each of the dozen-plus turtles sported its newly brightened number, now visible from airliners on their approach to LAX. And all of the partiers were feeling very good indeed.

When my family visited, Ray introduced them to the turtles. The kids, aged 12 to 17, immediately organized a turtle roundup, searching for all the turtles to place them in a row in order of their numbers. When the turtles weren't grazing on lawn grass or clover, or on some lettuce that Mildred put out for them, they were usually hiding under the shrubbery and vines that lined the inside of the surrounding wall, sometimes nearly buried in the dirt after scooting themselves as far underground as possible. It was like a combined treasure hunt and Chinese fire drill, with excitement added by each turtle when it headed for the bushes as soon the kid that found it placed it in the row and left to find the next one.

Ray was in stitches because it appeared that the turtles were winning. Then the kids gained on the turtles, getting them all in approximate order with only six or seven of them heading for the bushes.

A couple of years later, on my annual California sojourn, I was sitting on the back yard patio (Ray pronounced the word "pottio" in his quasi-senatorial voice) enjoying a martini with Ray and Mildred before we left for dinner at a restaurant, when Ray gave me a sly look and nodded his head toward the back yard, where three or four turtles were trimming the lawn. I looked in that direction.

"What?" I said.

"Look out there," Ray said, giving me a head-nod toward "out there."

"What do you mean?" I asked.

He pointed to where he wanted me to look, lowered his voice, and said, "Number four is trying to impregnate number nine."

I looked again, and by golly he was right. From where I sat, I couldn't see their numbers, but I accepted his identifications. After all, they were his turtles, and who could know better which was which? None of them were moving very fast, so I hadn't noticed their activities on my own.

Leaving for dinner, we stopped down the street to pick up my Aunt Helen, Mildred's sister, who had moved there when she retired from the Air Force a few years after the Korean War ended, where she had served in a MASH unit. Helen had joined the Army Air Corps as a nurse during WWII, and ended her career as a major and chief nurse at the March Air Force Base hospital in California, well after the War Department made the Air Force independent from its beginnings as part of the Army. Unmarried and living on her Air Force pension, she bought a registered apricot-colored toy poodle puppy named Taffy, and spent her days taking it to behavior school and to dog shows, where it won a wall-full of medals and plaques and shelves loaded with glistening trophies. The dog's trainer occasionally furnished dogs to the Disney organization for use in their movies. Taffy had always worked well with him, so he occasionally arranged for Disney or a TV commercial producer to use her in one of their productions. Taffy's most notable performance was in a 1968 Brian Keith-Doris Day movie titled *With Six You Get Egg Roll*. Taffy's portrait hung on our wall as our kids grew up, where they showed it proudly to their friends as "our cousin the movie star."

Taffy finally died, but not until she had given birth to one litter of pups, one of which was adopted by Mildred and Ray after their retirement but never entered in dog shows. Helen bought another toy poodle but by then didn't have the energy to train it as a show dog.

As we drove on I-10 westward through the I-210 interchange toward the Castaways Restaurant on a hillside above the freeway, Ray went into his pontification mode, lecturing us for a few minutes on how construction of the three-layer crossover had cost many millions of dollars and moved more dirt than the great pyramids. Other favorite subjects included his problems in convincing the ever-increasing Mexican immigrant and black populations in Pomona of the need for life insurance.

"Those people spend every cent they get and just don't understand the need for insurance," he said.

At the restaurant Ray had one more drink than he should have and got a little loud before we left to go home. On the way back into Pomona he ran the red light that caused Mildred to yell at him. Later, after their retirement, with less activity to occupy their time, they drank more, with Ray getting drunk each time we went out to dinner. Mildred got more irritated with his behavior, and, thankfully, convinced him to let me drive us home from the restaurant.

When I was in an exotic place on business or vacation, I occasionally sent Ray and Mildred a picture post card telling them where I was. Ray responded with some goofy post card of his own, and we kept in touch this way during the long intervals between my west coast trips. Once, from Phoenix, I sent them a post card with a beautiful color photo of an ugly Gila monster. My note said, "We're here observing the flora and fauna. Some of the fauna are not very attractive." The next day I sent a follow-up post card. The color photo showed a beautiful, nearly naked young lady. My note said, "On the other hand, *some* of the fauna are excellent." From Hawaii I sent a color post card showing a scantily clad hula dancer, with a note that remarked on the friendly residents.

The next year when I visited, Helen was suffering from colon cancer, or "the big C," as she called it. Most cancers defied early detection or treatment, and for many of that generation the word was too horrible to say out loud. She was too sick to go out to dinner, so the three of us went without her, but not before stopping by her house so I could see her. After saying goodbye at her door, I needed a few moments to blow my nose and dry my eyes so Mildred and Ray wouldn't think I had been crying. Mildred noticed anyway, but made a sympathetic comment about allergies being bad at this time of year. That was the last time I saw my Aunt Helen.

Mildred's many years of heavy cigarette smoking gradually gave her an enlarged heart, and put her for a while in the hospital, where she was sent home with an oxygen bottle to carry around for the rest of her life. Even in the hospital on continuous oxygen, she sneaked cigarettes when no one was looking. Back at home, she continued smoking and increased her drinking. After her death, Ray told me that he had found liquor bottles that she had hidden around the house.

In 1987 an earthquake in Illinois was felt across the entire Midwest. The quake was magnitude 5.1—small by California standards, but because it was in an unusual location, it was reported in newspapers across the country. Ray sent me a post card with a color photo of Death Valley. His note said, "I sure am glad I don't live in that damn earthquake country where your mother lives!"

I continued to take Ray out to dinner when I was in southern California, which by then was two or three times a year. A stroke had partially disabled him, causing him to cut back on his drinking, but leaving him with a speech impediment, making him sound as though he was drunk, even though he had only one vodka-on-the-rocks each time we met. His home remained neat and clean because he continued to employ the Mexican cleaning lady who had been with him and Mildred for many years.

When we went to dinner, he asked me drive his car to and from the restaurant, relieving me of the worry about his running red lights. Upon returning to his home, exhausted by the evening out, he made a beeline for the bedroom, shedding clothing on the way, in his hurry to get to bed. That signaled the end of our evening together. By then, my budgets were sufficient to eliminate the need to stay overnight at his house, so I drove back to my hotel in Studio City, ready to find a laundromat and do my laundry on Sunday, and then to show up at O'Halloran's office early on Monday morning for more sales calls.

I have wondered, in my more pensive moments, about the marks we make on this earth that remain after we are gone. For Ray, it was enough to have been a friend of many, convincing the poor to save money through the use of life insurance, playing music for others, and putting smiles on the faces of those around him. He did what he could, in the best way that he could, and that was sufficient.

Uncle Ray's health continued to deteriorate for a few more months. After he died his brother brought him back to his home town, Trenton, Missouri, where he was buried next to Aunt Mildred.

Chapter 35

First, Do No Harm

They had met while living in the same rooming house in college, and were clearly meant for each other. Both had come from small towns in rural areas, and both were the first in the family to attend college. They weren't raised to expect a college education as I was, but they each saw broader possibilities beyond their local lives. They wanted to make a difference in the world: Dad responded to his fascination with the new field of radio electronics, and Mom to the challenges of teaching children to realize the potential she knew they each had.

Dad and Mom were as perfectly matched as a couple could be. Both were upbeat and cheerful, their strengths complementing each other. They worked as a team throughout their life together, right up until the day Dad died of cancer.

When Dad landed his job in 1939 as a researcher in the Experiment Station of the Electrical Engineering Department at Purdue, his specialty was building experimental vacuum tubes for amplifying radio and television signals, as well as cathode ray tubes, which were the forerunners of TV picture tubes. His two patents covered ways to coat the inside of the tube with phosphor to allow the picture to be displayed.

Dad gradually worked his way into teaching undergraduate electrical engineering courses, first as a part-time teaching assistant, then as an assistant professor, followed by promotion to associate professor. His specialty was vacuum tube electronics, covering all the electronic circuitry that used vacuum tubes as amplifiers and modulators. When, in the early 1950s, he didn't get promoted to full professor because he didn't have a PhD and hadn't published many articles, he decided there was a need for a better book to use in the courses he taught. Together with George Happell, another associate professor of EE, he wrote that book. I was taking a mechanical drawing course as a high school sophomore and produced some of the charts and graphs for the early, self-published edition that was used in the third-year electronic circuits course he taught. In 1953 McGraw-Hill published the book, *Engineering Electronics*, and for several years it was one of the two most popular books in its field at universities around the country. This accomplishment was sufficient to earn him a full professorship.

Mom had grown up as the daughter of a small town mailman who knew everyone in town and chatted with many of them every day. She had inherited his friendly demeanor and applied it in her positive approach to classroom teaching and in her lifelong efforts never to embarrass, humiliate, or hurt anyone. Always mindful of whether her actions would set a good example for others, she made sure that we boys behaved that way as well.

Her October 1985 phone call told us that Dad was in the hospital for exploratory surgery and that cancer was suspected. Marianne and I hurried to Indiana to find him in his hospital bed with a large incision across his mid-section, and ugly, widely spaced stitches that looked as though the surgeon had been in too much of a hurry to do a neat job. Pancreatic cancer had spread to his liver and was inoperable. A couple of days later he came home, too weak to get out of bed or even shave himself, which I did for him with his electric razor. *Now make a mustache, Dad, so I can shave under your nose.*

In one private moment Mom and I cried in each other's arms.

"We're gonna lose him, aren't we?" I said, finally saying what we had avoided speaking about.

"I'm afraid so," she said. She straightened up, shook herself, and said, "I told myself I wasn't going to cry." And she stopped, never wanting to set a bad example by losing control of herself. She knew her responsibilities and would handle whatever happened.

Two days later, we left, expecting Dad to try chemo treatments in spite of the doctor's gloomy prognosis.

"I'll be back if needed," I said to Dad, trying clumsily to reassure him without starting up the tears again. He was taken for one chemo treatment, but was failing too fast, too weak to have more. The doctor began visiting at home, giving him daily shots to ease his pain.

In early December I got the call from Mom as I was taking down Spectracom's trade show display in Washington, DC.

"Mr. Hesselberth?" said the bellman when he found me. "You have a phone call. We'll switch it to a pay phone on a wall in the lobby."

"Bob? This is your mom. Dad died about an hour ago." My knees buckled and I couldn't speak.

"Bob? Are you there?"

From my crouch on the floor at the end of the phone cord I managed to say, "I'll call you back from my room."

When I could speak normally again, I found our local sales rep, Jim Ewing, who was with me at the show, and told him what the phone call was about and that I had to go find a flight to Indianapolis. He said he would finish packing up our equipment and get it back to East Rochester.

In my room on the phone, Mom told me that Dad had been in terrible pain at the end, but the doctor already was giving him the maximum pain-killer dosage. Any more would be deadly, and he couldn't do that. As he left the house the last time, he gave mom a syringe loaded with that lethal dose, saying that she could give it to Dad if things got too bad. Later, when they did get too bad and he was bleeding at both ends, throwing up, and writhing in pain, she gave him the shot that eased his pain and let him go to sleep for that final time. She never told me about the next few hours, but I would bet anything that after Dad's breathing stopped and before anyone else saw him, she had him all cleaned up and ready to go.

For a while I was furious with that damn doctor for making my mother, strong as she was, go through all that extra pain of her own. What was a doctor *for* if he couldn't provide his own medical services? What sort of rotten coward was he? How could he even call himself a doctor? I would have thrown furniture around the room if I could have seen it through my tears. Instead, I found a pillow and threw it.

I made my plane reservation and called Marianne to arrange for her trip to Indiana. I returned to the lobby to find that Jim had completed packing our display equipment. He took me to dinner while I waited for my plane, scheduled for later that evening. It couldn't have been easy for him, trying to keep my mind occupied and diverted from my problems during dinner.

At the funeral, our Presbyterian pastor spoke about Dad's cheerful, generous personality, and how he often kidded his friends and co-workers. He told of how Dad, in his basement shop after his retirement, had made special furniture and fixtures for hospital rehabilitation patients: A rocking chair that rocked sideways; a long-handled tool that a wheelchair-bound person could use to reach up, take the handset off the hook, and insert a dime into the slot of a payphone. He told of how, as he woke up after the surgery when the doctor first visited him, Dad had looked up at the clear plastic bag hanging above his bed, dripping yellow liquid into his veins, and said "That's lemon! I told them I wanted chocolate!"

By the time of the funeral, I had realized that the doctor had done as much for Dad as he could, right up until the end, when he had to obey his Hippocratic Oath: *Do no harm.*

Today, thanks to a combination of medical technology and enlightened thinking, hospice care for the dying avoids the terrible choice Mom had to make. The palliative care of hospice preserves the patient's dignity with humane and gentle treatment, and provides loving support for the family while continuing in the spirit of the oath. Hospice care-givers know that death is a part of the life we all signed up for when we were born. That message, humanely explained, makes the end of life easier for all.

Chapter 36

On Board Air Force One

"This is Sergeant Miller calling from the Air Force One crew," the voice said into my ear. The voice sounded official; self-confident, well-spoken, so I sat up a little straighter in my chair. The caller wasn't an officer and I wasn't a soldier, so I didn't jump up and stand at attention. In the mid-1980s Spectracom didn't yet have a sales manager, so I was taking all the sales calls when I was in the office.

"I'm the communications crew chief," Sgt. Miller said, "and one of our duties is to maintain the timekeeping system on board the aircraft. The system is old and hasn't worked well for a long time. The President gets annoyed when it gives him the wrong time, so we'd like to replace it. Can you come visit us to take a look at what we need to replace?"

I tried to imagine President Reagan getting annoyed, but the vision wouldn't play. I'd never seen him display anything but a pleasant demeanor and good humor on television. He was the most likeable President since John Kennedy, and I decided that if the people around him liked him as much as the public did, they would jump to do his bidding if he merely raised an eyebrow and asked, "Sergeant, why is that clock wrong?"

I had seen this effect work very well while on active duty in the army decades earlier. When a high-ranking officer asked or even hinted to a person of lower rank that something might need to be done, the resulting ripples escalated down the chain of command, amplified at each step until reaching crisis proportions. Thus, when the President, who was, after all, the highest ranking officer in the world, pointed out a flaw in the Air Force One clock system, there was immediate and firm response from the Air Force One crew.

By the time of the phone call, Spectracom was well-known in timekeeping circles as a premier provider of ground-based synchronized clock systems. We were not known for our *airborne* clock systems. The system on Air Force One may have been the only one in the world.

The sergeant described several problems. A half-dozen digital wall clocks were scattered around the aircraft in places such as the President's office, the press section, the cabin where the President's entourage sat, and in the first lady's quarters. All of the clocks were synchronized by a master clock system located on the bulkhead above the communications console just aft of the main entrance to the plane. A technician sitting at the console could look up and see three clock displays, each with its own push-button switches for adjusting the time ahead or back. One clock was always kept on Washington, DC time. A second clock controlled the slave time displays in the other parts of the aircraft, and was kept on local, or airplane, time. It was reset each time the plane crossed into a new time zone. The third clock displayed time at the destination.

When a trip started, each of the three clocks was set to its proper time, but due to faulty adjustment circuitry, the passengers could see the time on their cabin wall jumping around in strange and puzzling ways each time the crew tried to reset the time.

When the engines were shut down, the clocks lost power and required resetting each time the engines were started. Sometimes the resetting worked well, and sometimes it didn't.

The consensus at Andrews Air Force Base was that a new clock system was needed.

Within two minutes of ending my conversation with Sgt. Miller, I was on the phone to Jim Ewing, our sales rep in Silver Spring, Maryland, asking him to call Sgt. Miller and arrange for us to visit at a time when the plane was sure to be there. I had never had to coordinate my schedule with the President's before. It was as though the President had said, "Have your people call my people so we can take a meeting." A few days later I was in Washington with Jim, heading for Andrews Air Force Base. I, too, reacted to that raised Presidential eyebrow.

Sergeant Miller met us at the gate and drove us to the flight crew's day room, where we signed in. He then took us to the hangar where the plane was housed. The entryway resembled the security checkpoint at commercial airports, except that the examinations were far more thorough. Jim was the first to go through the gateway, and he set off the alarm. After he removed his belt, his glasses, and all the metal in his pockets, he still triggered the alarm. The guard got out his magic wand and ran it over Jim. The wand beeped in the vicinity of his shoulder, and the guard ran his hands over the area and found nothing.

"It's probably the pin in my shoulder where I was put back together after an airplane accident," Jim said. He had been a private pilot in his earlier days and, upon landing in gusty wind conditions, had ground-looped the plane and wrecked it. Among his injuries was a broken shoulder. The guard was skeptical, but finally satisfied himself that there was no bomb hidden in Jim's armpit and let him pass.

Then the alarm rejected me. One at a time, I removed my belt, the metal from my pockets, the pen from my shirt pocket, and my glasses, but the wand continued to beep. The cause was finally detected: a card of blister-packed decongestant pills that was foil-backed. The pills had been tucked between some note papers in my shirt pocket. My brief case contained all sorts of metal miscellany, including the steel ruler I would use to measure mounting dimensions and clearance spaces for the clocks. The guard rummaged through it on its way around the walk-through detector.

After being thoroughly de-metalized and with our privacy violated, we were allowed to proceed into the main hangar, where we beheld the shiniest Boeing 707 on the face of the earth. No new military recruit or gung-ho lieutenant had ever shined his brass or shoes to this level of dazzling brilliance. Not a single fly spec tarnished its glittering skin. No raindrop residue dulled its scintillescent surface. The gleaming craft stood majestically under the lights of the hangar, ready to leap to even more rigid attention should the President arrive to take a ride on his magic carpet.

The hangar was equally spotless. There were no oil slicks on the floor, no workbenches with scattered tools, and no dust anywhere. The air was pure, completely devoid of smoky smells and jet fuel haze. No sounds of outside life penetrated the walls. No vehicle traffic, no airport noises, nothing. If I were an airplane, I would have wanted to live there.

I gathered my composure and hurried to keep up with the sergeant, hoping that he hadn't caught me gawking like a first-time tourist. After all, I had been inside military missile bases, NASA satellite tracking stations, Drug Enforcement Administration laboratories, atomic power stations, and other secret places about which I shouldn't speak. This was not a sight-seeing trip—this was business. We were there to make the President happy about his clocks.

At the top of the stairs that we have all seen on television as the President and first lady descend so regally, we paused as the sergeant handed us each a pair of protective "footies" to pull on over our shoes before we stepped onto the plush wall-to-wall carpet that ran throughout the aircraft.

The cockpit was to our left as we entered, and turning to our right, the sergeant showed us the communications console where two operators would sit, all of the equipment for secure radio and telephone communications laid out before them. The master clocks were mounted at about our eye level as we stood there, but were overhead at a negative angle relative to the seated operators so they could look up and see them or reset them as needed. I recognized the designs as belonging to one of our peripheral competitors.

The sergeant showed us around the rest of the airplane so we could see the slave clocks that were synchronized by the master clock at the console. In the President's office the clock was mounted over the door, where he could view it as he sat at his desk. In the press cabin and other sections, the clocks were mounted on the walls, located for easy viewing.

At the console, the sergeant helped us unscrew the bulkhead panel where the master clocks were mounted so we could see the mounting details and measure how much room was available for replacement units. I made sketches of the bulkhead construction, the dimensions of all the relevant holes and mounting details, and the existing equipment and operating controls. I recorded the amount of room available for additional equipment, such as a battery backup system to keep the clocks running when the engines shut down.

After reassembling everything I took one last look around to make sure we had all our tools and notes and exited the plane. As we left, I looked wistfully through the nearby doorway into the President's office, wondering briefly if I should leave a business card for him, perhaps with a note on the back saying, "Sorry we missed you—will call again when you're not so busy. Give our best to Nancy." Outside the door we deposited our footies in a wastebasket and regally descended the stairs while straining to hear non-existent strains of "Hail To The Chief."

Nor was there a Marine guard waiting to salute us at the bottom.

The sergeant led us back to the crew's day room, where he opened a file drawer and pulled out a souvenir kit to give each of us containing an 8 x 10 photo of the plane, a descriptive pamphlet, and a few items with the Presidential seal printed on them, including a cocktail napkin, a dinner menu, and a book of matches.

Back in East Rochester at Spectracom headquarters, our crack engineering team went to work to prepare a technical proposal for Sergeant Miller. It showed how we would provide every function the customer needed, with ease of maintenance being a major focus. We threw in a few new technical features for good measure. It contained descriptions, block diagrams, mounting diagrams, and drawings of digital clocks with a more modern look, as well as a battery backup system and a better method of clock adjustment.

Three weeks after my visit to the airplane, we sent copies of the proposal off to Washington for Jim Ewing to hand deliver to the Air Force One crew.

Then we waited.

We had been told that it might take some time for them to find money to spend on the project, since it had not been provided in the last congressional appropriation, but they were confident they could work something out.

Weeks went by, then months. Telephone follow-ups provided no new information. Finally, when nearly a year had passed, the customer told us that a program had begun which would replace the old Boeing 707s with new aircraft. There would be no further upgrading of the 707s, thus eliminating the need for our system. A glimmer of hope remained, however:

There were two bidders competing for the order of new aircraft, Boeing and Douglas. The winning bidder might still need our clock system. More months of waiting followed, until it was finally announced that Boeing was the winner. Like hounds with our noses to the ground, baying at the sneaky fox, we headed for Seattle. There, we found that the electronic systems on the aircraft were to be provided by a single subcontractor in Texas. Again, we had found a newer, stronger scent to follow. More months went by while the system subcontractor got organized, planned their project, and made make-or-buy decisions.

Their decision was to make the clock system themselves, and the opportunity was finally gone. We filed our proposal in our "Dead" file and went on with the other aspects of our business. Boeing eventually delivered the new airplane, which went into service in 1990. In spite of our bitter loss and disappointment, we couldn't help feeling even sorrier for President Reagan, who had to endure his faulty timekeeping system for the rest of his time in office.

We could have consoled each other, if only I had left my card on his desk while on board Air Force One.

Chapter 37

Advanced Legal Training

In the mid-1980s Spectracom developed a product that turned out to be very profitable, but the patent we got on one of its features was potentially a lot more profitable. Then the legal battle that followed put its value in doubt.

Our existing Model 8161 Frequency Standard Oscillator required periodic manual adjustments to keep it accurate to within one part per billion. When we finally decided to add a feature that would automate those adjustments, we called the new product Model 8164. We hired Bill Schmidt, a brilliant local consultant, to help us design the microprocessor control loop that would automate the adjustment. We couldn't use a phase-locked loop for this because we wanted to be able to build in tiny frequency offsets that could be used in simulcast transmitter applications, so we used a frequency-locked loop in a unique way and patented the invention.

It was the beginning of a major legal adventure.

The 8164 was our most successful product to date. It was sold to calibration laboratories and was making inroads into the public safety two-way radio market to keep simulcast transmitters precisely on frequency. Then Schmidt came to us with an idea. He had identified a serious need in the paging market for an automated transmitter adjustment system, and Spectracom's patent was part of the solution.

Simulcast paging service companies had to maintain highly reliable service throughout their coverage area, or the customers would buy paging from a competitor. If a doctor, for instance, missed a page, it could be life-threatening for his patient. To maintain reliable, high quality service, the paging company had to send technicians around the coverage area from transmitter site to transmitter site to make frequent transmitter adjustments. The largest counties in the country are larger than Massachusetts and could require paging companies to keep a technician on the road continually, just making transmitter adjustments. Paging transmitters were typically located on the highest hills and mountains in their area, some of which were difficult or impossible to reach in bad weather. Spectracom had one customer on the west coast that had to use a helicopter to reach some transmitters in the winter.

Schmidt had conceived a system that would *automatically* adjust multiple paging transmitter frequencies and modulation delays *relative to each other* with higher precision than was ever before possible, thus keeping the transmitters from interfering with each other. His idea would improve paging reliability and simultaneously reduce costs for the paging companies.

Most things in life are trade-offs: To improve the reliability of your family's transportation, you buy a more expensive car. To have higher-quality meals, you might spend more on organically grown food. Higher reliability in electronic equipment usually requires more expensive parts. But here was an opportunity to make an enormous reduction in a customer's operating costs in return for a miniscule increase in the manufacturing cost of transmitters, and simultaneously improve paging reliability.

The decision to collaborate with Schmidt on the project was

a no-brainer: Spectracom formed a 50-50 partnership with his consulting company and named the partnership SimulComm. We provided access to our patent as well as much of the money for the development project, and Schmidt ran the project and provided the technical and market know-how to make it happen.

The development took more than a year, and in 1987 we took the product to a major trade show in San Francisco, where it created quite a stir among attendees from the paging industry. We had previously contacted potential licensees, including the two largest manufacturers of paging transmitters, Motorola and Quintron. Motorola had been decidedly uninterested, probably believing, as many large companies do, that if they needed new features in their products, they could develop them themselves and somehow work around our patent. Quintron was less than enthusiastic about the product, but at the show they turned around. Before the show even opened, Quintron said they wanted to meet to negotiate a license. They were so enthusiastic and so positive, we signed a letter of intent that night giving them exclusive rights to the technology in return for royalty payments that lasted several years, based on sales of products containing our system.

After the show opened, Motorola came to our booth to look. They went away, only to come back to offer us a similar deal, but we had to tell them they were too late. Over the next couple of years Quintron built our control system into all of their simulcast transmitters, and did all the manufacturing and sales. We just collected royalties.

A few months after the license agreement was signed, Schmidt closed his consulting business and went to work as Director of Advanced Development for Quintron. He moved to Quincy, Illinois and helped them integrate the SimulComm technology into their product line. At Spectracom we were uneasy about the potential conflict of interest in this arrangement, but we could do nothing about it, so we accepted it and went on with our lives. As Schmidt put it, "Wouldn't you rather have your fox in the other guy's henhouse where he can watch out for SimulComm's interests?"

Months later he came to us and said, "Look at this product data sheet that shows a new offering from Quintron that's made by another company. It has to be using our technology and we're not getting royalties on it."

Sure enough, it appeared as though that product was covered by our licensing agreement and that Quintron should have paid us royalties on it. When asked about it, Quintron claimed that it wasn't covered because it was made by another company. We thought that if they could get away with that kind of end run around our patent without paying royalties, they could do it again. We couldn't let that happen, so we took them to arbitration as provided for in our license agreement.

In the beginning of the controversy our patent attorney helped us try to negotiate a resolution, but our licensee was determined to not pay us any royalties that were not called for in our original agreement, even if it used our patent. We might have agreed to retroactively grandfather that first outside product since it may have been designed before our license agreement was signed, as long as they agreed to pay us royalties on any other products that used our technology. When those negotiations produced no results, we had no choice but to go to arbitration. The case would be tried in Chicago, a traveling midpoint between our plants, as called for in our license agreement. During this time we decided that our patent attorney shouldn't continue representing us in this case. He was a very good patent attorney and had obtained excellent patent coverage for us, but for this situation we needed an experienced litigator. We found a highly respected Chicago law firm with extensive technology litigation experience. Their lead attorney on our case, Larry Adler, had recently won a case involving a satellite launch that had gone bad, destroying the multi-million dollar satellite that didn't make it into orbit.

Because the attorneys on both sides and the arbitrator, who was a patent attorney in Chicago, had other active cases as well as ours, we all agreed to space our three-day hearings at three-month intervals until the case was finished. We had no idea that Schmidt and I would travel to Chicago every three months for a total of three years until the arbitration was finished.

The arbitrator had no incentive to move the case along. The longer it took, the more he got paid. He allowed several issues and spurious counterclaims into the case that had nothing to do with the subject we were there to litigate. At one point he ordered us to produce a witness over whom we had no control. We had no way of obeying his order. To solve that one, we had to go over his head to the American Arbitration Association. This was risky business. There wasn't a higher "court" to which we could appeal the order, so we felt that we had no choice but to appeal to the organization that had furnished him for our case. The AAA agreed with us and persuaded him to reverse his order.

In the middle of the series of arbitration hearings, Schmidt left his employment at Quintron to raise venture capital and found a company that would develop an all-digital system to compete with, and perhaps replace the SimulComm system. Of course Quintron was furious with him, and Spectracom wasn't happy that we weren't given a chance to participate.

At our last hearing both attorneys made their closing arguments, and the three-year case was over, except for the arbitrator's decision. We were on pins and needles for several days until the decision arrived: We had won! Our licensee had, in fact, breached our contract, which called for injunctive relief in the event of a breach. This meant that we had the right to stop them from using our system, which would, in effect, shut down their production. Much of their $80-million per year business was dependent on our system, and they were facing a major business disaster.

The same day the decision was announced, we got a phone call from Quintron asking us to negotiate a permanent license. Two days later Schmidt, Ed O'Connor from our company, and I were in Chicago again, in our attorney's conference room to meet with the Quintron CEO and two of his people.

Our attorney recommended that I do the talking for our side rather than Schmidt, who was a much better negotiator. But he had engendered so much hate during the arbitration that it was better to have someone else talk to the other side.

The discussion went very smoothly. They were willing to buy a royalty-free, non-exclusive license for $1.0 million, payable immediately. When we asked for them to add on our attorney's fees, they said they wouldn't pay them as a separate item, but might consider burying them in the total license fee. They apparently didn't want to go home and tell their board of directors that their transgressions were so heinous that they also had to pay for our legal expenses.

Our side went into another room to caucus. I sat down in a corner with my financial calculator to add up our lost income on the product for which they hadn't paid royalties, interest on that lost money, and the present value of our estimated future cash flow streams from our existing license agreement if it should continue. We included our attorney's fees, which by then were approaching $300,000. The highest we could logically make the total was $2.3 million, but that number was based on optimistic royalty estimates that favored us. We agreed that we didn't want to push the other side too hard, or they would go back home to reconsider their options.

Back in the conference room I presented our $2.3 million total to the other side, and explained how we arrived at it. Then I closed with a lower number, saying we would sell the license they wanted for a little under $2.0 million. They went out into the hall to caucus, and came right back and accepted our offer. The details were quickly worked out, and we waited for the lawyers to wordsmith the agreement and get it typed while the rest of us enjoyed a newly relaxed atmosphere in the conference room. We were all so relieved after three years of rancor and dissension that a sort of friendship broke out. After all, it was just business, and we were still in business together.

Our original patent attorney was delighted that we had won our case and said that he had never before patented an invention that made more than a million dollars for a client.

Spectracom's share of the proceeds of the license sale went right into the bank, and for several years it enabled us to finance the company's growth without dipping into our bank line of credit.

Schmidt completed the development of his all-digital product and soon sold his company to Motorola and moved with it to Dallas where their paging transmitter systems were manufactured. While at Motorola he convinced them to buy for $50,000 the residual patent rights that Spectracom and SimulComm still owned. He later left Motorola to found another start-up company that developed a different type of product for the communications industry. I invested a little of my own money in that effort. After I hadn't heard from Schmidt or his new company for a few years, I emailed him to ask how they were doing. He had gone to the well once too often and was unable to find a market for the product. His company had failed and was out of business, but he hadn't bothered to tell his stockholders.

Chapter 38

The Payoff

Tom Donaher and I were rapidly approaching 65, and Tom had decided to retire. We needed to decide what to do with Spectracom. I reviewed my options in early 1999:

1. Find a buyer and sell Spectracom so that both of us could retire.

2. Find a replacement for Tom and continue running the business for a few years.

In either case I would need to "sell" Spectracom. That is, someone must be convinced to invest in Spectracom—with money if we sold the company, or with a large part of their future if we hired an engineering VP.

What did we have to sell? Primarily, an excellent, profitable technology company, growing steadily at about fifteen per cent annually. Explosive growth, or just faster growth, would require either luck or a CEO with more horsepower than I had. We were dominant in two or three growing market niches; we were well-managed with a team of enthusiastic employees who liked their jobs (turnover was near zero); and we were in superb financial condition.

We had arrived at this enviable state of affairs for a number of reasons. We had chosen our market segments carefully, most of the time focusing on areas that matched our company capabilities. We had concentrated on excellence in everything that we did. And we had been willing to risk company resources on upcoming market needs, without a guarantee of success. As it turned out, we had developed a few product failures, but they were far outnumbered by the winners.

Our biggest failures were intended for the digital telecommunications market. We didn't understand the customer's needs. We had listened to the wishful thinking of AT&T and Bell Labs engineers without knowing enough about the requirements of the people running their networks—the people who would actually *buy* the products and use them. We had bitten off more than we could chew, and we paid for it by developing products that we couldn't sell and that never went beyond the prototype stage.

On the other hand, we had developed a lot of other products that met market needs and were sold in quantity to a variety of customers. The profits they provided far exceeded our losses on the failures. In some cases, we developed products that replaced existing ones. A lesson taught to me by Bill Stolze at RF Communications had sunk in, and I occasionally quoted him to my colleagues at Spectracom: He had said, "If we don't obsolete our own products at a high cost, our competitors will do it for us for free."

My decision process began with a search for Tom Donaher's replacement. After interviewing five or six possible candidates I found that locating a person with the right qualifications was very difficult. Tom was not easy to replace. There were some good managers available, but they either had insufficient technical depth or lacked specific experience in our markets and technologies. We needed someone who could "hit the ground running" in areas of both digital and analog circuit design, including feedback control systems, phase-locked loops, and imbedded microprocessor software and hardware design. Besides the difficulty of finding such a person, there was Tom's need to convert his part-ownership of Spectracom into income-producing investments so he could retire. Replacing him provided us no clear path to that result, unless the replacement, in addition to the required experience and talent, had a bucketful of money and could buy Tom's Spectracom stock.

In the second half of 1999 I decided that we would sell the company.

—✦—

Before we began contacting potential buyers, we announced our plans in a company meeting to forestall rumors. We had always been as open as possible about the operations of the business, and wanted to continue that policy. After the meeting our production manager told me that he wanted to buy the company and would try to raise the money. He seemed like an unlikely prospect, but we didn't discourage him.

We hired a small investment banking firm in New York City, Context Capital, to find a buyer. Over the next several months I spent nearly full-time on the project, getting almost no useful work done in running the company. First there were constant requests by the investment banker for financial and marketing information that would let him put together a "book" about Spectracom to use as a sales tool. Customer lists, supplier lists, dealers, sales reps, financial history — all had to be provided. Mailings were made to potential buyers, visitors were entertained, and competitors (all were possible buyers) were shown around the plant. A delegation from a British competitor flew in from London to look us over.

Because Spectracom was closely held, we had always been able to keep most of this information confidential, but now we were baring our corporate soul to the world. Although it was necessary, it was a new and unsettling experience. I remembered what someone had told me nearly three decades earlier: "You can't make an omelet without breaking some eggs."

We were elated when our closest competitor indicated serious interest. True Time Instrument Company would be a good buyer: Our products and markets were complementary, and the combined organizations would have a significantly lower cost of sales than True Time alone had. But it was not to be. Their owner gave us a ridiculous low-ball offer. It was clear that they weren't serious.

Several weeks later our production manager announced that he had put together a management team that could run the company and was working with a small venture capital firm who were prospective investors. They later produced a letter of intent that was signed by both parties, and we began a new phase of the process: Due Diligence. This is where the buyer tries to find skeletons in the closet and asks for every conceivable fact about the company and its history. For the next six months my assistant, Linda Dodd, and I dug through files, generated more files, made multiple copies of everything, and furnished the information to our attorneys and to the buyer. If skeletons were found, they would result in negotiated price reductions or, in the worst case, would kill the deal. None were found.

Tom and I designed ten-week training courses for the new management; prior to the company's sale, we would each meet weekly for two hours, Tom with his replacement, the new engineering VP, and I with my replacement, the new president. Tom would use his weekly meetings to review for his replacement each current product development program, the precision timekeeping technology behind each product and its engineering support, and all of our engineering systems and procedures. My weekly meetings would review for the new president all the major topics that the top officer of the corporation would need to know about: finance and accounting systems, marketing and distribution channels, personnel, front office operations, manufacturing, engineering, and customer base.

The new engineering VP came to two of his meetings, and the new president managed to attend four or five of his. Apparently the two of them felt they already knew enough about management that they didn't need familiarization with the specifics of running Spectracom.

Finally, as the letter-of-intent deadline approached, the due diligence process was completed, and a closing date was set. At the closing we all assembled around a large, expensive, polished wooden conference table in the offices of the buyer's attorney: the new management team, their venture capital company representatives, their attorney, our officers, and our investment banker, who had flown in from New York City. Except that our attorney didn't show up. After some phone calls he was located. He had forgotten the appointment. We all cooled our heels while he found his way to the meeting. After he arrived, the meeting began and the venture company announced that they hadn't been able to find enough investors. They were twenty percent short of the agreed upon selling price. The deal appeared to be dead. I was furious and was about to walk away from the deal, when Price Paschall, our investment banker, who was a superb negotiator, suggested a compromise: The buyer could give Tom and me a consulting contract that would make up the difference with five years of quarterly payments whether we did any work for them or not, if we would agree to the reduced price. After caucusing in private, both sides agreed, and the closing was completed. The investment banker had earned his commission.

✦

As we were closing on the sale of Spectracom in mid-2000, the dotcom market crash began. Over the next two and a half years, stocks lost a third of their value, drying up sources of venture capital and scaring investors out of the market. During that period it was next to impossible to sell technology companies.

Our timing had been perfect.

Chapter 39

Spectracom Epilogue

When the new management team took over the company, the president asked me to stay away from Spectracom for the next thirty days. That way the new management could establish their authority without the distraction of old loyalties to the founders. We were happy to have a vacation but were insulted by the insinuation that we would have a negative effect on operation of the business. The new management's arrogance and fear of continuing old loyalties prevented their acceptance of our help during the transition.

Our national sales manager had decided that he didn't want to work for the new management team and resigned just before the sale was finalized. He reported that our production manager had been harassing him with threats of tighter supervision and less operating freedom. Months later he filed a lawsuit against Spectracom, claiming $60,000 of unpaid commissions and management bonus. In selling the company we had agreed to remain responsible for any liabilities incurred before the closing. This lawsuit fell under that provision. The sales manager had never been on a commission, and the entire management and incentive bonus that we owed him had been carefully calculated and paid after he left. The case remained on the court docket for three years while the other side's attorney gradually reduced their demand to entice us to settle out of court. In the meantime we followed our new attorney's bad advice to not insist on summary judgment right away. During that time we accumulated tens of thousands of dollars in legal fees. On the day before the trial was to begin, the lawyer for the other side called us and agreed to settle for four thousand dollars. He apparently had concluded that they had no case. We agreed to settle in order to avoid the cost and uncertainty of a court battle.

By four years after the sale of the company, each of the new management team had been fired by the venture capital firm that controlled Spectracom, and sales were only marginally higher than when we sold the company. A new president was imported from the west coast. She had most recently been the president of our competitor, True Time Instrument Company. Under her leadership, Spectracom prospered and grew.

As this is written, about twelve years after our sale of Spectracom, the company is now a subsidiary of a French corporation, Orolia. Spectracom has divisions in three other countries and sales have grown, through internal growth and acquisitions, to about five times what they were when I retired.

Two Shakes of a Lamb's Tail

V

Sunset over the Vineyard

Old Time, in whose banks we deposit our notes,
Is a miser who always wants guineas for groats;
He keeps all his customers in arrears
By lending them minutes and charging them years.

Oliver Wendell Holmes, Sr.
Poems of the Class of '29

"You mean now?"

Yogi Berra
In response to being asked what time it was

Chapter 40

A Medical Adventure

The entrance to the Westfall Surgical Center in Rochester comprises three sequential, double-wide, automatic, motion-sensing doors. Sensing our approach, the first set of doors slid open, floating on whisper-silent bearings. Then the second set opened to Marianne and me, then the third. Beyond was a sculpted reception desk in a lobby that didn't resemble any hospital or doctor's office I'd ever seen. Maybe the reception area of a national stock brokerage or a high-class law firm, but certainly not a hospital or clinic. Two young ladies sat behind the artfully designed reception desk, and I showed my filled-out forms to the nearest one. Not touching my papers, she directed me back through the last set of automatic motion-sensing doors to the elevator on my left and told me to take it to the basement, where I would find people who wanted to see my papers.

As we exited the elevator, which was as silent as the front doors of the building, a smaller, more conventional reception desk appeared through a door on our right. Now we were in a doctor's waiting room with fifteen or twenty others. The woman at the desk took my papers, checked them against some other papers she took from a file folder, asked for my name and birth date, checked my answer against her papers, and told me to take a seat and wait to be called. Before she let me go, I had to hold out my wrist so she could put an ID bracelet around it. Marianne and I took seats next to each other, comforted by the knowledge that anyone who felt the need could now identify me by reading the bracelet that peeked from under the cuff of my shirtsleeve with red-orange blast furnace intensity.

✧

My preparation for this day began when I got out of bed the morning before. The calendar was completely empty except for a meeting with a drywall contractor quoting some repairs. I had already canceled my 6:00 p.m. racquetball league match. By 6:00 p.m. I expected to be busy at home.

During a routine annual physical exam my family doctor had said, "What, you've never had a colonoscopy? The time has come." The appointment was made, and the day arrived.

As I read my printed instruction sheet for the sixth or seventh time that morning, I was again instructed that "The day before the examination for breakfast, lunch and dinner you are asked to have *clear liquids* only." Hmmm... The instructions hadn't changed. No food all day. OK, I could handle that. I would think of it as a Lenten sacrifice that I forgot to make until a week after Good Friday. Then the instructions said, "Mix half the bottle of MiraLax in *each* of two 32-oz bottles of clear Gatorade until dissolved and chill."

A recent trip to the pharmacy had made me the proud owner of a big bottle of MiraLax powder, and the grocery store was the source of two one-quart bottles of clear Gatorade. I already had a case of the stuff at home in the pantry, but it didn't qualify for this project. My own taste in Gatorade, which I guzzle during breaks in my racquetball matches, runs toward the "Xtremo" family of flavors: Mango Electrico, and Tropical Intenso, one orange, and the other red, both of which contain Red Dye #40. I had to settle for the only *clear* Gatorade flavor to be found on Wegman's shelves: Watermelon, a sissy flavor most likely preferred by croquet players and little girls.

At 1:00 p.m. I was to begin drinking the magic mixture at the rate of "8 oz every 15 or 30 minutes until *both* bottles are finished." Let's do some math here. There was no way I could drink eight ounces of *anything* every fifteen minutes for more than a quarter of an hour. To drink, at that rate, 64 ounces of a concoction that was expected to have deleterious and explosive effects on me was an instruction produced by a demented mind. A rate of eight ounces every *30* minutes just *might* be possible, especially since I didn't have to take time out for dinner. Even at that rate I would be fully occupied for four hours, not counting bathroom time.

Because I hadn't pre-mixed the ingredients (What could be so difficult about mixing some powder and some Gatorade that I had to do it the day before?) I sat down in the kitchen at 12:30 p.m. to begin polluting the Gatorade with MiraLax powder. On the label, in parentheses underneath the trade name, was the chemical name of the powder: polyethylene glycol. *Isn't that what's in my car's radiator to keep it from freezing? Oh, well, if I take a nap in a snow bank, I won't need to worry about frostbite.*

I opened the first bottle of Gatorade and sampled it. It tasted like a cross between watermelon and bubblegum, but at least it was drinkable. I started pouring polyethylene glycol into the bottle and stirred it with a long-handled iced tea spoon. Each time I poured more powder into the bottle, the level of liquid in the bottle rose until it was spilling over the top as I stirred. I hadn't yet put more than about six tablespoons of the stuff in there, and there was no more room in the bottle. Getting a drinking glass from the cupboard, I poured some of the doctored Gatorade into it and continued pouring the powder into the Gatorade bottle and stirring. Again it filled to the brim, and I had to pour more into the glass to make more room in the bottle.

By now, the glass was full and I had to get another from the cupboard. As I closed the cupboard door, a glance at the clock told me that it was well past one o'clock already and I still had three quarters of the powder in the bottle it came in. I'd better hurry. Three quarters was a guess, because the bottle was opaque and I couldn't see the level of powder in it. How would I know when to start pouring the second half of the powder into the second Gatorade bottle? Even worse, how would I know how much powder to pour into the drinking glasses of weak mix to bring them up to the same strength as what was in the Gatorade bottles?

In a flash of inspiration I decided to ignore the strength of the mix in each container. Just get the powder all dissolved somewhere, and then mix them all together. This required that I empty half of the mix from one of the bottles so I would have room to pour mix into it from one of the glasses or the other bottle. I got more glasses from the cupboard. The clock said 2:00 pm, and the kitchen table was covered with glasses, bottles, bottle caps, and paper towels for wiping up my spillage. At this rate it would be morning before I finished my mixing, and by the time I got to my appointment I would still have unfinished business, which would teach the doctors and nurses not to make me mix my own drinks the next time. It would serve them right.

I quickly poured the now slimy liquid from bottle to glass to glass and back to bottle several times. By now it was surely mixed evenly. I poured as much as I could back into the Gatorade bottles, but still had two full ten-ounce glasses of the stuff left over. That now made a total of 84 ounces of liquid. I was already an hour late beginning my drinking, and now it would take me over *five* hours to swallow the increased amount.

As I began drinking, I wished that I had done the mixing the night before so the blended liquid could have cooled more in the refrigerator. The slimy taste and texture would have been more palatable. However, I was only mildly nauseated after swallowing the first few glasses, and managed to finish the last glass by 7:00 pm. The last dash to the bathroom was completed by the time I went to bed, ravenously hungry, at 10:00 p.m.

The next morning I staggered out of bed, weakened from hunger, at 7:00 a.m. Using the last few drops of moisture in my body, I drooled while my wife ate her breakfast of nourishing cereal soaking in milk, healthful cranberry-apple juice, and succulent toast covered with cinnamon-sugar. I read the paper and tried to ignore the growling in my stomach while we waited for our departure for my ten o'clock appointment. I would drive to the Surgery Center, and she would drive me back home, since I wouldn't be allowed to drive in my still semi-sedated and hunger-crazed condition.

"Robert?" called a stout, stern-looking nurse from the doorway to the inner sanctum of the Surgery Center.

"Robert who?" I ask. There are lots of Roberts in this town. I don't want to say, "Yes, that's me," only to find out as I emerge from the anesthesia that I had just gotten a tonsillectomy.

She stumbled over my last name with sufficient clarity, and I admitted to her that I was the person in question. As I followed her through the door, I saw two young female orderlies spray something from a bottle onto a gurney-bed, covering not only the bed, but the pillow as well, and wiping it off with a paper towel. I followed the nurse down the hall into the preparation and recovery room, where she interrogated me to make sure I was who I said I was. She then told me to strip and put on a backwards hospital gown, and for the first time I realized why those gowns were open in back: Access.

When I returned to my compartment from behind the dressing booth curtain, she checked my ID bracelet against her records, inserted a catheter into the crook of my arm, and told me to lie down on the gurney-bed which the two orderlies had wheeled into my cubicle.

"Is that the bed I saw you spraying with noxious chemicals?" I ask the girls.

They giggled and one of them said, "Yes, that's our validator. It's good stuff."

Another orderly wheeled me into the operating room where I was greeted by some attendants and by the doctor, whom I berated for making me drink all that vile antifreeze. Everyone had a good chuckle, and I felt someone fiddle with the catheter in my arm....

"Time to wake up, Robert!" said the nurse as she patted me on the chest to get my attention. I didn't want to wake up. The nurse told my wife that I might be woozy for a while because they gave me "a little extra" anesthesia. She also told us that the test showed me to be free of polyps and tumors, and gave us a computer printout containing three high-resolution color photos of the inside of my colon, suitable for framing. It included a map showing exactly where each photo was taken. As Marianne helped me dress I noticed the bed I was sitting on and the privacy provided by the curtains that surround it, and in my stupor, I made a lewd suggestion and asked if we have time. She shot me with a look that said, "Probably not ever again in this lifetime unless you button your lip." As we made our way out to the parking lot I still wore my ID bracelet in case I got lost. On the way home Marianne bought me two sandwiches and a milkshake at Arby's, which I consumed in front of the TV set before flopping into bed where I slept until dinnertime.

Chapter 41

Sunset Over the Vineyard

The weather in Niagara-On-The-Lake was perfect. The sun was out and the temperature just right. The profusion of flowers lining the streets was blooming at its peak with no visible wilted blossoms. It was too early to check into the Shannaleigh Bed and Breakfast, but the proprietors let us leave our car in their parking area while we wandered Queen Street, window shopping and people watching before the start of the noon-hour one-act play.

We were in Canada to enjoy the Shaw Festival that attracts thousands every summer to this idyllic town. It was the way we had celebrated our wedding anniversary in recent years, and after we saw three plays in a day and a half, Marianne and I were ready for a nice quiet dinner out by ourselves.

The River Bend Restaurant was in a brand new plantation mansion that also housed a small boutique hotel in the middle of a vineyard. "Fine dining" would have to be part of its description if you accept my definition: Real cloth napkins and tablecloths, butter not wrapped in foil, and meals that are "presented" instead of just plopped onto the plates. The diners, however, instead of being formally dressed, were garbed in either elegantly casual, or casually elegant attire. There was no candelabrum on our table, only a single long-stemmed, bright red Zinnia in a tall, skinny vase, held erect at eye level by an extra-long soda straw encasing its stem.

We were seated one table away from the large picture window on the west side of the room. The view of the approaching sunset included a vast expanse of vineyard, at the far end of which was the Peller Estates Winery, looking like a homey, modern hotel, or perhaps an even larger and more modern plantation mansion than the one we were in. Above the winery the sun was directly in our eyes, but the window shades, adjusted for us by our waiter, filtered the glare without completely blocking our view.

While we drank our cocktails, a younger couple in their thirties was ushered to the table between us and the window. They took seats with their backs to us so they, too, could view the sunset. The young lady was beautiful, garbed in casually elegant attire. She wore simple black slip-on shoes, shiny black leather pants, and a black, long-sleeved sweater that she filled spectacularly. The lady was far too young to have known Howard Hughes, so it was a mystery how she achieved the construction of such well-engineered cantilevering. Perhaps she had attended a Sotheby's auction of items from the Jane Russell estate. The décolletage was tastefully displayed, and the curves exhibited by her profile, two perfectly drawn intersecting parabolas, were as exquisite as the sunset that we expected soon to see through the window over her shoulder.

Her sweater had a curiously stylish frill: Its long sleeves dangled below her wrists as though, when she pulled them on, she found them to be ten inches too long. Realizing this, she used her perfectly manicured and sharpened nails to poke her hands through the top of each sleeve at the point where the sleeve should have ended, and thereby created the dangles.

If our parabolic lady wasn't careful when she reached for the bread basket, her sleeve dangles would upset her wine glass, which had just been delivered. She leaned over the table to sniff the wine, exposing at the small of her back a gap of skin between the bottom of her sweater and the top of her stylish leather pants. Along the lower edge of the gap a narrow strip of crimson underwear peeked out at me, which, in my estimation, lowered her sartorial standing from casually elegant to merely elegantly casual, and simultaneously enhanced her allure, as though she stepped out of a Frederick's of Hollywood window display and threw on some street clothing for dinner. I realized with disappointment that her pants were more likely to be vinyl than leather.

She inspected her wine while we sipped our cocktails and ordered dinner. The sun sank lower over the vineyard, leading us to speculate that the sunset would be worth the wait. By then, I was concerned that my lack of intelligent conversation with Marianne would be blamed on my ogling of Ms. Parabola, so I concentrated my thoughts and eyes on the developing sunset, while flashing only an occasional glance at the next table where she sat, apparently discussing her wine with the waitress. When the waitress left with the glass of wine in hand, I wondered: Could Parabola be both a fashion plate *and* a wine snob? Perhaps her pants really were leather.

Our dinner arrived as the sun sank below the horizon, leaving only a few wispy clouds lit up in shades of orange, pink, maroon, and fuscia and a jet plane contrail against a background of deepening blue. Someone raised the window shades, letting us see the sunset's complete detail, an abstract painting that would be worth thousands of dollars if it were on canvas.

The waitress brought a different glass of wine to the next table, and both the lady and her husband (she wore a wedding ring) were served salads. Parabola ignored her salad and studied her new glass of wine as intensely as an entomologist trying to identify a bug floating in it. She picked it up by the stem, tilted it, stared at it, held it up to the light, stared at it, swirled the wine around in the glass, and studied it some more. Abruptly, she put it down and took from her purse a pen and a pad of paper, and began taking notes, describing the insect, no doubt. She wrote, put the pen down, and picked up the wineglass for more study. Then more note taking and more studying.

Again I worried that my wife would think I was ignoring her, so I tried to limit my attention to her, my dinner, and the sunset. We had our usual contest to see who could be the first to put titles on the jazz piano renditions of several songs that came from somewhere in the stratosphere of the room.

"Is that one 'Cherokee'?"

"No, I think it's 'Avalon'."

The mysterious behavior at the next table still intrigued me, and, like bombsights, my eyes again locked onto the action there. After more studying and note taking, Parabola's investigation entered a new phase. After vigorously sloshing the wine around in the wineglass, she set it on the table in front of her, and kneeled with one knee on her chair, the other foot on the floor, and her elbows on the table. Hiked up over the wineglass, she inserted her nose into it. Marianne was focused on the sunset, so she didn't see me stop eating and stare. I wondered if this wasn't the moral equivalent of the way a dog laps water from his dish. Could she not lift the glass to her nose rather than bringing her nose and much of the rest of herself to the glass? The nose was not merely waving around over the glass, gently searching for ketones and pheromones that might escape from it; it was *in* the glass. *All the way* in the glass. I watched, expecting that when the nose emerges, it would be encircled by a red ring imprinted there by the rim pressed against her skin, a huge circular zit that she would run to the restroom to cover with makeup.

She did come up for air now and then, to enable more note-taking before again leaning over the table to plunge her proboscis into the glass, each time flashing that sliver of crimson underwear at me. In a stunning show of generosity, she let her husband share the aroma, and he plunged *his* honker into the glass. Thoughts of sanitation flitted through my mind. At times like this did men ever shed nose hairs? I myself had never done so, but I couldn't speak for others. Or maybe while his schnozz was in there, he'd blow some bubbles. If so, I expected the end of it to display a deep purple hue, like someone in a "Got milk?" ad who, after picking up the wrong glass, missed the target when he tried to drink from it.

My disappointment was boundless when his nose appeared unmarked as he handed the glass back to his wife. He didn't bother to take notes.

"Is that 'Honeysuckle Rose'?"

"No, but wait a minute… It's 'Ain't Misbehavin'.'"

We finished our meal as the sunset faded to streaks of gray, and Parabola completed her notes. As she put them into her purse, she was careful not to catch her sleeve dangles in the zipper.

We found our car in the gloom of the parking lot, and found our way back out of the vineyard to the road and into town. We were already anticipating our next spectacular meal, a three-course breakfast with real cloth napkins and tablecloths, no foil-wrapped butter, elegantly served by the proprietors of the Shannaleigh Bed and Breakfast. Dress would be merely casual, and conversation with my wife would occupy my entire attention.

Chapter 42

Running Under the Fan

"Unzip your pants," she said, "and pull your shirt up." I pulled out my shirt and unfastened my pants while she watched. Nurses don't usually watch after they tell you to disrobe. They leave the room or turn away and act busy with some paperwork. Since this was only a partial disrobing, I supposed that being watched was okay.

"Now sit up on the edge of the examining table," she said. I hiked myself onto the table.

She reached behind herself and picked up a miniature, stainless steel AK-47 with a needle-like bayonet on its business end. With her finger on the trigger, she said, "Now this will sting a little. It's going just under the skin and into the fat of your belly. Do you want it in the left side or the right side?"

I couldn't imagine why it would matter. I'm right-handed, so I said, "The left side." With her free hand she gathered a wad of hairy lard three inches east of my belly button, pressed the muzzle of her weapon against it, and shoved. She was right. It stung.

After the third shove she let go of my belly flab, grabbed some folded gauze, and clapped it over my puncture wound. As she withdrew the instrument, leaving the pellet inside me, she said, "Press your finger over the gauze." I tore my eyes away from the ceiling and did as she instructed.

"That's it," she said. "You'll have a little bruise there, but it'll go away in a few days." She took my finger away from my wound and peeked under the gauze. "Still leaking," she said, and then stuck onto the gauze a six-inch piece of depilatory tape, rubbing it down over the hair for three inches on each side. I wondered how much carcinogenic solvent it would take to get it off.

As I put my clothes back in order, she put away her tools and told me about side effects. "For a while you'll become impotent and your libido will decrease. You may also have some hot flashes, but they're usually not too bad."

Swell. I wracked my brain to remember the difference between potency and libido: The former is what you're *able* to do, and the latter is how earnestly you *want* to. The two are not always linked, but she had just launched an attack on them both.

"And how long does this last?" I asked.

"It's a ninety-day shot," she said.

The "ninety-day shot" was a pellet of female hormone designed to leak into my system to shrink my prostate. When the prostate was small enough that none of it was hiding behind part of my pelvic bone, the urologist/surgeon would implant radioactive "seeds" in it to kill some cancerous cells found lurking there during a biopsy a few weeks before. The biopsy had been done because the PSA (short for "prostate-specific antigen") level in my blood had doubled since the last measurement two years before, but only one of the twelve needle samples had shown a tiny speck of cancerous cells. The tests had apparently found the cancer early, and it was not an aggressive type. I had plenty of time to decide on a treatment.

It was a time in my life when every doctor whose office I entered wanted to put his finger into my nether regions to check my prostate by giving it artificial peristalsis. First was my family doctor who had started the whole thing by ordering the blood test in the first place. His finger was the size of a garden hose with the nozzle still connected, but he could feel no tumor. The next one was the urologist to whom I was referred. He called the process his "finger wave." His finger was of normal size, and he also felt no tumor, but said he should do a biopsy.

A few days later the biopsy was done using a mechanical, ultrasonic transducing, needle-shooting "finger" that was only mildly discomforting. When the positive results came back, my options were explained to me and I was sent to a radiology oncologist who also did a finger wave before going over my options once again. Instead of doing nothing, external radiation, or surgical removal of the organ, I chose radioactive seed implantation, a "one-time process" that would end the treatment.

The next step was to get an accurate ultrasonic measurement of my prostate. It was performed by a nurse-practitioner, who, after teaching me what the examining table stirrups were for, did yet another mechanical, ultrasonic finger wave (no needles this time), and determined that hormonal treatment was necessary to shrink the gland to a size that would allow seed implantation. A few days later, in the urologist's office, the hormone pellet was implanted by the nurse, and I went home to spend a half-hour peeling and cutting her tape off, trying to avoid scalping my belly. A new phase of my life had begun.

I called my brother and said in a falsetto voice, "Hi, I got my ovary implant today."

A couple of weeks later the hot flashes began, one or two a day at first, accelerating to one every thirty minutes. My reaction, when at home, was to run to the nearest room with a ceiling fan and stand under it for five minutes. If I was in bed and awake, I either threw off or flapped the covers. Awaking in the morning with sweat-soaked pajamas was a regular event. In a car or a restaurant, or sitting in a meeting, I was limited to removing my sweater and mopping my brow. Each event brought forth giggles and smiles from any family members or friends in the vicinity. My wife, Marianne, thought it was hilarious. Her 71-year-old husband had PMS.

Another side effect was the 18 pounds I gained over the next three months, far more than just the additional weight of my new ovary. Most of it was concentrated in my burgeoning pot belly. That and a higher cholesterol count caused my family doctor to put me on Lipitor for the duration.

Some of the hormone effects were beneficial. There seemed to be fewer whiskers to knock out of my electric razor each morning. *Could the growth of my beard be slowing?* I could always tell that it was time for my haircut when I had three or four bad hair days in a row. Just before the surgery it took six weeks instead of the usual four before the bad hair days began, saving me the cost of half a haircut.

Several weeks after the hormone shot, I went back to the oncologist's office, where the nurse-practitioner gave me more practice using the stirrups while she did some ultrasound measurements.

"How are you getting along with the hormone shot?" she asked.

"Pretty good," I said, "but they were right about the hot flashes. And I prefer to think about the loss of libido as perpetual satiation."

She tried not to smile as she said, "I never thought of it that way before."

She then declared my prostate sufficiently shrunken to have the radioactive seeds implanted. She asked Marianne to come into the examining room and delivered a lecture on what to expect. Marianne was to accompany me to the hospital, where the surgery would be done under general anesthesia. Later the same day she would drive me home, as I would still be woozy.

The half-life of the radioactivity was said to be 60 days. I later calculated that in a year the radioactivity would be down to less than 1.6% of its original strength. I was to be given a card to show at airports or international borders that would explain to the guards why I was driving their Geiger counter into such a frenzy. The nurse practitioner told me not to hold pregnant women or grandchildren on my lap for a few months. She showed us a vial containing some of the titanium seeds that hadn't yet been made radioactive. They looked like smooth, shiny, quarter-inch pieces of paper clip wire. The urologist would insert them using only a large needle guided by ultrasound images (no incisions). The radiation oncologist would be there, along with a physicist, presumably to manage the radioactive material and to prevent core meltdown if I started to glow. I didn't ask who would manage the building evacuation.

For two weeks afterward, my wife was to sleep in a separate bed. I inferred that this was so I could avoid temptations—as though this restriction was necessary, given my already hormone-sodden, perpetually satiated body. I later learned that it was only to protect her from getting irradiated by me until those pesky radioactive seeds were well-started into their decay process.[*]

---

[*] This was a silly requirement. If the radioactivity half-life was sixty days, the decay would have barely started by the end of two weeks, and my wife could still have been injured. The head of the Radiation Oncology Department later left the city for another job, and his replacement immediately removed the requirement. Separating me from children and pregnant women for six months might have been more reasonable.

On the appointed day we followed the green line to the green hospital elevators and took them up one floor to the outpatient admitting office. The secretary signed me in and turned me over to a nurse who parked me next to a hospital bed. She pulled the curtains around it while telling me to get undressed, put my clothes in the plastic bag, put on a backwards hospital gown that was impossible to fasten shut except at the neck, and climb into the bed. I did so and waited while various announcements came over the PA system, along with occasional Morse code beeps: Three dashes (long beeps), a pause, followed by two dashes. No dots (short beeps). O-M. *Aha! I was onto them!* Maybe I could learn something that would help me escape from this place where they made me submit to impolite insertions of various instruments into orifices that were not designed to receive them. Little did they know that I knew the entire Morse code alphabet by heart. I would beat them yet! There it was again: three dashes followed by two dashes. Definitely O-M.

I had learned Morse code back in my scouting and amateur radio days, but the hospital wardens had no way of knowing this, and I wasn't about to tell them. Now if I could only figure out what O-M meant.

Lying in my bed, the code speed I was receiving from the hospital's stratosphere was in the range of five words per minute, so it was easy to read. O-M. What could it mean? Was it the mantra of the spirits of dead or dying prostate cancer patients? Or was it a signal for the hospital staff to be on the lookout for a still-living one who was about to jump out of his bed and run from the building with his backwards hospital gown flapping in the breeze behind him like Superman's cape? If I did that, I could stay cool longer and wouldn't need a fan to stand under.

I was spared the need to solve this puzzle as the curtains around my bed parted and Marianne appeared to sit by my bedside while I waited. After she complimented me on my new wardrobe, we watched the activity around the room. Nurses came and went, visiting other patients. A nurse came to my bed with a machine that squeezed my upper arm like a mechanical gorilla, automatically measuring my blood pressure. Another took my hand and stuck an I-V catheter into the back of it and fastened a connecting tube from it to a transparent bag of liquid that hung over the head of the bed. Doctors came and went, wearing green pajamas and a green hat that made each of them look like they were hiding a Rastafarian hair-do. One of them introduced himself to me, saying that he was to be my anesthesiologist. After he explained his plan to render me insentient, he looked at my red allergy wrist-band and said, "What happens when you take penicillin?"

"I get red spots all over me," I said.

"Oh," he said. "How did you find that out?"

"After being put on Ampicillin pills for a sinus infection, I got spots all over my body. Benedryl and Prednisone cured it."

Next my urologist-surgeon visited, looking out of place in street clothes. He told me what to expect and said, "I need to put on my pajamas now, but we'll see you again in a few minutes."

"While I'm in there with you, could you also fix my toenail fungus?" I asked.

"Sure," he said, and gave me a thumbs-up sign.

Then a very large man in green pajamas introduced himself to me as the nurse who would take me into the operating room. I immediately forgot his name, but thought of him as "Igor." He couldn't find my chart, which should have been hanging on my bed by then, so he went off somewhere to look for it, which filled me with confidence that these people really knew what they were doing.

A staff person came through emptying waste baskets. He was dressed in a smock and a hat like the doctors', except that the hat was multi-colored and said "Puerto Rico" across the back. He filled two large garbage bags, tied them shut, and dragged them out into the hall.

Marianne said, "They're about to take you out, so I'd better kiss you now." It was as though I was going off for another day at the office, except that I was prone on a hospital bed.

Igor returned with my chart, laid it on the bed at my feet, and wheeled me away.

The operating room was filled with green pajamas, all of whom turned from what they were doing and looked at me. I said "Hi" to both of my doctors and asked the room, "Which one of you is the physicist?"

A green pajama sitting at a computer screen raised his hand and said, "That would be me."

"I'm impressed," I said. "I've never had my own physicist before."

After Igor shifted me from the bed to the operating table, another green pajama fiddled with the tubing that connected to the catheter in my hand. Igor looked at my allergy wrist-band and asked what happened when I took penicillin. "Red spots all over me," I said. He then told me a story about a horse he once had, who broke out all over in huge welts when the vet gave him a penicillin shot.

"How could you tell?" I asked. "Didn't his fur cover them?"

"Oh, you could see them. They were really big." Sure they were. And *my* horse sired a really big unicorn. He was vamping until their chemicals went to my brain.

"Are you comfortable now?" Igor asked. "Turn your head a little this way............"

"Wake up, Robert. You're back in the recovery room. It's time to wake up," a nurse said. I knew it wasn't Igor because this one was dressed in white and sounded more female. I looked through the fog at Marianne and said I had a sore throat.

"That's caused by the breathing tube they put down your throat," the nurse said. "It'll feel better in a little bit." I wondered why the breathing tube was made of sandpaper. *Couldn't they lubricate it somehow before they insert it? After all, the implements they had inserted into my other end were smooth enough.*

A while later, the nurse came back and said, "I'll pull out your catheter now, and when you have to pee, you just let me know and I'll walk you over to the restroom and we'll see if you still can."

Still can? Catheter? How many catheters do I have in me? And what if I can't? And it's not ladylike to say pee. Urinate, or maybe micturate, would be more professional.

She dove under the covers with both hands, made me squirm as she pulled out some tubing and quickly dropped it somewhere out of sight.

"Now you just let me know when you need to go," she said. She was far too cheerful. Here I was, facing a major urinary crisis, and the nurse, my lifeline, was calmly walking away.

By then I had a long list of questions to ask, but she had already deserted me. I decided not to wait too long, because if there were problems I wanted to give the medical staff plenty of time to solve them or alert the ER before I blew up like a balloon. I felt a little better when the doctor came in and said everything had gone well. "While I was in the region I checked you for bladder tumors and polyps. No problem, you're clean," he said.

A half hour later the nurse walked me across the room to the john. "Here you are," she said, and closed the door as she left. I resisted the urge to ask her to stay and watch in case of an emergency, but I needn't have worried. Everything was fine. I theorized that they try to scare the patients because it diverts their attention from the real problems and the patient feels so good to learn that there was no problem after all. Sort of like that hilarious riddle we learned in kindergarten. Question: Why did the little moron keep hitting his thumb with a hammer? Answer: Because it felt so good when he stopped.

Back at home, things went as predicted, and a couple of days after the surgery I worked up enough courage to inspect myself with the magnifying mirror in the bathroom. Various parts looked like I had contracted the heartbreak of psoriasis, but I had no pain or itching. "Oh, yeah, that bruising happens," said the doctor during my follow-up exam two days later. "It'll go away soon." And it did.

The wallet-sized card explaining my radioactivity came in the mail as promised. It informed the reader about the radioactive implants I had received, along with radiation exposure level, decay rate, and the name of the doctor who had done it. Security checkpoint guards would know the card was authentic because the handwriting was barely legible—it had to have been written by a real doctor.

My life gradually returned to normal, and five months after the hormone implant (two months after the surgery) I could again enter a room without looking around for the nearest fan.

Chapter 43

Steely Street Revisited

While visiting my mother in West Lafayette for a long weekend in 2005, I slipped out of the nursing home while she was napping and drove around town to visit some old haunts and stir up a few ghosts. After we had moved to the north end of town, there was little reason to return to my old neighborhoods over the years. Most of my friends lived in the north half of town, and I had no college classes in the Purdue School of Agriculture in the south part of town. This time, back in my hometown with a couple of hours to kill, curiosity led me southward.

We had moved to Evergreen Street after we came back from Connecticut at the end of WWII. I was ten. Now, the neighborhood was nearly the same, but the front porch of the house where we had lived for five years had been removed and a two-story addition extended toward the street in its place. The driveway beside the house still was there, but it ended at a newer, more modern garage behind the house. I didn't look to see if the clothesline was still in the back yard, where we had fastened Rip's leash so he could run. I had my doubts. Likewise with the ground-level basement window that looked out onto the driveway from the coal bin, but I could almost see the portable chute guiding the coal as it was shoveled from the delivery truck into the bowels of the house by the driver. If the sour cherry tree was still in the back yard, I didn't see it, either. Do cherry trees live to be eighty years old? It was probably less than twenty when my mother worried that I would fall as I showed off for her, climbing as high as I could picking its cherries each summer. Now, I wished that she was still healthy enough to worry about the risks I took. Her worries about my endangering life and limb among the flexible upper branches of a cherry tree were preferable to my current concerns about her future in the nursing home.

The rest of the Evergreen Street neighborhood was entirely as I remembered it, except the huge Dutch Elms that made tunnels of the streets were gone. The elm trees had died of Dutch Elm Disease as it spread across the country in the 1950s. It is estimated that over 100 million trees died of the disease. New trees of another kind had been planted, now grown nearly as large, and the street looked much the same as in the early 1950s. It was the same neighborhood where I had chased butterflies with a net the summer before my ninth grade biology class. We had been expected to assemble a butterfly collection to show the class, but alcohol or benzene on cotton in the bottom of a jar didn't kill the butterflies quickly enough. Before they died, they beat their wings to shreds trying to escape. Near the end of Evergreen Street beside the Purdue campus, at Arth's Drug Store, Mr. Arth poured plaster of Paris laced with plenty of cyanide into the bottom of an empty Skippy peanut butter jar for me. For the entire summer the residual fumes killed butterflies instantly.

Every fall those elm trees dropped truckloads of leaves onto the neighborhood streets and yards. People raked them into long rows in the street gutters and burned them. On cool, sunny afternoons, the air was filled with smoky smells of burning autumn leaves and the distant sound of Purdue's marching band practicing on the athletic field beside the field house at the far end of the street. The drum major's whistle and the beat of the giant bass drum accompanied all those brass instruments and flavored the smoky air all over town. One of those bass drummers in later years was Neil Armstrong, well before his name was a household word around the world.

The alley behind our house, where garages and garbage cans stood, was still there. I replayed in my mind the experiment I had performed six decades ago to see if David could have actually slain Goliath with a stone. I had made a sling out of twine and attached a piece of cow leather that held a large rock. I twirled the sling and tried to fire golf-ball-sized stones down the half-block to the end of the alley. The power generated by the sling certainly could have slain anyone that got his head in the way of its projectile, but *my* shots scattered all over the landscape. Some stones went almost straight up and came down twenty feet away and others skipped along the ground. Those that went far came down in a distant neighbor's shrubs.

When a woman working in her garden figured out where the rocks were coming from, she yelled at me.

"You stop that! You'll hurt someone!"

I stopped. But I concluded that David was either well-trained or lucky. If he had needed to reload for a second shot, Goliath would have had time to grab him and end his biblical career.

The alley behind Dodge Street, where I had shot myself in the thumb with a pellet gun, was still there, too. I ran my forefinger over the old scar as I drove by.

Further back in time, Steely Street beckoned from the south end of town, and the neighbor kids there yelled at me to come back and play. I drove a couple of miles to the south end of Grant Street, past the Mays' house where I took piano lessons from my mother's best friend, until I reached Bob Kriebel's house. Both houses were smaller than they had been when we moved away to Connecticut in 1943. I turned right into Steely Street at the intersection where the pavement had jumped up at my face and left scabs when I fell off my bike. Steely Street, where for four years I had started my daily one-mile walk to grade school and back, without parental accompaniment, school bus rides, or armed guards.

Unlike Evergreen Street, Steely Street had been replaced by a strange neighborhood that didn't belong there. The area, once teeming with children who had to stand aside when a new 1939 Plymouth or an old Ford Model A drove by, where an airplane had once dropped advertising leaflets chased and collected by those same children, was now a different place.

Our house and those beside it were gone, replaced by a parking lot, and it made me angry. I drove into the parking lot—after all, it was my yard, and I could damn well stop there and look around if I wanted to. The back yard and the wild cherry tree holding my tree house that Dad had built for me were gone. The slide wire from the tree house down to a telephone pole by the cow pasture fence was gone. The pasture behind the fence and the cow with the stomach-inspection hole in its side were gone, replaced by the new Purdue power plant and an adjacent substation, bristling with cables, insulators, and transformers, moved there from the center of the campus. The farm land at the west end of our block-long street was now covered with new buildings, parking lots, streets. And Mom wasn't there, that young and cheerful housewife, standing on the porch with me, waiting for Dad to walk up the street from work.

Across from our house, the north side of Steely Street was partly as it had been. Four of the original houses were there, seedier than before, needing paint, now part of the student ghetto. I swore out loud at the gods of progress and destruction and was glad the car windows were closed.

Then the ghosts started chasing me away, blaming me for not coming back, for not preventing the loss of our neighborhood. As I drove away on other streets where I had once walked and run and ridden, I peered at signs on corners, reminding myself of street names now hidden behind five or six decades of mental mist. Finally, I headed north through campus and neighborhoods more recently familiar to find refuge in Mom's nursing home, fleeing the ghosts, haunted by memories.

Chapter 44

The Case of the Missing Chapeau

The music ended and my wife said, "Bob, do you still have your hat?" I checked under my left armpit, where I last remembered holding it: No hat. My stomach dropped an inch as I scanned the floor around me. It was my favorite hat that kept the sun off both my sunglasses and my bald spot. It was a neutral grey color, and its maroon and dark blue piping was so unobtrusive that I could wear it with anything. It didn't fit well and I looked like a doofus in it, but I wore it anyway. Marianne, in a rare moment of benevolent flattery, had said, "Well, it looks better on you than your other hats."

The building we were in was huge, and the Lightner Museum it housed, elegant. Built around a courtyard with water-spitting fish that kept the pool full, its Spanish architecture fit the mood of the historic district of St. Augustine.

We had arrived early for the demonstration of music-making machinery. While waiting with the other tourists, we snooped around among the exhibits like curious cats. As the hour drew near, we joined the others and headed for the Music Room.

A woman with an official-looking nametag came in and made sure that a tourist in a wheelchair was positioned in front of everyone else, and began the demonstration.

A half-hour later, the demo over and my ears ringing with nickelodeon music, my wife asked if I still had my hat.

Sunset over the Vineyard

"That guy behind you has one just like yours," she said. The man was rotund, shorter than I, but his head was pointier than mine, so the hat fit perfectly. I took a closer look. The neutral grey color was the same. The shape was the same. Even the maroon and dark blue piping was the same. He was asking questions of the lecturer in a Scottish accent. When I asked him if, by any chance, he had found the hat here in the museum, he said no, it was his.

Since we had been only on the first floor while waiting for the demonstration, we retraced our route, looking under display cases, behind doors, and in every nook and cranny we could find: No hat. I went to the ticket desk near the entrance, and to the souvenir shop through which we had entered: No hat had been turned in.

Back into the museum I went for more searching: No hat. By now, the museum staff probably thought we were casing the joint for a burglary. Then down the street to the restaurant where we had eaten lunch. As I left the museum, the gift shop clerk said that the lecturer had told her that the Scotsman had come into the museum without a hat; she had seen him on the second floor prior to the music box demo, and he had no hat. Contemplating that revelation on my way to the restaurant, my blood pressure rose. If the hat wasn't at the restaurant, I would search the entire museum for him and confront him more forcefully this time. It didn't matter if they thought I was planning a caper. Maybe it would motivate the staff to find my hat just to get me out of the place.

My hat was not at the restaurant. On the way back to the museum I decided that the pointy-headed Scot was a liar. He *had* to have found my hat and liked it so much he wasn't about to give it back. After all, he could wear it with anything. I didn't need that kind of sartorial flattery. I wanted my hat back.

At the museum once more, I searched the second floor for the rotund Scotsman. Then the third floor. No Scotsman.

Finally giving up the search and, collecting my wife, I headed for the door.

On the way through the gift shop I said to the clerk, "I feel obliged to leave a message for the Scotsman. Would you deliver it if you see him again? Tell him I feel a little guilty and hope I haven't inconvenienced him. You see, I'm just getting over a really bad case of scabies."

Chapter 45

A Gift for Earl Butz

When Dr. Earl Butz was sent to jail, much of the nation, especially all of West Lafayette, was shocked. How could such a respected and successful man have neglected to report so much income on his tax return?

I first knew of Dr. Butz when he was head of the Agricultural Economics Department at Purdue University and I was in high school. He then served three years as Assistant Secretary of Agriculture in the Eisenhower administration, and about the time I graduated from Purdue, he returned to Purdue as Dean of the School of Agriculture. He and my dad had been Purdue graduate students and met while they lived in the Cary Hall student residence complex. Their careers at Purdue were quite different, with Dad in Physics and then Electrical Engineering, and Earl Butz on the Agriculture side of campus.

Eventually Dr. Butz left Purdue and joined President Nixon's administration, where folks in Indiana said he was the best Secretary of Agriculture ever to serve in that position. By the time he was booted from office for telling one too many dirty jokes, having been ratted out to the press by John Dean, he had succeeded, according to my father, in eliminating all but two of the federal government's crop price support programs: peanuts and tobacco. Farmers could now grow their other crops based on economic and business considerations without also worrying about what the government would or wouldn't allow them to grow. A significant step in this accomplishment was the sale to the Russians of the American grain surplus stockpiles. When Dr. Butz left Washington under a cloud of adverse publicity, Dad remarked that "Earl always did like to tell dirty jokes."

Apparently disillusioned and bitter—at least that's my guess—at having suffered public humiliation that far exceeded the malevolence of his transgressions, Earl Butz failed to report the income from his speaking engagements. The result of this $148,000 oversight was a plea of guilty and a sentence of five years in jail, reduced to 30 days in jail, five years of probation, and fines and penalties of more than $70,000. Mom said she "felt so sorry for Mary Emma having to put up with that humiliation while Earl was away."

Eventually, the Butzes moved into the Westminster Village retirement community, where Mom had lived since the year after Dad died. In 1995, Mary Emma Butz died, and Dr. Butz remained in their apartment for several years.

About the time Mom moved to her retirement apartment, I read a novel by Jane Smiley titled *Moo*, a story about people and events on the campus of a Midwestern agricultural college. Presumably, the college in the book was patterned after Iowa State University, where Ms. Smiley taught. In the book, a student secretly raises a prize pig in an unused part of a campus building. The pig's name is Earl Butz.

As I read the story, I wondered whether the real Earl Butz had read it, or if he even knew about the appearance of his namesake in the plot. If he knew about it, was he insulted that a pig was named after him? Or did he consider it an honor that a famous novelist had named such a fine specimen of livestock after him? I concluded that, given his well-developed sense of humor, the latter was more likely.

I took the book to West Lafayette on one of my trips to visit Mom and asked Dr. Butz to autograph it. His famous sense of humor being still intact, he agreed and signed the book. During our conversation in his apartment, he told me at some length how lucky he had been in his selection of his wife. Years after her death, he was still very much in love with her, and, I suspect, more than a little ashamed of the humiliation he had inflicted on her.

A couple of years later I attended a writers' conference in St. Petersburg, Florida, where Jane Smiley was the keynote speaker. I took along my copy of *Moo* to ask her to autograph it. During her book-signing session, I bought her Pulitzer prize-winning book, *A Thousand Acres*, as well as another copy of *Moo* for her to autograph. I explained to her that I knew Earl Butz and was planning to give him a copy of *Moo* if she would autograph it for him. Amused by the prospect, she signed my copy of *Moo* right under Earl Butz's signature. She also signed my copy of *A Thousand Acres*, and the new copy of *Moo* with the inscription, "Best wishes to the *real* Earl Butz."

The next time I was in West Lafayette I gave him the book.

Butz's legacy in the world of US agriculture is considerable. He led the transformation of our family farm culture into one of big agriculture, resulting in lower food prices and improved standard of living for many. The grain surplus in the US had been a millstone around each administration's neck, causing ever increasing government subsidies that sometimes paid farmers not to plant, and huge government stockpiles of grain surpluses. Butz promoted grain exports and engineered the sale of government stockpiles to the Russians, who had food shortages.

In their later years, both Mom and Dr. Butz lived in the nursing home at Westminster Village, as chance would have it, directly across the hall from each other. Both were in wheelchairs, with failing health.

Ever since my high school days, whenever Mom didn't like one of my friends or someone I dated, I could sense it. She never said anything negative about them, but the atmosphere in the room got a tiny bit chillier when the person's name was mentioned. I got the same feeling when Earl Butz's name came up in conversation. She never said anything negative about him, but I sensed that she didn't approve of his humor, and wasn't interested in cultivating a friendship with him, even though he lived right across the hall.

Mom died in January of 2007 at 99. Earl Butz died a year later in February 2008 at 98. He holds the record for the Cabinet member with the longest lifespan.

Chapter 46

Teacher

"And then September came and I entered Mrs. Hesselberth's classroom. And everything changed. Years later, my mother talked about this time in my life. Of Mrs. Hesselberth, she simply said, 'She saved your life.'"

From behind the pulpit, the speaker, John Hutchings, went on to eulogize my mother, Merno Hesselberth, in a way that I had not heard before. The occasion was her funeral on the afternoon of January 12, 2007.

Marianne and I were enjoying some winter sunshine on the Gulf of Mexico beach of Longboat Key, near Sarasota when I got the call. The head nurse told me that my 99-year-old mother had told her in no uncertain terms that she would no longer eat, drink, or take her daily doses of a dozen or so pills. Her body had gradually failed her in recent years, until she could no longer see, feed herself, walk, speak clearly, or get in and out of her wheelchair unassisted. Her once-sparkling mind worked more slowly now, but not to the point where she was unable to make that final decision. Years earlier, while walking through the nursing home to visit a friend who was in bad shape, Mom had told me "I do *not* want to live that way." Now, her time had come: She would no longer live that way.

We had known it was imminent. Our daughter Sue Geraci had brought her two sons from Honeoye Falls, New York, to visit their great grandma between Christmas and New Year's. From Raleigh, North Carolina, our son Dave had flown in for an overnight visit two days before we got the call. His wife, and their three-week-old baby, Amber Grace Merno Hesselberth, were unable to make the trip. And our northern Virginia daughter, Mary Jo Clark, was already on the scene. Two days later, I was at the Tampa airport, on my way to West Lafayette, Indiana when the nurse called my cell phone with the news that Mom had died. Marianne made plans to follow me as soon as she could get on a plane.

At the funeral, later that week, John Hutchings got up to speak. Hutchings was the brother of my brother's sister-in-law's ex-husband. I had never met him, but my brother John had and knew of his experience as a student in Mom's fourth grade class in 1957. Hence, the invitation for Hutchings to speak at the funeral. His tribute gave our family a new perspective on Mom. We knew she was a very good (and very strict) teacher, but we had never heard specific stories from her students that told us why.

Hutchings told of moving to town and entering an unfamiliar new school as a third-grader, and of feeling unwelcomed by his teacher and disconnected from his classmates. He used words like "increasingly miserable... unhappy... isolated and withdrawn... After enduring a dreary winter and spring at [school] I spent an endless, friendless summer.

"And then September came and I entered Mrs. Hesselberth's classroom. And everything changed..."

Hutchings doubted that she did anything other than what she did every day of her teaching career: "She created an environment where everybody counted and where everybody learned." He went on to share some anecdotes showing why

316

everybody liked the teacher, including the artful way she put her entire body into the effort of blowing a note on her pitch pipe, and the sketches she drew of each class member as they presented an assigned solo report to the class.

Then he said, "More than specific memories, however, I remember the climate...in Mrs. Hesselberth's classroom. It can be summarized in just one word: *Positive*. She treated us in a way that made us want to do well, that made us want to please her. Because she was so positive that we were smart, we were. Because she was so positive we would behave well, we did. Because she so positively believed that each of us was a valued member of the class, we believed that of one another. She was very sure of herself and very sure of us, positive that everything we did was exceptional. She made us believe in ourselves. How could a confused and unhappy kid remain that way in the presence of this overwhelmingly positive force? How could any of us not succeed in the face of those positive expectations and confident support?"

—◇—

Growing up with her as our mother, my brother John and I got multiple doses of her positive demeanor, but we took them for granted: Didn't all mothers display a perpetually positive outlook after our little failures and disappointments? Didn't all mothers offer cheery encouragement to their sons when a hateful teacher gave us impossible homework? And weren't all mothers overbearingly cheerful every morning when their sons got out of bed, even though we desperately wanted to remain grouchy and miserable?

Hutchings' words brought back to us those fading memories and reminded us of how truly lucky we were to have such a remarkable mother.

Her upbeat attitude included an imperative to avoid and prevent discomfort for others. Confrontations were carefully avoided by well-crafted diplomacy. If I wanted to play tennis with Rich Bauman, she asked, "Would he be available after your homework is finished?" If I wanted to take on another after-school activity or responsibility, she asked, "How will it cut into your Scout meeting time?" or, more importantly, "Can you still get your homework done?" Disapproval of a questionable activity or a not-so-responsible friend was similarly disguised in terms that cast no aspersions, but somehow let me know that I should think twice before continuing. It was the best kind of training in quality decision making.

Her consideration for others extended to planning for her own death. Well before she moved into the nursing home, she told us that her notebook contained instructions on who was to perform the funeral ceremony, where it was to be held, and what poems and music were to be used. The poem that was to appear in the service program was "A Parting Guest" by James Whitcomb Riley:

What delightful hosts are they —
Life and Love
Lingeringly I turn away,
This late hour, yet glad enough
They have not withheld from me
Their high hospitality.
So, with face lit with delight
And all gratitude, I stay
Yet to press their hands and say,
"Thanks.—So fine a time! Good night."

And so, luminous in memory I still see her, halfway into her one-hundredth year: She pauses, face lit with delight as in the poem, and says, "Thanks.—So fine a time! Good night."

Chapter 47

Perfect Timing

"It's a cyst or a tumor, we don't yet know which," Dr. Kukfa said. "But until we know whether it's malignant, we'll have to act as though it is. The good news is that it's only a little over a centimeter long. We usually don't see these on the pancreas until they're over three centimeters."

The ultrasound image that had provided this bit of intelligence had been made because routine quarterly tests, done as follow-up to my prostate cancer treatment, had found my blood sugar to be three times normal. After the doctor saw the report and before I left his office, he taught me to inject myself with insulin. I left with an order in my hand for the ultrasound scan and a suspicion that my pancreas was in trouble. In 30 minutes, I had been transformed from a healthy retiree with no symptoms whatever, to a diabetic requiring daily insulin injections and blood sugar measurements.

It seemed that, once again, the timing of events in my life had worked out in my favor: If I hadn't been getting regular blood tests to monitor my PSA, the thing growing in my pancreas would have been much larger before it was found. (Having an alert doctor also helped. Thank you, Dr. Michael Kukfa.) My propensity for good timing had stuck with me. Instead of a little cloud over my head all the time like Joe

Btfsplk in the Li'l Abner comics, I was afflicted with fortunate timing coincidences.

It had started when I was young. My birth was delayed until the invention of penicillin, so that when I later contracted trench mouth and pleurisy as a child, I was readily cured. The timing of my birth also let me avoid combat in wartime. I was too young for World War II and Korea, had already served when Vietnam heated up, and was too old for the Gulf War, Afghanistan, and Iraq. Rapid transportation by automobile and airplane developed just in time for me to take advantage of them, as did a host of technology items like the transistor and the computer. A new little pill made birth control a snap just as we decided that our family was large enough but hadn't yet figured out what was causing it. My master's degree in business was completed at just the right time to apply it at work and later in starting and running Spectracom—whose business turned out to be providing good timing to others. The need for precision timing in 9-1-1 call centers around the country developed just as we became able to help it along.

My retirement and sale of Spectracom occurred at just the right time, just as the US economy began one of its periodic nosedives in the "dot-com crash." Venture capital sources dried up, and had we waited, we wouldn't have been able to retire until a few years later.

Now, in retirement, another lucky (ironic?) coincidence had plunged me into a round of medical tests and doctor appointments. The next step, after the ultrasound test, was a CT scan. Yes, the ultrasound picture was correct, and the tumor was displayed in high resolution for the doctors to puzzle over. It was in the head of the pancreas and was interfering with my insulin production. A biopsy was scheduled, but the ultrasonic endoscope that went down my gullet to near the pancreas was unable to shoot its sampling needle at the tumor because a large blood vessel was in the way. In any case, the tumor would have to come out. I would need six hours of the surgery known as a Whipple Procedure to remove the afflicted half of the pancreas, and along with it a few other miscellaneous parts—the duodenum, 40 percent of my stomach, the common bile duct, and the gall bladder (no worries about future gall bladder attacks!). This decimation would be followed by a thorough re-plumbing job to make sure that food and insulin could still find their way through the construction site among the stubs of newly abbreviated organs.

After the surgery, the tumor and its immediate surroundings were tested. The pathologist said it was probably not malignant, but the cells were a rare type (one in perhaps 600,000) that needed to be sent to Sloan-Kettering in New York City for a second opinion. I envisioned the errant half of my pancreas packed in dry ice, its airliner seat paid for by my insurance company as it hurried to the Big Apple for analysis.

After I was back home, our daughter Sue came to visit. She took a picture of me without a shirt so we could record for posterity the 23 stainless steel staples that decorated my torso and held me together while my ten-inch incision healed. I posed like a body builder with a vicious look on my face, my newly emaciated muscles flexed, and my staples gleaming menacingly under the living room lights. Later, when I could use my computer again, I found on the internet a photo of a real body builder in a similar pose. I replaced his face with mine and used the resulting composite as the "Before" half of a Before and After pair on the editorial page of our annual Christmas newsletter to show how seriously the surgery had debilitated me. The caption explained that the surgery had also removed those annoying ripples from my abdomen.

After ten days in the hospital, recovery was slow, but I no longer needed insulin shots. My January and February weeks of recovery at home were spent fighting a case of *c. diff.* acquired in the hospital, wrapped in a blanket in an overstuffed recliner chair in our living room, staring out the window and across a neighbor's back yard at a porch light that was never turned off. Occasionally I was distracted by a fox that wandered from the underbrush onto the snow to sun himself, or a hawk in a tree that tore apart and ate a smaller animal, but like the green light across the harbor on the end of Daisy's East Egg dock, that porch light mesmerized me. Why was it always on? Didn't those people care about their electric bill? Did they know it was on? Should I call and tell them? No one ever went in or out of the back door next to that light, so maybe they were just waiting for my arrival. If so, someone should tell them I had already arrived right where I wanted to be.

Four weeks after my surgery the biopsy confirmation came back: Not yet malignant. We had gotten it in time and no chemo treatment would be needed.

Six months later I was back on the racquetball court, wearing, against Marianne's wishes, a full beard that had sprouted in the hospital, and I gradually gained back some of the 25 pounds lost during the ordeal. When I was healthy enough to again take orders from Marianne, I shaved off the beard just in time to forestall the threat of a divorce.

Once again—perfect timing.

Acknowledgements

I owe special thanks to those who gave me invaluable help along the way:

First of all, to my parents, whose aura was with me every step of the way.

To my teachers at West Lafayette High School, especially Mr. Donald Fites, my math teacher, whose mentoring boosted my confidence as well as my interest in math; and to my high school gang, *The Buzzards*, who helped me grow up in ways that never got us in trouble.

To my wife, Marianne, who has put up with my foibles for all these years, and who always helped me tend the fires in my belly.

To my bosses and colleagues, who taught me how to be an engineer and manager: Don Cooke, Harold Higgs, Floyd Koontz, Walt Zarris, Bill Stolze, Elmer Schwittek, Roger Bettin, Guy Numann, Joe Huie; and to Marc Broda and Clyde Washburn, whose technical expertise was invaluable during the Spectracom start up.

To my business partners, Tom Donaher and Gene Dorland, who were essential team members and leaders in building Spectracom; to Ed O'Connor, a peerless model for all aspiring sales and marketing executives; to Linda Dodd, my sparkling assistant, without whose help Spectracom's business and my office would have been hopeless messes (My insolent partners felt that my office was a wasteland in spite of Linda's heroic efforts.); to Jim Rall, Debbie Strauss, Bob Cole, Sandy Fitzsimmons, and many other dedicated Spectracom team members who were every bit as responsible as I was for the success of Spectracom; and to Chick Lewis, a business consultant who coached us and rubbed our noses in our mistakes.

To those who helped me along the way with the writing of this book: Barbara Murphy, Carol Samuel, and Flo Smith at the Osher Lifelong Learning Institute; workshop leaders at *Writers and Books*; the members of my writing group, *The Night Writers*, who coached me during endless revisions and edits; Terry Lehr, my editor, whose knowledge of tense consistency, pronoun antecedents, and compound predicates astounds me (Any remaining errors are mine; I was probably too dense or stubborn to take her advice.); and the Bob Wright Creative Group, the graphic designers who adapted their original Spectracom brochure art for use on the cover of this book.

Thank you, thank you, one and all.

-RJH

Made in the USA
San Bernardino, CA
23 May 2014